MACHINE SCORING OF
STUDENT ESSAYS

MACHINE SCORING OF STUDENT ESSAYS

Truth and Consequences

Edited by

PATRICIA FREITAG ERICSSON
RICHARD H. HASWELL

UTAH STATE UNIVERSITY PRESS
Logan, UT

Utah State University Press
Logan, Utah 84322

Printed on acid-free paper

Cover design by Barbara Yale-Read

Library of Congress Cataloging-in-Publication Data

Machine scoring of student essays : truth and consequences / edited by Patricia Freitag Ericsson and
Richard H. Haswell.
    p. cm.
    Includes bibliographical references and index.
    ISBN 0-87421-632-X (pbk. : acid-free paper)
    1. English language–Rhetoric–Study and teaching–Evaluation. 2. Report writing–Study and teaching
(Higher)–Evaluation. 3.
    Grading and marking (Students)–Data processing. 4. Educational tests and measurements–Data pro-
cessing. I. Ericsson, Patricia
Freitag, 1950- II. Haswell, Richard H.
    PE1404.M33 2005
    808'.042076–dc22
                                            2005031304

CONTENTS

INTRODUCTION

Patricia Freitag Ericsson and Richard H. Haswell

We're in the fifth year of the twenty-first century and the Parliament of India, several universities in Italy, and four Catholic churches in Monterrey, Mexico, all have bought cell-phone jammers. Meanwhile in the State of Texas, USA, the State Board of Education has decided that students who fail the essay-writing part of the state's college entrance examination can retake it either with ACT's COMPASS tests using e-Write or with the College Board's ACCUPLACER tests using WritePlacer *Plus*. Though dispersed geographically, these events have one thing in common. They illustrate how new technology can sneak in the back door and establish itself while those at the front gates, nominally in charge, are not much noticing. All of a sudden cell phones are disturbing legislative sessions and church services and allowing students to cheat on examinations in new ways. All of a sudden students can pass entrance examination essays in ways never allowed before, with their essays scored by machines running commercial software programs. How did this technology happen so fast?

And where were educators when it happened? We will leave the MPs in India and the deacons in Mexico to account for themselves, but as for automated essay scoring in the State of Texas, college educators can only throw up their hands. The decisions on e-Write and WritePlacer *Plus* were made by state government officials and industry lobbyists with no input from writing experts or administrators in higher education. The Texas step toward machine grading may not be typical so far. But in the near future there will be plenty of like steps taken everywhere in academe.

The analysis and scoring of student essays by computer—the history, the mechanisms, the theory, and the educational consequences—is the topic of this collection of essays. It is an understatement to say that the topic is rapidly growing in importance at all levels of the educational enterprise, and that the perspective on it has been, up to this point, dominated almost exclusively by the commercial purveyors of the product. Other than the notable exceptions of articles by Dennis Baron in the *Chronicle of Higher Education* (1998), Anne Herrington and Charles Moran in *College English* (2001), Julie Cheville in *English Journal* (2004), and Michael Williamson in the *Journal of Writing Assessment* (2004) and the occasional sparsely attended conference presentation, the response on machine scoring from the academic community, especially from writing teachers and composition scholars, has been silence.

This book adds some voices from the academic community to the conversation, hoping thereby to jump-start a productive debate from educators about the machine assessment of student essays. With contributions by pioneers in writing assessment and by other scholars, the volume opens the discussion to broader audiences and to nonproprietary voices. It considers theory, practice, experiences, trials, lore, and data from the postsecondary side of machine scoring, especially from teachers and students. The essays focus largely on the postsecondary scene, but their implications move in all educational directions. Educators, administrators, and academic researchers provide background and understanding of machine scoring that will make productive sense of it to colleagues, students, administrators, legislators, and the interested public—to better shape, we hope, the way this new instructional technology will be used at all levels.

We even dare to hope that the entrepreneurs might benefit from these pages. Before the publication of this volume, the only book-length treatment of machine assessment came from the machine scoring industry. Mark Shermis and Jill Burstein's edited collection, *Automated Essay Scoring: A Cross-Disciplinary Perspective* (2003), advanced arguments supporting machine assessment technology—arguments from a group of authors almost all involved in the production and sale of the machinery. Despite the subtitle's promise of a "cross-disciplinary perspective," the voice of the academic world is almost completely muted, and largely omitted from discussion are many educational issues impacting higher education—historical, linguistic, social, ethical, theoretical, pragmatic, and political. Our volume seeks to fill in these lacunae. Our primary goal, however, is not to counter industry viewpoints, solely to cast a con against their pro. This volume does not propose some countertechnology to jam the current industry software. It just questions the "truth" that industry publicizes about automated essay scoring and problematizes the educational "consequences." It takes the discussion of machine scoring to a broader level and a wider audience, to the kind of polyvocal discussion and critical analysis that should inform scholarly study and civic discourse.

The need for a wider audience is urgent because machine scoring programs are making rapid inroads into writing assessment. Teachers at every level are encouraged to use online writing software so their students can pass standardized tests that will be graded, at least in part, by assessment machines. Web-based promotion for Educational Testing Service's Criterion (2004) promises student writers "an opportunity to improve skills by writing and revising in a self-paced, risk-free environment" and suggests that Criterion is a perfect tool for testing and assessing writing as well. Vantage Learning's Web site (2005a) touts its product benefits: from learning to write to assessing writing. Vantage "offers several solutions to aid educators in meeting NCLB [No Child Left Behind] requirements, from MY Access!, our online writing environment that has been proven to increase students' writing proficiency, to our customized solutions that are used in statewide assessments in the states of Texas, Oregon, Pennsylvania and Virginia." Claims by both these companies are accompanied by glowing praise from administrators and even from some teachers.

Two- and four-year colleges and technical schools are turning to online computer essay scoring in large numbers in order to place incoming students. One of the most popular of these placement machines is the College Board's ACCUPLACER, whose fact sheet (2005) claims its technology will "test students more accurately, with fewer questions in less time, and with immediate results"—and thereby make the whole campus happier!

ACCUPLACER appeals to all members of your campus family.

- Students find it less stressful and time-consuming, more accurate and immediate.
- Faculty have more options, and find it more reliable, valid, and accurate.
- Test administrators need ACCUPLACER because it is easy to use, accurate, reliable, and valid.
- Institutional researchers appreciate the easy access to student and performance data.

ACCUPLACER's marketing campaign has been remarkably successful. In October 2004, Suzanne Murphy of the College Board told us that although she could not reveal which college and universities are using ACCUPLACER, she could tell us that "there are over 900 colleges that use ACCUPLACER in all of the U.S. states as well as a number of Canadian colleges and other colleges around the world." In addition, she was willing to let us know: "Last year over 5,000,000 tests were administered." Although ACCUPLACER once offered "traditional" (i.e., human) as well as electronic assessment of writing samples, that option is no longer available, and all ACCUPLACER scoring is done electronically through the WritePlacer *Plus* technology.

University teachers across the curriculum are using commercial computer evaluation programs to grade essay exams and term papers. With funding from a Pew Grant in Course Redesign, Florida Gulf Coast University (2005) recently implemented an "automated essay assessment capability" for a general-education course, Understanding the Visual and Performing Arts. This automated assessment is provided by Knowledge Analysis Technologies (the creators of the Intelligent Essay Assessor) and allows for what the Pew Grants demanded: a redesign of "instructional approaches using technology to achieve cost savings as well as quality enhancements." These grants were focused on "large-enrollment introductory courses, which have the potential of impacting significant student numbers and generating substantial cost savings." This Florida university is not alone in its use of the Intelligent Essay Assessor or other programs like it in content area courses.

Two-year schools especially have been attracted to the technology. In 2000 Elisabeth Bass, a college teacher in New Jersey, informed writing program administrators of her intuition that "virtually every community college in the state has moved to ACCUPLACER." Bass's guess proved not far wrong. In a 2004 study of the placement practices in twenty-four New Jersey colleges and universities, Ramapo College testing coordinator Wanda G. Kosinski (2003) found that 70 percent of the institutions used computerized assessment for placement. Of those 70 percent, ACCUPLACER was used by fifteen (or 62.5 percent). Of the institutions in her study, Kosinski found that 69 percent of the two-year schools were using ACCUPLACER, Criterion, or COMPASS (all testing batteries containing computerized assessment machines). But many four-year schools have also been attracted to the "substantial cost savings." Of the four-year schools Kosinski gathered data from, 54 percent were using ACCUPLACER, giving ACCUPLACER over 62 percent of the computerized testing share in this study. Hers is not the only state where this is happening, and ACCUPLACER is not the only product available. ACT's COMPASS tests will probably be outselling ACCUPLACER in a few years.

Machine scoring no longer has a foot in the door of higher education. It's sitting comfortably in the parlor. In K–12 schools, machine scoring has become even more of a permanent resident, heavily promoted for use in grade-promotion examinations, in graduation examinations, in practice for mandated state testing, and in grading and responding to course writing as a relief from the "burden" put on teachers. But that is a topic for another book.

At whatever academic level, machine scoring of student essays has been admitted with hardly any questioning of its true academic credentials. We stress *academic*. The entrepreneurs have thoroughly validated their software in terms of instrument validity, test equivalency, interrater reliability, and cost efficiency. What they have not done and what educators have little done is validate the software in terms of instructional adequacy, viability, and ethics. We have intentionally avoided providing much "how-to" advice, believing that this volume will serve as a sourcebook and a springboard for those interested in a critical look at the educational impact and implications of machine assessment of essays. Specific institutional circumstances will impact how administrators and teachers will respond to machine scoring. Our hope is that this book provides the critical resources for those responses. It will make a start in answering hitherto unbroached questions about the history of machine scoring, its consequences in the classroom, the ease with which writers can fool it, the reaction to it by students and teachers, and the authenticity of its "reading" of student writing. But we think this volume will do more. Even a quick glance through the chapters reveals that they raise questions that will help set the future agenda for debate and action on automated essay scoring.

- Who are the stakeholders, what are their interests, and why have some—teachers and students—largely been left out of the conversation? (McAllister and White)
- Can machine analysis programs understand the meaning of texts? (Ericsson)
- What are the capabilities and limits of a computer's ability to interpret extended discourse? (Anson)
- Why have composition teachers been so blasé about computer analysis of writing? What has been their complicity? (Haswell)
- How easy is it to fool the machine? (McGee)
- How closely do the score results of grading software match the careful evaluation of writing teachers? (Jones)
- How do students react when they find out their placement essays are being graded by a computer? (Herrington and Moran)
- What is the actual success, the adequacy, of automatic scores in placing students? (Matzen and Sorensen; Ziegler; and Maddox)
- How does use of machine scoring for placement affect the role of the writing program coordinator? (Corso)

- Are there ways that computer analysis of student writing can be effectively used in composition classes? (Whithaus)
- Are their legitimate spaces for machine analysis in a curriculum devoted to teaching higher reasoning and critical thinking? (Brent and Townsend).
- What is the educational or language ideology promoted by the machinery? (Rothermel)
- What do we lose if we let computers score student writing? (Condon)
- Where will machine scoring lead the teaching profession: to greater or less control over our courses, to more or less success in instruction? (Broad)

Although we have presented these essays without topic partitions, the book moves from historical and theoretical issues through concrete applications and problems to future ramifications. It ends with two pragmatic tools that we think will help everyone move toward a productive continuation of the discussion: a bibliography of the machine scoring literature, 1962–2005, and a glossary of terms. We think the questions that our authors raise and answer wrestle with the main truths (theoretical and empirical) and the main consequences (instructional and ethical) of machine scoring of student essays.

It is worth asking, finally: what have been the consequences of the lopsided production of discourse seen so far on automated scoring of essays? Our authors' questions are most readily asked by teachers and students, not by politicians or business people. None of these topics are explored by Shermis and Burstein's *Automated Essay Scoring* (2003), which, for instance, reports not one completed study of the instructional validity of machine scoring. In fact, on the issue of automated essay scoring teachers and students have not been encouraged to ask questions at all and sometimes have been systematically excluded from forums where their opinion should have a voice and might have an appeal. In *The Neglected "R": The Need for a Writing Revolution* (2003), authored by the National Commission on Writing in America's Schools and Colleges and published by the College Board, teachers and students are excluded from the agenda for "revolution." Instead it is recommended that "the private sector work with curriculum specialists, assessment experts, and state and local educational agencies to apply emerging technologies to the teaching, development, grading, and assessment of writing" (30). The essays in this volume stand as a response from the very stakeholders that the National Commission on Writing omits. We hope they mark the start of a different revolution, in which the people most affected by this particular "emerging technology" have a say in that future.

1

INTERESTED COMPLICITIES
The Dialectic of Computer-Assisted Writing Assessment

Ken S. McAllister and Edward M. White

She knew how difficult creating something new had proved. And she certainly had learned the hard way that there were no easy shortcuts to success. In particular, she remembered with embarrassment how she had tried to crash through the gates of success with a little piece on a young author struggling to succeed, and she still squirmed when she remembered how Evaluator, the Agency of Culture's gateway computer, had responded to her first Submission with an extreme boredom and superior knowledge born of long experience, "Ah, yes, Ms. Austen, a story on a young author, another one. Let's see, that's the eighth today—one from North America, one from Europe, two from Asia, and the rest from Africa, where that seems a popular discovery of this month. Your ending, like your concentration on classroom action and late night discussion among would-be authors, makes this a clear example of Kunstlerroman type 4A.31. Record this number and check the library, which at the last network census has 4,245 examples, three of which are canonical, 103 Serious Fiction, and the remainder ephemera. (Landow 1992, 193–194)

This excerpt from George Landow's tongue-in-cheek short story about "Apprentice Author Austen" and her attempts to publish a story on the international computer network, thereby ensuring her promotion to "Author," suggests a frightful future for writing and its assessment. The notion that a computer can deliver aesthetic judgments based on quantifiable linguistic determinants is abhorrent to many contemporary writing teachers, who usually treasure such CPU-halting literary features as ambiguity, punning, metaphor, and veiled reference. But Landow's "Evaluator" may only be a few generations ahead of extant technologies like the Educational Testing Service's e-rater, and recent developments in the fields of linguistic theory, natural language processing, psychometrics, and software design have already made computers indispensable in the analysis, if not the assessment, of the written word. In this chapter, we approach the history of computer-assisted writing assessment[1] using a broad perspective that takes into account the roles of computational and linguistics research, the entrepreneurialism that turns such research into branded commodities, the adoption and rejection of these technologies among teachers and administrators, and the reception of computer-assisted writing assessment by the students whose work these technologies process.

Such a broad treatment cannot hope to be comprehensive, of course. Fortunately, the field of computer-assisted writing assessment is sufficiently well established that there exist numerous retrospectives devoted to each of the roles noted above—research, marketing, adoption, and use—many of which are listed in the bibliography at the end of this book. Our purpose here in this first chapter of an entire volume dedicated to computer-assisted writing assessment is to offer readers a broad perspective on how computer-assisted writing assessment has reached the point it occupies today, a point at which the balance of funding is slowly shifting from the research side to the commercial side, and where there is—despite the protestations of many teachers and writers—an increasing acceptance of the idea that computers can prove useful in assessing writing. This objective cannot be reached by examining the disembodied parts of computer-assisted writing assessment's historical composition; instead, such assessment must be treated as an extended site of inquiry in which all its components are seen as articulated elements of a historical process. This complex process has evolved in particular ways and taken particular forms in the past half century due to a variety of social and economic relations that have elevated and devalued different interests along the way.

In the following sections we trace this web of relations and suggest that theoretically informed practice in particular circumstances—what we will be calling "praxis"—rather than uncritical approbation or pessimistic denunciation ought to guide future deliberations on the place of computer-assisted writing assessment in educational institutions. Our hope is that by surveying for readers the technological, ideological, and institutional landscape that computer-assisted writing assessment has traversed over the years, we will help them—everyone from the greenest of writing program administrators to the most savvy of traditional assessment gurus—develop some historical and critical perspective on this technology's development, as well as on its adoption or rejection in particular contexts. Such perspectives, we believe, make the always difficult process of deciding how to allocate scarce resources—not to mention the equally dizzying process of simply distinguishing hype from reality—considerably more straightforward than trying to do so without some knowledge of the field's history, technology, and "interested complicities."

INTERESTED COMPLICITIES

The process of designing computers to read human texts is usually called natural language processing, and when these techniques are applied to written texts and specifically connected to software that draws conclusions from natural language processing, it becomes a form of writing assessment. Raymond Kurzweil (1999), an artificial intelligence guru specializing in speech recognition technologies, has a grim view of natural language processing, asserting as recently as the end of the last century that "understanding human language in a relatively unrestricted domain remains too difficult for today's computers" (306). In other words, it is impossible—for now at least—for computers to discern the complex and manifold meanings of such things as brainstorming sessions in the boardroom, chitchat at a dinner party and, yes, student essays.

The disjunction between the desire for natural language processing and the current state of technology has created a territory for debate over computer-assisted writing assessment that is dynamic and occasionally volatile. It is possible, of course, to freeze this debate and claim that it is divided into this or that camp, but such an assertion would be difficult to maintain for long. To say, for instance, that there are those who are for and those who are against computer-assisted writing assessment might be true enough if one examines its history only from the perspective of its reception among certain articulate groups of writing teachers.[2] Such a perspective doesn't take into consideration, however, the fact that there are a fair number of teachers—and perhaps even some readers of this book—who are undecided about computer-assisted writing assessment; such people, in fact, might well like there to be a technology that delivers what computer-assisted writing assessment companies say it can, but who are ultimately skeptical. Nor does it consider the fact that natural language processing researchers frequently occupy a position that may be termed "informed hopefulness." Such a position neither denies the current limitations and failings of computer-assisted writing assessment nor rejects the possibility that high-quality (i.e., humanlike) computer-assisted writing assessment is achievable.

Another way the debate could be misleadingly characterized is as a misunderstanding between researchers and end users. Almost without exception, the researchers developing systems that "read" texts acknowledge that the computers don't really "understand" what they're seeing, but only recognize patterns and probabilities. Of course, the process of reading among humans—and virtually every other sign-reading creature—also depends on pattern recognition and probabilistic reasoning, but the human brain adds to this a wealth of other types of interpretive skills—sensory perception, associative thinking, and advanced contextual analysis, for example—that makes a vast difference between how computers and humans read. Nonetheless, end users see the fruits of natural language processing research, which is often very compelling from certain angles, and declare such computer-assisted writing assessment systems either a welcome pedagogical innovation or a homogenizing and potentially dangerous pedagogical crutch. This misunderstanding is often exacerbated by the people who commodify the work of researchers and turn it into products for end users. The marketing of computer-assisted writing assessment algorithms and the computer applications built around them is an exercise in subtlety (when done well) or in hucksterism (when done dishonestly). The challenge for marketers dealing with computer-assisted writing assessment is that they must find a way around the straightforward and largely uncontested fact that, as Kurzweil (1999) said, computers can't read and understand human language in unrestricted domains—precisely the type of writing found in school writing assignments.[3]

Rather than trying to tell the story of the history of computer-assisted writing assessment as a tale of good and evil—where good and evil could be played interchangeably by computers and humans—we prefer to tell the history more dialectically, that is, as a history of interested complicities. The evolution of computer-assisted writing assessment involves many perspectives, and each perspective has a particular stake in the technology's success or failure. Some people have pursued computer-assisted writing assessment for fame and profit, while others have done it for the sake of curiosity and the advancement of learning (which is itself often fueled by the pressure of the promotion and tenure process). Some have pursued computer-assisted writing assessment for the advantages that novelty brings to the classroom, while others have embraced it as a labor-saving innovation. And some people have rejected computer-assisted writing assessment for its paltry return on the investments that have been made in it, its disappointing performance in practical situations, and the message its adoption—even in its most disappointing form—seems to send to the world: computers can teach and respond to student writing as well as humans. In its way, each of these perspectives is justifiable, and for this reason we believe it is important to step back and ask what kind of conditions would be necessary to sustain such a variety of views and to attempt to ascertain what the most responsible stance to take to such a tangle of interests might be in the first decade of the twenty-first century.

The development of computer-assisted writing assessment is a complex evolution driven by the dialectic among researchers, entrepreneurs, and teachers. The former two groups have long been working to extend the limits of machine cognition as well as exploit for profit the technologies that the researchers have developed. Teachers, too, have been driven to shape the development of computer-assisted writing assessment, mainly by their understandable desires to lighten their workloads, serve their students, and protect their jobs and sense of professional importance. All of these people have motives for their perspectives, and some have more power than others to press their interests forward. As a dynamic system—as a dialectic—each accommodation of one of those interests causes changes throughout the system, perhaps steeling the resolve of certain opponents while eliminating others and redirecting the course of research elsewhere. In general, all of the participants in this dialectic are aware of the interests at stake—their own and those of others—and have tended to accept certain broad disciplinary shifts (from computer-assisted writing assessment as research to computer-assisted writing assessment as commodity, for example) while fighting for particular community-based stakes that seem fairly easy to maintain (like having a human spot-check the computer's assessments). It is for this reason that we see computer-assisted writing assessment as being a dialectic charac-terized by interested complicities: each group—researchers, marketers, adopters, and users—has interests in the technology that have become complicit with, but are different from, those of all the others.

The remainder of this chapter briefly narrates this dialectic begin-ning in the English department. It is there that the analysis of texts has been a staple of scholarly activity since long before the advent of the computer and where, despite its reputation for textual conservatism, innovative academics have more consistently acted as the hub of activity for the inherently interdisciplinary work of computer-assisted writing analysis and assessment than anyplace else on campus. Additionally, many readers of this book will be members of English departments seeking to engage their colleagues in discussion about the meaning and implications of computer-assisted writing assessment. Such readers will be more able to talk with their colleagues, almost all of whom have a background in literature, if they are aware of the literary theories—theories of reading, as others may call them—that underlay response to and assessment of all texts.

NOTES FROM THE ENGLISH DEPARTMENT

When Lionel Trilling criticized V. L. Parrington in his 1948 essay "Reality in America," he did so in language that to proponents of computer-assisted writing assessment must now seem simultaneously validating and dismissive. Trilling notes cuttingly that Parrington's work is "notable for its generosity and enthusiasm but certainly not for its accuracy or originality" (1950, 15). To illustrate this criticism, Trilling complains that Parrington uses the word *romantic* "more frequently than one can count, and seldom with the same meaning, seldom with the sense that the word . . . is still full of complicated but not wholly pointless ideas, that it involves many contrary but definable things" (17). In this barrage of barbs, Trilling implies that accuracy, accountability, and stability are crucial characteristics of all good writing.

Further, Trilling here, as elsewhere, articulates the formalism that had come to dominate American literary criticism in the late 1940s and 1950s. Though based on older models of European formalism, this innovation in literary analysis was optimistically termed by American critics "the new criticism" because it eschewed such impressionistic matters as morality, biography, and reader emotion for intense study of texts as objects containing meanings to be discerned through detailed examination and close reading. Such reading, with particular attention to metaphor, irony, ambiguity, and structure, would reveal the deep meanings within the text and allow the critic to announce those meanings with a certain scientific accuracy based wholly on the words in the work of literature.[4] The few opponents of this approach complained that this dispassionate analysis was altogether too aesthetic and removed from the real and passionate world of literature and life, and that it rendered students passive before the all-knowing teacher who would unfold the meaning of a poem or a play as if solving a complicated puzzle that only initiates could work through. The charge of mere aestheticism, made fervently by Marxist and other critics with social concerns about the effects of literature, rings with particular irony now, as we look back to the new criticism as providing a kind of theoretical ground for computer assessment, an "explication de texte" also based on the belief that meaning—or at least value—resides wholly in the words and structure of a piece of writing.

Within twenty years after the publication of Trilling's essay, numerous articles had been published in the United States and Europe that treated literary texts as immutable objects available for semiscientific study; the characteristics that were projected onto the texts by a new breed of high-tech scholars—so designated because they eschewed the stereotype of the English professor by taking up computer programming and statistical analysis—were remarkably similar to the characteristics that Trilling and others had propagated a generation or two earlier. Rosanne Potter (1991), in her retrospective of the statistical analysis of literature, observes that early computer-using textual critics "took pride in discovering answers based on countable features in texts rather than on impressions" (402)—a phenomenon still quite apparent in the advertising literature for today's student essay evaluation software.[5] This pride came to its fullest fruition in 1968 when the Catholic University of Louvain opened its Centre de Traitement Electronique des Documents (CTED), an academically funded and staffed institution that had as its basic functions "developing automation in the field of the study of documents" and to act "as a training centre for the application of computing science to the human sciences" (Tombeur 1971, 335). By 1976, fueled by the early and ongoing successes of Ellis Page and the Centre de Traitement Electronique des Documents, early and encouraging developments in the field of artificial intelligence were potent enough to move prominent computational linguists Gerald Salton and Anita Wong (1976) to call for "a full theory of language understanding . . . which would account for the complete stated and implied content of the texts" (69). In other words, Salton and Wong, who were by no means alone, wanted an accurate linguistic model that could be superimposed by a computer, via a series of algorithms, over any given text to generate viable interpretations.

The post-structural theories of reading that have largely replaced formalism have done so by rejecting the narrowness and simplifications that restricted its reading of literature. Deconstruction, for instance, though fully committed to close reading of texts, emphasized the contradictions in them, the places where different meanings existed simultaneously, and replaced serious scientific analysis (or expanded on it) with new versions of reading as play and contest, both as a kind of insouciance (a book on Hegel opens with a chapter on eagles, or *aigles*, pronounced the same as Hegel in French) and as performance, in the sense that a musician "plays" and hence brings alive a musical composition. In fact, the performance of the critic virtually replaces the performance of the author: authors die so that readers may live, according to one summary of the approach. Reader-response criticism restores the reader's role in creating meaning from a text, rejecting the new criticism's axiom that criticism should discover the best reading in the text; in this approach, every reader is entitled to—indeed, must eventually come up with—his or own text, since every reader is different from all others. And new historical readers proposed that textual meanings were to be obtained by situating the text in its social and historical contexts. In short, the limits that the new criticism placed on the experience of reading a literary text—limits that allowed those critics to reveal hitherto hidden meanings and connections within the text—were seen by the 1970s as far too restrictive for the reading and study of literature. But it was those very limitations, restrictions, and mathematical facts that ultimately provided the definition of reading that the early proponents of computer "reading" could use as they began to experiment with machine encounters with texts.

Consider the opportunity for computational analysis unwittingly pointed out by Richard Chase, an intellectual descendant of Trilling and the other exponents of the new criticism. Chase (1957) fortified Trilling's largely successful attempts to cement together a definition of "Romance" in his book *The American Novel and Its Tradition*. Chase expeditiously decrees romance characters to be "probably rather two-dimensional types, [and they] will not be complexly related to each other or to society or to the past" (13). In radically simplifying the meaning of romance characters, Chase observed that they were isolated from any real relationship with culture, history, or humanity. To most lovers of literature, such a withering review would be a lighthouse, warning unsuspecting readers away from the treacherous rocks of bad writing. But for literary hackers searching for ways to decode a living language, the flat characterizations in second-rate romance novels could prove a perfect schoolroom for computers learning to read. And so too, it might be argued, could the often formulaic writings of students. At the same time, deconstructionists expanded the range of critical attention to such texts as advertising, popular culture, television sitcoms, and, inevitably, student writing. Such texts, of no interest whatever to the new critics, offered much simpler writing for analysis than the Keats odes or Shakespeare plays favored by the formalists, and so allowed relatively simplistic readings to appear as critical insights. Computer-assisted writing assessment experimenters could use these apparently more simple texts for machine analysis while maintaining the limited scientific approach to texts they inherited from the new critics. In this way, student writings came to be seen as a sort of proving ground for new reading and assessment algorithms, which could not approach the sophistication of aesthetic literary analysis. Nonetheless, computer-assisted writing assessment is a sophisticated project from a technical, if not an aesthetic, perspective and it is to some of these technicalities—and the researchers who pioneered them—that we now turn. In so doing, we hope to provide readers with a rough sketch of the principles and procedures upon which computer-assisted writing assessment began and upon which it continues to build, as well as to briefly characterize the historical and material conditions that provided the loam for this emerging bond among mathematicians, computer scientists, linguists, and writing teachers.

THE RESEARCHERS

Computer-assisted writing assessment is a subdiscipline of natural language processing, which is itself a subdiscipline of the field of artificial intelligence. The history of artificial intelligence research is a long and tragicomic one that involves a host of colorful characters, bitter enmities, stunning successes, humiliating failures, and more than a few hoaxes and practical jokes. Barring a look back at precomputer automata—chess-playing machines and mechanical fortune tellers, for instance—the field of artificial intelligence emerged and grew wildly during the cold war, from the 1940s through the 1980s. Natural language processing followed this same trajectory, though because of its more modest claims—and price tag—along the way, it did not suffer to quite the same extent that artificial intelligence research did when what is now commonly referred to as "AI Winter"—the period when federal funding for artificial intelligence (AI) projects was cut to a sliver of its former glory—hit in the 1980s.

During the cold war, there was a high premium on developing any and all technologies that could promote one side over the other; high-level military strategizing and force deployment occupied one set of artificial intelligence priorities, and natural language processing—in the form of universal language translation—was another. While these technologies did advance in important ways—pattern-recognition systems, neural networks, and the rudimentary translators found on the Web today are all fruits of this research—they never quite gave the return on investment promised by researchers.

With the collapse of the Soviet Union and the fall of the Berlin Wall, governmental urgency and the relatively lush funding that accompanied it for developing highly advanced technologies fell away, and researchers were left to find new sources of funding, a situation that forced many researchers to become entrepreneurs. Thus, researchers became complicit in the interests of business—namely profit generation—and turned their attention to practical problems such as data mining, the automated translation of business and technical documents, and evaluating student writing. This move from largely self-directed research within the context of the military-industrial complex to the business world also made researchers complicit with the interests of adopters, who were, after all, their sponsors' clients. The consequences of these complicities included a new research focus on analyzing the genre of the student essay (instead of literature and documents secured by intelligence agencies) and a focus on interface design (the front end).

Ellis Page's research, with its successful trajectory from the 1960s into the 1980s, then its virtual disappearance until the mid-1990s when his Project Essay Grade (PEG) reemerged as a commercial product, exemplifies the spectacular rise and fall of artificial intelligence and its subdisciplines. There were certainly many others—Terry Winnograd, Henry Slotnick, Patrick Finn—who exemplify this history and whose work had to be adapted or abandoned in the face of this sudden funding shift. But before we describe how the entrepreneurs leveraged this change to their advantage, we wish to offer here a brief sketch of how natural language processing works, that is, of the research that underlies today's commercial writing-assessment products. It is fitting to include this here because, as noted earlier, a detailed description of the processes of commercial computer-assisted writing assessment applications is impossible to provide, not only because they vary from one implementation to the next, but also because virtually all of the most popular systems are protected intellectual property. Shermis and Burstein (2003) acknowledge this fact in the introduction to *Automated Essay Scoring: A Cross-Disciplinary Perspective* and also observe that this fact causes problems when one sets out to describe the details of such systems: "[T]he explanations as to why [computer-assisted writing assessment] works well are only rudimentary, subject to 'trade secrets,' and may not correspond well to past research" (xiii). Shermis and Burstein's book demonstrates this problem unfortunately well; despite the book's status as "the first book to focus entirely on the subject" of computer-assisted writing assessment, only three of its thirteen essays contain detailed descriptions about how their computer assessment applications work (see Larkey and Croft 2003; Leacock and Chodorow 2003; Burstein and Marcu 2004).

In our view, the technical details of computer-assisted writing assessment are an important component of its history because the technical details are the primary site of struggle for all of the players in the computer-assisted writing assessment game. Without an understanding of how these systems work generally, the work of effectively assessing the systems and their advocates and critics requires one to forego any claim on situational knowledge and rely almost entirely on instinctual and anecdotal evidence. For this reason, we offer here a brief overview of how computer-assisted writing assessment systems work in general, drawing from a single but highly influential source: *Natural Language Information Processing: A Computer Grammar of English and Its Applications* by Naomi Sager (1981). Sager, currently a research professor at the Courant Institute of Mathematical Sciences of New York University, is recognized as one of the founders of the field of natural language processing. Although she published several important studies in the early 1960s, her 1981 book *Natural Language Information Processing* is now one of the field's canonical texts and is considered the first relatively complete accounting of English grammar in computer-readable form. While many advances have been made in the field since the 1980s, Sager's computer English grammar remains the keystone in numerous computational linguistics projects around the world.[6] Sager and her team of researchers developed the Linguistic String Program, an application designed to read and analyze scientific and technical articles. Several medical research institutions use the Linguistic String Program to track patterns in everything from articles in the *Journal of the American Medical Association* to physicians' daily reports.

One of the original aims of natural language processing projects such as Sager's was not to assess writing but rather to gather content information from it. Because computers are able to process enormous amounts of data very rapidly, natural language processing researchers hoped that by making an automated system that could "understand" language, they would simultaneously create a tool capable of retrieving any sort of information from any sort of text faster than even an expert in the field could. Projections for the future of natural language processing have long included systems able to read and evaluate vast quantities of literature in a particular field—say all the articles that have been published in the *Journal of Astrophysics*—and then establish connections between all the articles, perhaps even discovering what D. R. Swanson terms "undiscovered public knowledge" (7).[7] Another natural language processing project that has long been energetically researched is mechanical translation, the ability of a computer system to translate the prose of one language into the prose of another. And while it was Ellis Page's early work that is traditionally acknowledged as the starting point of the subdiscipline of computer-assisted writing assessment for the purposes of evaluating students, it was Sager's research that has led to some of today's most sophisticated natural language processing systems. The ubiquity of Sager's research in subsequent natural language processing projects from the 1980s forward suggests that at least some of that research lies at the heart of current proprietary student-writing assessment systems.

Sager's computer grammar of English is similar to the structure of transformational-generative grammar developed by—among others— Noam Chomsky. Sager and her team parsed out and coded hundreds of T- and PS-rules into their computer, depending on a single basic assumption about how natural language works, namely, that language is linear on the surface and this linearity is determined by grammar. Thus, if researchers could construct all the rules that dictate how "elements in well-formed sentences" may be combined, then in principle those rules may be translated into the artificial language of computers, thus enabling computers to understand natural languages like English, Cantonese, or Malayalam (Sager 1981, 4).

The way the Linguistic String Program, Sager's computerized grammar system, works can be briefly described as follows: first, the system identifies the "center sentence," or what we might call the basic sentence, as well as adjunct and nominalization strings (modifiers of one sort or another). It does this by proceeding one word at a time through the sentence from left to right. The Linguistic String Program applies the restrictions that are appropriate for it, as dictated in the lexicon, then it diagrams all possible syntactic forms and functions that term could be acting as; this diagram is called a "parse tree," and it is not unusual for the computer to generate numerous trees for each word. When the computer has finished making all the possible parse trees for one word, it moves on to the next word. Here the computer first generates all possible parse trees then compares this set of trees to the trees of the previous word(s). At this stage, the computer applies other restrictions that try to manage "local ambiguity," that is, semantically nonsensical but grammatical readings. By applying all these restrictions, the number of parse trees for each word is reduced. This process repeats until the program reaches an end mark, such as a period or question mark. At this point, the number of parse trees is usually very few, perhaps one or two for each word. A final set of restrictions is applied to the sentence, which determines its final "meaning." This process of generating hundreds, even thousands of parse trees per sentence is very computationally demanding, and in 1981 it was necessary to run the Linguistic String Program on a Control Data 6600 minicomputer—among the fastest machines available at that time—just to get the syntactic positions of each word sorted out in a reasonable amount of time.

Finally, the Linguistic String Program analyzes the whole set of parse trees for particular meanings that a human user has asked the program to look for. The computer does this analysis by using the semantic entries in a digital lexicon and by using more restrictions that help the computer determine context. For example, consider the word "pulse." During the previous stage, the lexicon would have told the program that "pulse" can be either a noun or a verb, and the program, upon analysis of the sentence "The nurse recorded the patient's pulse as 75/120," would have marked "pulse" as a noun. But the lexicon also indicates that the noun "pulse" can refer to something physiological or astronomical. Now the computer must use the advanced selection restrictions to look at all the words in the current or previous sentences for signs about which "pulse" is meant; in this example, terms like "patient" and "nurse" indicate that "pulse" is physiological, not astronomical. The Linguistic String Program was also programmed to recognize the use of back-reference terms like "this," "the foregoing," and "thus," which stand in place of ideas mentioned in previous sentences. The reference rules made the Linguistic String Program both more complicated and much more versatile and powerful than any previous language-analysis program, because back reference is an extremely common trope in formal and informal communication.

A few years after Sager's landmark work and a few years before Ellis Page returned to his development on Project Essay Grade (a return made significantly easier by the now-easy access to powerful desktop computers), Yaacov Choueka and Serge Lusignan (1985) set out to develop software that would automate "the process of disambiguation," that is, software that could determine context. When they had completed their program, they used it to analyze Lionel Groulx's *Journal de Jeunesse.* Groulx was an early-twentieth-century Quebecois historian and ardent nationalist. Rosanne Potter (1991) describes their process and results this way: "The text [Groulx's] consists of 215,000 types, 17,300 different forms; the simple step-by-step process started when 31 ambiguous words were chosen as a test set; of these 23 words (75%) have two different lemmatizations; seven (22%) have three, and one (3%) has four. . . . In 9 out of 10 cases, a two context is sufficient for disambiguation; even a one-context is sufficient in almost 8 out of 10 cases" (412).

George Landow, whose short story excerpt opened this chapter, never mentions the year in which "Jane Austen's Submission" takes place, but the response given by his fictional Evaluator program seems not much different from the actual response provided by Choueka and Lusignan's analysis program. Indeed, these responses do not differ markedly from the statistical outputs of current commercial applications such as e-rater, IntelliMetric, WritePlacer *Plus*, or the Intelligent Essay Assessor.

While there are numerous problems with Sager's (and others') natural language processing research—for example, their reliance on the examination, deconstruction, and reconstruction of "the well-formed sentence," and their exclusion of "colloquial or purely literary" usages of words (Potter 1991, 414; Landauer, Laham, and Foltz 2003, 108)—we have included this brief technical description only to give readers a sense of the basis upon which the rhetoric of the computer-assisted writing assessment discussion is founded. When writing assessment is reduced to tasks such as identifying "the relative frequencies of function words (expressed in words per million), [then] articles, pronouns, auxiliaries, prepositions, conjunctions, *wh-* words, [and] adverbs" become very important (Potter 1991, 412); their sheer number and the linguistic functions they serve become important in ways that seem startling to a human reader, for whom they tend to be more or less transparent. This importance has recently become marked by the proprietary ways in which such statistics are generated and processed, information that is increasingly kept under lock and key so as to protect the future revenues these algorithms might generate. Toward the end of Potter's retrospective, she suggests: "Each new generation of computing machines leads to increases in knowledge of linguistic regularities" (428). Similarly, Ellis Page, Dieter Paulus, Jakob Nielsen, and others have shown that each new generation of computing machines also leads to increases in knowledge about linguistic *irregularities*, a crucial element of writing-assessment software, from the simplest grammar-checker to the most sophisticated digital parser. It is the ability of researchers to corral and manage the regularities and irregularities of language, coordinated with the increasing demands on teachers and students alike and the defunding of artificial intelligence and natural language processing projects in the post cold war era, that paved the way for entrepreneurs to enter the picture and begin to turn writing assessment into a capital venture.

THE ENTREPRENEURS

Driving computer-assisted writing assessment's shift from federally funded to corporately funded research were entrepreneurs like Ellis Page, Jill Burstein, and Thomas Landauer (among others), and companies such as Educational Testing Service, Vantage Learning, Knowledge Analysis Technologies, Pearson Education, and Text Analysis International (TextAI). The dialectical shift their work represents is easily seen in the marketing materials they present, both in print and on the Web. Consider, for example, this blurb taken from TextAI's online corporate history: "Text Analysis International, Inc. (TextAI) was founded in 1998 to bring to market a new and pragmatic approach for analyzing electronic text. TextAI is a privately held software development company poised to take advantage of the surging demand for effective text analysis solutions with its groundbreaking VisualText technology. VisualText is the culmination of years of research and development in the field of natural language processing. The Company's products are based on software tools for developing accurate, robust, and extensible text analyzers" (2005).

Seeing a business opportunity in the abandoned work of government researchers, a raft of natural language processing entrepreneurs began writing business plans and designing practical applications and friendly interfaces to their (or their partners') complex work. The National Language Software Registry (2000) lists no fewer than 171 computer applications to analyze written text, for example, and lists dozens more in areas such as "spoken language understanding," "corpus analyzers," and "multimedia information extractors."

Ellis Page, traditionally recognized as the progenitor of computerized writing assessment with his 1966 Project Essay Grade, was a former high school teacher who saw computers as an opportunity to help struggling instructors: "Teachers in the humanities are often overworked and underpaid, harassed by mounting piles of student themes, or twinged with guilt over not assigning enough for a solid basis of student practice and feedback" (1968, 211). Page's work eventually became sponsored by the Educational Testing Service and the National Assessment of Educational Progress and has been proved to be both a reliable and valid way to assess certain aspects of student writing. We cannot speak to the differences between the current version and the 1966 form of Page's program, because, as we noted earlier, the code is proprietary. But the advertising is certainly more sophisticated. In Page's recent summary of PEG's migration to the World Wide Web, he notes with understandable satisfaction that, in addition to the system's high correlation to human judges, a separate study had assessed PEG itself as a "cost-effective means of grading essays of this type" (2003, 50).

Similarly, the developers of the Intelligent Essay Assessor (IEA) (Knowledge Analysis Technologies/Pearson Education) and e-rater (ETS Technologies, Inc.) have capitalized on the federal funding crash of natural language processing research and developed their own successful commercial ventures. IEAs users include several major textbook and test-creation companies (Holt, Rinehart, and Winston; Harcourt; Prentice Hall) as well as an increasing number of defense-related customers. Knowledge Analysis Technologies' former president, Thomas Landauer,[8] is also a professor at the University of Colorado Boulder, and he has been deeply involved in computational linguistics for more than thirty years. The recent purchase of Knowledge Analysis Technologies (KAT) by Pearson Education (billed as "the largest education company in the world") promises to fund KAT's particular stripe of computer-assisted writing assessment for years to come, and is, says Landauer, "a dream come true for KAT. The founder's vision was to bring the enormous educational potential of our unique text-understanding technologies to the service of educators and students worldwide. The technology is now mature. The market is now ready. With the vast and varied strengths of Pearson Education and the other Pearson companies joined in the effort we now feel certain of success" (2005). KAT has found a lucrative niche that allows its research in the field of computer-assisted writing assessment to continue, albeit in directions probably unimagined in Landauer's early days.

Jill Burstein, codirector of research for Educational Testing Service's subdivision ETS Technologies, is another former English composition teacher. Unlike Page and Landauer, however, Burstein comes from a new generation of scholar/entrepreneurs, one in which the corporate context of natural language processing research is assumed. ETS has, of course, a very long history in writing assessment, dating back to the 1940s and 1950s. Despite this long history, however, it was not until the late 1990s—just like its competitors—that ETS fully committed to computer-assisted writing assessment by adopting e-rater "for operational scoring of the GMAT Analytical Writing Assessment" (Burstein 2003, 113). Due to falling computer costs and the rising expense of doing large-scale writing assessment with human labor alone, ETS began to invest in researchers like Burstein to find a way to cut costs and maximize profit. In a 2001 GRE Professional Board Report, Burstein and several of her colleagues acknowledge this fact: "One hope for reducing the cost of essay scoring comes from longstanding efforts to develop computer programs that can, by modeling trained essay readers, evaluate essays automatically" (Powers et al. 2001, 1). The dialectic of computer-assisted writing assessment evolves at ETS in the same ways it does at Vantage Learning and Knowledge Analysis Technologies: rather than being driven by cold war politics and ideologies, marketability, usability, and profitability become the watchwords guiding research as well as funding its advancements and deployments in the public and private sectors.

Entrepreneurs, whether they are also researchers or are only funding the researchers, see the market potential for essay-assessment software and fill the void left by the National Science Foundation and other federal funding agencies. This reinvigoration of natural language processing research gives many scholars both some new liberties and some new constraints: there is money to pursue the sometimes highly abstract work of computational linguistics, but the upshot of this work must always be a significant return on investment. One practical consequence of this has been that unlike in other more academy-exclusive types of research, researchers doing corporately funded computer-assisted writing assessment must attend to the feedback given them by the adopters of the technologies they've developed. And because it is these adopters whose money ultimately funds their research, entrepreneurs are required to develop front ends and sets of documentation that make their systems "friendly"—that is, easy to use, cheap relative to some other assessment mechanism (such as human labor), and accurate according to some explicable standard—to both the adopters (who administer the assessments) and the users (whose work is assessed).

The language of the entrepreneurs' promotional materials suggests these constraints quite baldly through their easy-to-understand claims about validity, reliability, affordability, and accessibility. The consequences of the complicities among researchers and entrepreneurs are that (1) computer-assisted writing assessment and natural language processing research is channeled toward commodifiable ends (which may not be optimal from a research perspective); (2) the product is sold as a proven, rather than an experimental, technology; and (3) the assessment results (i.e., the results of the computer algorithms) must mimic human graders and appease the expectations of users rather than aim toward real interpretive complexity. In the last two sections of this chapter, we raise some of the issues these complicities catalyze with the adopters of computer-assisted writing-assessment systems—that is, university and other institutional administrators—as well as for the people whose work is assessed by applications like e-rater and the Intelligent Essay Assessor.

THE ADOPTERS

Some teachers and administrators turn reflexively to technological solutions when funding for human labor is in crisis, as has been the case for education at all levels in recent years. They gain support from those who turn to technological solutions for other reasons, such as a genuine interest in new methodologies as well as the novelty and "coolness" factors they bring. In the majority of cases, however, educators ready to adopt computer-assisted writing assessment see it in terms of cost-effectiveness, efficiency, and perhaps in certain cases "customer satisfaction" (though this seems like an imposition of entrepreneurial rhetoric). The adopters' interests are complicit with those of researchers in that adopters need reassurance that they're getting what they pay for, that is, valid and reliable results (hence all the white papers on entrepreneurial Web sites). The adopters' interests are complicit with those of entrepreneurs in that adopters need effective solutions to labor and funding shortages and probably, in some cases, need lower-cost alternatives to continued levels of funding (i.e., the "downsizing" model). And adopters are complicit with the interests of users in that as education itself is increasingly commodified, students (and their parents) want evidence that their money is being well spent (or at least is not being wasted). Since a considerable amount of school funding is now tied to standardized tests and to the pressures of the job market, adopters and users share an interest in meeting those expectations by the most efficient and economical means possible. The consequences of these complicities may include a forfeiture of institutional control over writing assessment, a heightened sense of responsibility to users, who are suddenly subject to assessments delivered by a somewhat suspect source, and a decreased labor pool (which may temporarily reduce institutional pressure and minimize, for instance, the possibility of labor organizing or other mass-protest actions).

As this book goes to press, we can see these complicities at work in the introduction of written portions to the two tests taken by almost all applicants to American four-year colleges and universities: the SAT and the ACT. Both of these tests included short essay portions for the first time in 2005, with scores intended for use in the postsecondary admissions process. A perhaps unintended side effect is that the scores produced by these tests (mandatory for the SAT; optional for the ACT) are replacing local tests designed for placement of students into various levels of first-year writing courses. Since the "writing" scores (derived from a combination of multiple-choice items, contributing three-quarters of the score, and a brief impromptu essay) are paid for by the student and are claimed to be valid, the expense and trouble of local testing seems unnecessary. That a single test can serve all students in all colleges for placement into all writing programs seems improbable, even with human scorers reading the essays. And although neither Pearson Education nor the American College Testing Service have declared that they will use computer-assisted writing-assessment technologies, and while both are actively recruiting human readers, it seems obvious that computer-assisted writing assessment will be pressed into service sooner or later (probably sooner) for the two million or so essays that their companies will need to score.

The adopters will be colleges and universities eager to have information on student writing abilities for admission deliberations and willing to abandon their own placement procedures—designed for their own students and their own programs—for a one-size-fits-all test of (at least to some) dubious validity. The entrepreneurs of the two large testing firms will be promoting the convenience and cost savings of the new tests, while the writing program administrators and the faculty will be raising questions about the cost-effectiveness of scores that may not relate to a particular campus writing program or its particular student profile. The entrepreneurs will tout the savings to adopters, because the scores will be delivered to the campus at no cost to the institution (though the students will pay and the testing services will make large profits), and we suspect that the faculty and the users will not have much of a voice in the final assessments or admissions decisions.

THE USERS

Students are the users whose writing is assessed and whose lives are affected by the results of these assessments. Their main interest, presumably, is to become better writers or at least to perform sufficiently well on their tests and in their classes to achieve the level of success they desire. Their interests are complicit, then, with the researchers through their desire to have their writing evaluated in a manner consistent with the expectations of the test writers or assignment givers. Users' interests are complicit with the entrepreneurs in that they need the costs of education to remain reasonable and under certain circumstances might be willing to sacrifice a certain amount of validity for a decrease in educational costs—as long as it doesn't cut into the bottom line of successful testing. Finally, users' interests are complicit with those of adopters in that users recognize their dependence on the success of adopters and also recognize the obligation that adopters owe to them; these recognitions mean that users must both cooperate with and correct adopters' decisions—this is an integral part of the feedback process. The consequences of these complicities may include low user resistance to ineffective computer-assisted writing assessment, an inability to effectively assess computer-assisted writing assessment itself (and thereby effectively participate in the feedback process), and a sense that writing—as with Landow's Jane Austen—is not the art of saying something well but rather of saying something new using a set of preexisting rules.

CONCLUSION

The history of computer-assisted writing assessment, viewed dialectically, shows how there are a variety of sometimes contesting but always complicit interests that have shaped the direction of the discipline. These interested complicities are still at work, and writing teachers need to adopt a model of praxis—a process of critical (including self-critical) reflection and informed practice toward just ends—as they pursue their interests concerning computer-assisted writing assessment. This means that all complicit parties, but most particularly the faculty (which ultimately owns the curriculum), need to be aware of the history and profundity of the issues behind computer-assisted writing assessment. Those in the humanities should become informed of the ways literary formalism has laid the theoretical ground for computer-assisted writing assessment and also begin to understand the sophistication and complexity of modern computer-assisted writing-assessment algorithms. The time has passed for easy dismissal of (and easy jokes about) computer-assisted writing assessment; the time has come for reasoned and critical examinations of it. For instance, the questions about the validity of the SAT and ACT writing tests will not go away if, or when, the student essays are scored by computer. It will be up to humanists to demand or institute studies on their own campuses to answer these questions. At the same time, some local writing assessments may be so unreliable that computer scoring may have a role to play in improving them. If humanists do not take this step of critique, painful as it may be for many, they will be sent out of the room when serious discussion gets under way between the entrepreneurs and the adopters. If we fail to imagine the application of computer-assisted writing assessment to radically improve education, we may simply forfeit computer-assisted writing assessment to those who prioritize lucre above literacy.

2

THE MEANING OF MEANING
Is a Paragraph More than an Equation?

Patricia Freitag Ericsson

Several chapters in this collection allude to or deal briefly with issues of "meaning" in the controversy about the machine scoring of essays. This chapter's intent is to explore extensively the "meaning of meaning," arguing that, although they may appear to be esoteric, considerations of "meaning" are central to the controversy about the machine scoring of student essays and important to include as we make arguments about it. Foregrounding of the "meaning of meaning" in this chapter establishes a foundation for other chapters that may allude to the importance of meaning in the machine-scoring controversy. Discussion in this chapter can also serve as a vital, integral part of the argument when machine scoring is being considered.

The meaning of meaning is critical when advertisements of machine-scoring products make claims that their products actually can ascertain meaning. Although Knowledge Analysis Technologies' Web-based advertisements for the Intelligent Essay Assessor have recently been revised, in May 2003 their Web site proudly proclaimed that they were providing "[m]achine-learning technology that understands the meaning of text." This provocative claim has now been moved to a less prominent place in the site. In its place is the claim that the Intelligent Essay Assessor operates based on a "machine-learning algorithm that accurately mimics human understanding of language" (2004a). Although this claim may be less shocking, the contention that a machine "mimics human understanding of language" is fallacious and misleading.

IntelliMetric, another popular machine-scoring program, is similarly promoted. The August 2004 Vantage Learning Web site defines IntelliMetric as an "intelligent scoring system that relies on artificial intelligence to emulate the process carried out by expert human scorers" and describes the five main features of writing that IntelliMetric is purportedly capable of determining. One of these is "Focus and Meaning," which is described as "cohesiveness and consistency in purpose and main idea; maintaining a single point of view" (2005a). If these are the elements of "meaning," then meaning is indeed a very simple concept.

Conceptions of meaning articulated in publications about these scoring machines are as troublesome as their Web-based advertising. For example, Thomas Landauer, the chief researcher and founder of the company that sells the Intelligent Essay Assessor, claims: "The fundamental idea is to think of a paragraph as an equation: its meaning equals a combination of the meanings of its words. Then the thousands of paragraphs in a textbook are just a huge set of simultaneous equations." Intelligent Essay Assessor is based primarily on an algorithm that equates meaning to "*meaning of word$_1$ + meaning of word$_2$ + . . . + meaning of word$_n$ = meaning of passage*," working on "the basic assumption . . . that the meaning of a passage is contained in its words" (Landauer, Laham, and Foltz 2003, 88). Although Landauer and his associates do admit that this conception "is by no means a complete model of linguistic meaning," they still believe that "for practical purposes" this kind of analysis "simulates human judgments and behavior" adequately (or in their words, "quite well") (89).

Vantage Learning guards the inner workings of its scoring machines closely. Almost every publication by Vantage Technologies describes Intellimetric as a system that depends on the "proprietary" technologies of "CogniSearch" and "Quantum Reasoning." Researchers interested in finding out more about these technologies hit a dead end. Impressive-sounding names and volumes of research conducted exclusively by Vantage Learning are the only assurances that anyone has about Intellimetric. Independent researchers cannot replicate this research or verify Vantage's claims, since the technologies used are not available to anyone else. (Edmund Jones's chapter 6 in this volume provides insights into how Intellimetric works, despite having no access to the actual algorithms used in the program.) Scott Elliot of Vantage Learning says that Intellimetric is based on a "blend of artificial intelligence (AI), natural language processing and statistical technologies" and claims that through this blend of technologies the program "internalizes the pooled wisdom of many expert scorers" (2003, 71).[1] Besides this gloss of what technologies are behind the interface and the unsupported claim that the program is wise, very little about the actual workings of Intellimetric can be found. Since Vantage Learning's promotional material defines "focus and meaning" as "cohesiveness and consistency in purpose and main idea; maintaining a single point of view," we must assume that their understanding of meaning is somehow encompassed in those fourteen words and that their technologies depend on this simplistic definition.

WHY DO WE TEACH STUDENTS TO COMPOSE?

Considering the meaning of meaning is vitally important not only because some machine-scoring promoters advertise their products as able to ascertain meaning, but also because most people believe that conveying meaning is the most important goal of the written word. During discussions of the machine scoring of writing, participants must carefully consider why we ask students to compose essays and what we expect them to gain from knowing how to compose such texts. To begin this consideration of meaning and composing, the work of Ann E. Berthoff in *The Making of Meaning* is particularly helpful. In this 1981 volume, Berthoff argues for a theory of composing as a meaning-making activity, not just composing for the purpose of regurgitating specific content-knowledge information in a predetermined form. She emphasizes the need for composing as a process fueled by imagination consisting of "abstraction, symbolization, selection, 'purposing'" (4). This process "requires or enables us to coordinate and subordinate, to amalgamate, discard, and expand; it is our means of giving shape to content" (4–5). In this kind of composing process, learners are discovering, interpreting, and coming to know—they are making meaning. Later in the same book, Berthoff argues that if we teach composition "by arbitrarily setting topics and then concentrating on the mechanics of expression and the conventions governing correct usage," our students cannot learn to write competently (19). Composing, Berthoff says, works in "contradistinction to filling in the slots of a drill sheet or a preformed outline—[composing] is a means of discovering what we want to say, as well as being the saying of it " (20). Unfortunately, using computers to evaluate and score student compositions does exactly what Berthoff claims will not teach students to write competently. When composing for a machine, students are given arbitrary topics and are judged by a machine that concentrates on mechanics and conventions, plus the addition of a few important content words—not content ideas.

Although Berthoff's understanding of composing is decades old, it still underlies the "best-practice" models in composition theory and practice. Writing in 1998, Sharon Crowley asserts that composition "focuses on the process of learning rather than the acquisition of knowledge" (3). This focus continues Berthoff's emphasis on composition as a project of discovery and meaning making rather than a project of repeating facts and figures. Composition, Crowley maintains, "encourages collaboration" and "emphasizes the historical, political, and social contexts and practices associated with composing rather than concentrating on texts as isolated artifacts." Again, computer scoring of student compositions has nothing to do with collaboration and everything to do with texts solely as "isolated artifacts."

THE MEANING OF MEANING

If we agree that we teach students to compose so that they can make sense of isolated facts and figures, so that they can make meaning, and so that they understand the social nature of meaning making and convey meaning to others, we are obligated to consider the meaning of meaning. Even though machine-scoring promoters tout their programs as being able to discern meaning, the scholarly areas they depend on have little truck with the meaning of meaning. In the introduction to their 2003 book *Automated Essay Scoring: A Cross-Disciplinary Perspective*, Mark Shermis and Jill Burstein claim that perspectives on machine scoring should come from "writing teachers, test developers, cognitive psychologists, psychometricians, and computer scientists" (xv).[2] Although I strongly agree that writing teachers should be involved in discussions about machine scoring, I must protest the way Shermis and Burstein include this perspective in their book. The only chapter in the book that acknowledges a teacher's perspective is written by a person who has led the National Council of Teachers of English but is decades removed from teaching or researching writing. He can hardly be considered a "writing teacher." The others areas listed by Shermis and Burstein—test developers, cognitive psychologists, psychometricians, and computer scientists—are less concerned with what is at the core of writing—making meaning.

Which other "perspectives" need to be considered if making meaning is central to what writing and composing is all about? I would argue that we need to include writing teachers (real teachers in the trenches, not figureheads), composition scholars, rhetoricians, linguists, philosophers, and a host of others in such an inquiry. To remedy the shortcomings of depending only on Shermis and Berstein's limited list, I begin with Ann Berthoff, whose understanding of writing as a meaning-making project underpins this chapter. While she was writing *The Making of Meaning*, Berthoff was an in-the-trenches writing teacher as well as a scholar (which qualifies her in Shermis and Berstein's view as well as mine). Since she defines composing as a meaning-making project, Berthoff is obligated to explore what the term "meaning making" entails. She argues that "meanings are not things, and finding them is not like going on an Easter egg hunt. *Meanings are relationships: they are unstable, shifting, dynamic; they do not stay still nor can we prove the authenticity or the validity of one or another meaning that we find*" (1981, 42; emphasis added). Berthoff warns composition teachers and others of the danger of conflating the terms *meaning* and *information*. Citing support from engineers and logicians, she argues that "*information* has nothing to do with *meaning*" and bemoans the fact that the word "information" is regularly and erroneously "used as a synonym for meaning." She urges readers to resist this conflation, arguing, "We should continually be defining the meaning of meaning, but instead we consider that there is no need since we are using a scientific term" (53).

Many machine-scoring programs, according to ETS's Jill Burstein, treat student compositions like a "bag of words" and go on a virtual Easter egg hunt to find the right words (Phelan 2003). These programs treat essays as pure information that can be mined for some abstracted set of words that, at least to their promoters, equates to meaning. The shifting, dynamic relationships that these words have to each other, to society, and to different readers is invisible to these information-seeking machines. The machines can tell users whether writers have matched the words in an essay with words in a database (or a triangulated database matrix), but they cannot assess whether this mix of words conveys any meaning.[3]

In 1988 Berthoff argued that ideas can be flattened so that any "generative power" they might have had is lost. Words fed into a scoring machine are flattened this way, stripped of their generative power; thus the possibility for "interaction" with ideas is reduced to only "transaction." A machine that equates meaning to a combination of *word* + *word* + *word* reduces the reader/word relationship to a one-dimensional "stimulus-response" connection. The machine responds to the stimuli of words, not concepts or ideas. The machine responds with limited experience—only that experience the programmers have been able to feed it. The machine has no understanding, no sense of the concepts and ideas that underlie the words, no ability to bring to the words what Berthoff claims is important in discerning meaning, "what we [humans] presuppose and analyze and conjecture and conclude"—all of this adding up to a human sense of what a text might mean (p. 43).

Considering the meaning of meaning is not a newfound intellectual pursuit, especially in philosophical circles. We have access to thousands of years of consideration of the meaning of meaning—dating at least from 360 BCE and the Platonic Dialogues. In *Theaetetus*, Socrates asks

Theaetetus (a young aristocrat) to define the meaning of the term *knowledge*, claiming (in his inimitable Socratic way) that the meaning of this term was something he could never solve to his satisfaction. Theaetetus takes the bait, answers, and (to his credit) states that if he is incorrect, he knows Socrates will correct him. Thereupon, Socrates and Theaetetus embark on a classic Socratic adventure that considers not only the meaning of knowledge but considerations of perception, true and false beliefs, the mutability of knowledge, and the meaning of meaning. In this dialogue, Socrates asks, "How can a man understand the name of anything, when he does not know the nature of it?" Later he states, "[N]othing is self-existent." Certainly Socrates would agree that a word or collection of words has no meaning without some knowledge of the nature of the social, historical, and political context within which those words are being used.

Fast-forwarding nearly 2,300 years (and countless considerations of meaning during those centuries) we find rhetorician I. A. Richards and linguist C. K. Ogden studying the meaning of meaning in a 1923 book aptly titled *The Meaning of Meaning*. In this book, Richards and Ogden explore misconceptions about meaning and coin the term "proper meaning superstition," which is the mistaken idea that every word has a precise, correct meaning. They argue convincingly that different words mean different things to different people in different situations. Computer-scoring enthusiasts fail to comprehend what Richards and Ogden understand about meaning: "Meaning does not reside in the words or signs themselves; to believe that it does is to fall victim to the 'proper meaning superstition,' the belief that words have inherent meaning" (Bizell and Herzberg 1990, 964). Richards and Ogden argued (in 1923) that "everyone now knows" that words "'mean' nothing by themselves," although that belief was once "universal" (968). Unfortunately, their proclamation was premature. The belief that words have meaning on their own still holds sway with many, as evidenced by the public claims of the machine-scoring industry. That industry ignores scholarly considerations like those of Richards, who in 1936 claimed that "the stability of the meaning of a word comes from the constancy of the context that gives it its meaning" (11).

Philosopher Mihailo Markovic's 1961 volume on meaning, *Dialectical Theory of Meaning*, illustrates just how complex meaning is. In part 3 of this book, Markovic offers four possible general definitions of meaning. Definition A is particularly appropriate to concerns in this chapter. "When a group of conscious beings, witnessing the appearance of a material object, is disposed to think of an object (or an experience any other mental state whose external correlate is an object), and that thought (experience) may be expressed objectively using some means which all the members of the given social group can understand and use, we may say that in that case that the given material object is a sign and it has a definite meaning" (363).

Markovic limits meaning to "conscious beings" and deliberately adds the "social group" to the definition, thus making any claim that a computer could discern or understand meaning highly questionable. Although the goal of artificial intelligence might be the creation of a sentient machine, few (if any) honest experts in that field would claim that this goal has been reached. Despite fictional presentations in futuristic books and movies, the idea of an artificial-intelligence machine being part of a social group is hardly in the realistic future. Some machine-scoring companies may claim that they are simulating an artificial sort of social group when they feed volumes of words on a topic into a computer, but the database of words created this way is a far cry from even the most broadly construed definition of a "social group." It takes a huge leap to imagine that a machine fed word after word after word would have any relationship to a real social group made up of conscious beings who have experienced the word with their senses. Markovic's succinct claim that "social, practical meaning is greatly dependent on context" (1961, 365) is worth committing to memory as we carry on the debates about meaning and machine scoring.

Because of his background in both science and language studies, Jay Lemke's (1995) perspectives on meaning are particularly appropriate for consideration. Lemke earned a Ph.D. in theoretical physics in 1973 but turned to linguistics, semiotics, and language studies in the 1980s to help him better understand the teaching of science. He argues that the meanings of words, phrases, sentences, paragraphs, and bigger chunks of texts are all dependent on context and that the meanings of these parts change from one social situation to another. In an idea that has Socratic echoes, Lemke argues that "[l]anguage does not operate in isolation"; it is part of the "whole 'dance' of meaning-making (a dance that always assumes a partner, that always helps to create one)" (8).[4] In what could be taken as a caution to the computer-scoring enthusiasts, Lemke counsels, "We are not likely to understand the role of language in our culture or in our society if we divorce it from its material origins or from its integration into larger systems of resources for making meaning." He argues that "all meanings are made within communities" and that "analysis of meaning should not be separated from the social, historical, cultural and political dimensions of these communities" (9).

THE CONSTRUCTION OF MEANING IN DISCOURSE COMMUNITIES

In addition to his perspectives on meaning, Lemke's work can help us understand the complications and disjunctions created when different research and language communities meet. According to Lemke, scientific discourse is built on the "language of truth" (an objective view, usually based on numerical proofs). Lemke argues that scientific discourse's power is "the power to compel belief in the truth of what they [scientists] are saying" (1995, 178). When other discourse communities (like the linguistic or the rhetorical) try to advance their ways of thinking—ways of thinking that "include elements of the language of feeling or of the language of action and values," ways of thinking that "argue from values or the implications of propositions for action and social consequences"—they are discounted as being nonscientific, beyond proof as *true*, and therefore not believable. In the machine-scoring world, the scientific discourse community depends on a limited, numbers-based meaning of meaning that holds currency for some in the general public. However, other discourse communities, those that do not rely on a numbers-based meaning of meaning, hold compelling views that must be brought into the discussion as a counterbalance.

As an example of this counterbalance, we can contrast information theory with semiotics. The approach to scoring student essays used by the scoring machines is based largely on an information theory that "looks for the common denominator in all forms of information and quantifies information in common units." In contrast, language studies (especially semiotics) looks at "the significant ways in which units that carry information differ from one another" (Lemke 1995, 170). This remarkably different way of looking at information (in this case the information in a student essay) at least partially explains the problems that ensue when information theory is used as a basis for finding meaning in a text. The differences between an information theory approach that tries to determine "the amount of information that a text could contain" is remarkably different from a linguistic, semiotic, or social constructionist theory that is interested in discovering "the possible meanings that a text could have in a community."

Literacy theory is also valuable in helping us bring the views of a different discourse community into discussions about machine scoring and the meaning of meaning. Drawing on the work of James Gee, literacy scholars Colin Lankshear and Michele Knobel (2003) offer more on the community or sociocultural perspective. In contrast to an information or artificial intelligence perspective, the sociocultural perspective holds that it is "impossible to separate out from text-mediated social practices the 'bits' concerned with reading or writing (or any other sense of the 'literacy') and to treat them independently of all the 'non-print' bits." The non-print bits, which may include "values and gestures, context and meaning, actions and objects, talk and interaction, tools and spaces," are "non-subtractable parts of integrated wholes." In a sociocultural perspective, meaning cannot exist in isolation from the social and cultural milieu in which those meanings are made. Lankshear and Knobel argue that "if, in some trivial sense they [literacy bits] *can* be said to exist (e.g. as code), they do not *mean* anything" (8).

Machine-scoring programs "see" student essays as code. They take students' words, sentences, and paragraphs out of their social/cultural contexts, process them as meaningless "bits" or tiny fragments of the mosaic of meaning, and claim to have "read" these essays for meaning. They claim to be able to "mimic" the way a human reader would read them. And they base these claims on uninformed, possibly fraudulent, understandings of meaning. If we bring a broad spectrum of discourse communities into discussions about the machine scoring of student essays, perhaps we can insist that the machine-scoring industry account for the severely limited capabilities of their programs. Perhaps we can even convince them (since the industry is peopled by highly educated, and hopefully educable, researchers) of what we know about students' communication needs and of the serious disservice they are doing to students with their limited understanding of why we teach students to write and how students become better writers.

IF WRITING IS MORE THAN *WORD* + *WORD* + *WORD,* THEN WHAT?

The machine-scoring industry is misleading the public with untenable claims about what their machines can do—claims that state these machines can evaluate student writing and even help students become better writers. If we agree that we teach students to write so that they can make and communicate meaning, we need to promote an appropriate understanding of both those goals and thereby undermine the claims made by the industry. In their 2000 book, *Multiliteracies: Literacy Learning and the Design of Social Futures,* Bill Cope, a communication and culture scholar, and Mary Kalantzis, an education and language scholar, argue that students need to be taught how to be successful communicators in a world that is marked by "local diversity" and "global connectedness" (14). This world is not one that can be virtually simulated by a computer program. Cope and Kalantzis contend that "the most important skill students need to learn is to negotiate regional, ethnic, or class-based dialects; variations in register that occur according to social context; hybrid cross-cultural discourses; the code switching often to be found within a text among different languages, dialects, or registers; different visual and iconic meanings; and variations in the gestural relationship among people, language and material objects."

For Cope and Kalantzis, language is a "dynamic representation resource" that is continually remade by writers and speakers as they endeavor to accomplish their goals in various cultural projects (2000, 5). Students who write to and for machines will not develop any sense of the dynamics of language; they will not acquire an understanding of diverse audiences and the need to adapt to those audiences; and, like those who program and promote machine scoring, they will be oblivious to and uninformed about the meaning of meaning.

Assuming that we agree with composition scholars, rhetoricians, linguists, philosophers, literacy scholars, and others that writing is a process of learning, that it is about making meaning rather than spitting out a series of facts and figures, that it is about analyzing, integrating, and understanding historical, political, and social contexts in which we are located, then we need to challenge machine scoring on these counts. Machine-scoring machines "see" texts as isolated artifacts. These machines cannot understand texts as social instruments, as organic entities that work to help writers and readers make sense of social and political environments. If composition is about making meaning—for both the writer and the reader—then scoring machines are deadly. Writing for an asocial machine that "understands" a text only as an equation of *word* + *word* + *word* strikes a death blow to the understanding of writing and composing as a meaning-making activity. Students who learn to write for these machines will see writing and composing as a process of getting the right words in the "bag of words" without a concern for a human audience or any legitimate communicative purpose. Students deserve better than this dumbed-down version of writing and composing. We need to take responsibility for getting them what they deserve.

3

CAN'T TOUCH THIS
Reflections on the Servitude of Computers as Readers

Chris M. Anson

> *Yo! I told you*
> *U can't touch this*
> *Why you standing there, man?*
> *U can't touch this*
> *Yo, sound the bells, school is in, sucker*
> *U can't touch this*
>
> —M. C. Hammer, "Can't Touch This" (1990)

Consider, for a moment, what's going on. First, you're in a multidimensional context where you and I, and this text, share a presence, a purpose, and knowledge that delimit the interpretive possibilities and let you begin fitting into boxes what little you've seen so far, or maybe shaping a box *around* it: academic genre, essay in a book, trusted editors, a focus on machines as readers, the common use of an opening quotation (lyrics, or a poem, or a proverb, or a line of text from a famous work). This one's in a vernacular. Does its style provide the meaning you'll eventually construct as you read, or is there something important about the direct-address question? Or school bells? Or is it about M. C. Hammer—a rapper launching a most un-rap-like text?

Curious, you move on, absorbing each new bit information, activating memory and prior experience to make something more of this than random words or the mutterings of the mad. After all, the text is validated by its context; it's been what Pratt (1977) calls "preselected." And just then—that reference, with its scholarly-looking date, adds a soupçon of authority. *Soupçon*. A bit of high-minded lexis. Will there be a thesis? Possibly. Is it emerging here, toward the end of the second paragraph? Doubtful; it wasn't at the end of the first. But there is a *cumulative* sense of direction and purpose—the text is adding up to something, and you move on to test various hypotheses as you automatically forgive the intentional sentence fragments. Meanwhile, that old reflective turn, *metacognition*, has been disturbed and awoken from its usual reading slumber: the text is calling attention to your relationship with it and making you think, *what's going on here?*

In reading and interpreting the lyrics and introduction to this point, you have employed a dazzling array of conscious and tacit, cognitive and social, discursive and structural, temporal and historical, linguistic and intertextual knowledge, tangled and interdependent. If you're a machine, our condolences: you'll need far more than a latent semantic analysis program to say anything of *significance* about the text—to interact with it, to converse with yourself through it. Alas, more information alone won't help: even if your data bank boasts a domain that includes M. C. Hammer, what in cyberspace will you do with the reference except spit out a response that there is no relationship between the chunk of his song—no doubt already flagged as "poor" on the grammar and sentence pattern scale—and the rest of the text? And what about the possibility of irony, of self-consciousness?

This essay argues that the processes humans use to read, interpret, and evaluate text can't be replicated by a computer—not now, and not until long after the written ideas of the current generation of learners and teachers are bits of archaic-sounding print losing their magnetic resonance on the disks and drives of antiquity. Machines are incapable of reading natural discourse with anything like the complexity that humans read it. This assertion—though obvious to all but the most impassioned believers that Hal is just on the horizon—suggests several important consequences for the push to create machine-scoring systems for writing, among them the relegation of meaning, audience, and rhetorical purpose to the trash icon of human literacy. In an unexpected turn of direction befuddling the coherence parameters of anything but a human reader, I'll then argue *for* the continued exploration of digital technologies both to analyze human prose and possibly to provide formative information that might be useful to developing writers. Unlike the use of computer technology to make judgments on writing for purposes of ranking, sorting, or placing students, such applications are neither premature nor of questionable value for the future of composition in general and reading, responding to, and evaluating student writing in particular.

AI: WHAT WE LEARN FROM ITS BRILLIANT FAILURES

A number of goals have been proposed for the development of machine-scoring systems that can "read" essays produced by humans and analyze, rate, or evaluate the essays. The results could be used, for

example, to provide information about applicants for positions requiring some degree of writing ability, to place students into writing or
other courses appropriate to their skill level, or to yield one of a number of indices that can decide whether a student should be accepted
to a particular college or university or should pass from one level to
the next in elementary and secondary education. The allure of such
programs is obvious: computers could scan and evaluate an unlimited
number of brief texts written by novice writers and provide the same
results as human readers but with greater consistency and much greater
efficiency. So optimistic are the advocates of some machine-scoring programs that they even flirt with anthropomorphic descriptions of these
programs' capacities. Streeter et al. (2002), for example, assert that the
Intelligent Essay Assessor "*understands* the meaning of written essays" (1;
emphasis added). If such a claim were true, there would be no further
need for teachers to read and respond to student writing—ever. In place
of human readers, machines could understand texts in dozens of different settings. The government could rate entire school systems on the
basis of machine-scored performances and allocate funding accordingly.
Computers might even be able to read the transcripts of court hearings
and reach verdicts that would determine the fate of human defendants,
and do so without all the usual interpretation, discussion, and negotiation—all those messy subjectivities to which humans are prone.

But before we can speculate about such applications (or horrors), we
need to explore what is meant by the capacity to "understand." What is
involved in understanding written text? What are some of the processes
humans use to do so, and does it seem likely that computers could be
programmed to replicate those processes? Some answers to these questions can be found in the pioneering work of artificial intelligence (AI)
and natural language, whose cycles of failures and successes did much
to illuminate human language and reveal some of its astonishing complexity.

The development of AI in natural language has focused on different but related goals: to simulate the human *production* of language
and to simulate the human *comprehension*—or, more commonly termed,
"processing"—of text (see Wagman 1998). Throughout the 1970s, as
burgeoning technologies inspired new speculation and experiments, AI
experts investigated whether computers could do anything meaningful
with "natural language," the text produced and interpreted by human
beings in the course of daily life. In a series of fascinating explorations
at the Yale Artificial Intelligence Laboratories, Roger Schank and his

colleagues and students set out to simulate the processes of both human language production and interpretation. As Schank (1984) articulated it, the goal of getting computers to begin "understanding" language was as much about coming to a fuller description of what humans do when we make and use language: "If we can program [a computer] to understand English and to respond to sentences and stories with the kind of logical conclusions and inferences an average human would make, this would be quite an achievement. But before we even tackle such a problem we will have to learn how humans understand such sentences and form their responses to them. What is language and how do humans use it? What does it mean to understand a sentence? How do humans interpret each other's messages?" (14).

To answer these questions, Schank and colleagues began creating sophisticated programs designed to use and manipulate natural language. Some programs worked with simple, prototypical characters and plots in order to create brief but coherent narratives. *Tale Spin*, for example, created fable-like stories using a stock set of animal characters, props, scenes, and motives. As Schank and Abelson (1977) describe it, this program, created by Jim Meehan, "makes up stories by simulating a world, assigning goals to some characters, and saying what happens when these goals interact with events in the simulated world" (210; see Meehan 1976). Each time the program created a story, however, its mistakes revealed certain kinds of knowledge fundamental to human language processes that computers lacked and had to be given. Although the chronicle of these failures is too extensive to be summarized here, a few examples are instructive.

In an early iteration, *Tale Spin* produced the following story from its many programmed roles, actions, and scripts:

> One day Joe Bear was hungry. He asked his friend Irving Bird where some honey was. Irving told him there was a beehive in the oak tree. Joe threatened to hit Irving if he didn't tell him where some honey was. (Schank and Abelson 1977, 83)

In this output, it became clear that the system needed to know what it had just said. The computer "was capable of answering the question *Where is honey found?* But it could not look back at *beehive* and see that is where honey can be found" (83). When we use language, our texts are not linear; the assertions and ideas represented in each bit of text cumulatively (and exponentially) complicate and inform both further text and prior text. In reading (or listening), we look to previous text to interpret incoming text and make predictions about text yet to come. We move backward and forward at the same time.

A later attempt yielded the following tale:

> Once upon a time there was a dishonest fox and a vain crow. One day the crow was sitting in his tree, holding a piece of cheese in his mouth. He noticed that he was holding the piece of cheese. He became hungry, and swallowed the cheese. The fox walked over to the crow. The end.

This time the program, which had been set up to create an Aesop-like plot, had been given the knowledge that the animal characters could be aware that they were hungry, and that would activate a goal to satisfy their hunger. But this awareness is not automatic, or else every character would try to satisfy its hunger immediately whenever food is present. The program had to allow the crow to hold the cheese but not eat it.

Natural language processing experiments at Yale also produced a number of programs designed to read and "interpret" existing text for routine purposes, such as taking a full news story and condensing it into its essential ideas. For example, SAM (Script Applier Mechanism) was a prototype designed to answer simple questions about texts it had processed. In the many false starts in this and other programs, the researchers uncovered dozens of types of world knowledge applied by humans to natural discourse: actions, roles, causal chains, properties, possibilities, and plans. Schank and colleagues had stumbled on a central problem: the need to account for the linguistic and psychological ubiquity of *inferencing*. Inferencing occurs in natural language constantly, providing the connective tissue between assertions and yielding meaning and interpretation. It works all the way from simple word-level semantics to the level of entire discourses in context. For the former, Schank offers the following example of the need for computers to "know" almost limitless permutations of word meanings.

> John gave Mary a book.
> John gave Mary a hard time.
> John gave Mary a night on the town.
> John gave up.
> John gave no reason for his actions.
> John gave a party.
> John gave his life for freedom. (1984, 93)

Or, to use another example, consider what a computer programmed to understand "hand" (in, say, "Hand me a cookie") would do with "John had a hand in the robbery" or "John asked Mary for her hand," or "John is an old hand" (94). Simply programming the computer with alternative meanings of a word wasn't sufficient to get the computer to know what meaning to apply in a given case—which requires knowledge of the word's surrounding sentential and discursive context.

While such word-level semantic puzzles were not a major programming obstacle, work in AI at the level of discourse began revealing that humans bring to text a vast, complex storehouse of prior knowledge and experience. To simplify and categorize some of this knowledge in order to continue programming computers to work with natural language, AI researchers proposed several domains of inferencing, such as scripts, plans, and goals. As Robert Abelson conceived them (Schank 1984, 143), scripts constitute stereotypical world events based on typical experiences within a known culture or context. A common example is the restaurant script activated in the following narrative:

> John went to the new fancy French restaurant. He had coq au vin, a glass of Beaujolais, and mousse for desert. He left a big tip.

Most readers who have dined at fancy restaurants will fill in many times more information than is presented in this brief text by accessing scriptual knowledge. A fancy restaurant script includes certain roles, props, and actions. A diner is seated, often by a host or maitre d'. A waiter brings a menu. (Sometimes multiple waiters play different roles; a sommelier might provide advice on the wines.) Ordering is done from the table, where the check is also paid and tips are left. Assumptions about John's experience—that he ate with a knife and fork, or that the wine was poured into a glass and not a plastic cup or a chalice—come not from the text on the page, but from knowledge the reader brings *to* the text. No one reading this text would infer a scenario in which John leaves only the tip, without paying the bill, or leaves the tip in the bathroom sink, or goes into the kitchen to order and pick up his food. "John heard a knife clatter to the floor" will activate certain further interpretations and responses (for example, it's a mild social gaffe to drop your silverware in a fancy restaurant).

But compare the script for a fast-food restaurant, where the roles, props, and actions are altogether different: ordering at a counter, paying before eating, taking your own food to a table, and so on. No one reading a text about John going to Burger King would infer a scenario in which John waits at his table for someone to show up with a menu. The line, "John heard a knife clatter to the floor" will, in the context of a fast-food script, lead to a different set of interpretations (someone is up to no good, for example, since only plastic knives are found in fast-food restaurants). Unless something explicitly contradicts it, a script creates a mass of inferential knowledge literally not present in the assertions of the text, invisible to a parser and simple decoder. Without this knowledge, a computer can't begin to work with even simple narratives or accounts of events, much less sophisticated academic arguments or other essays expected of students in schools and colleges.

As Boden (1977) points out, interpretation "is largely a creative ability of filling in the gaps" (310). Yet although it seems to require more cognitive effort for humans to "read between the lines," inferencing also appears to be desirable in many kinds of texts. When humans are provided with all the information needed to fill in a script, the resulting text is unappealing. A text such as "John wanted to marry his friend's wife. He bought some arsenic" is rendered horrendously boring when the considerable inferencing is filled in, but this is precisely the level of detail that a program needs in order to make sense of the text. Even the following more explicit version leaves out much necessary information:

> John wanted to marry his friend's wife. To marry his friend's wife, John knew that he had to get rid of his friend. One way to get rid of his friend would be to kill his friend. One way to kill his friend would be to poison his friend. One way to poison his friend would be to give his friend arsenic without his knowing. John decided to get some arsenic. In order to get some arsenic, John needed to know where arsenic was sold. In order to find out where arsenic was sold, John had to consult the Internet. In order to consult the Internet, John had to go to his computer. In order to go to his computer. . . .

Although it is possible to program computers to work with simple scripts such as going to a restaurant or riding a bus, interpreting natural language also involves making inferences that don't rely on scriptual knowledge. Schank offers the following narrative as illustration:

> John knew that his wife's surgery would be very expensive. There was always Uncle Harry. He reached for the phone book. (1984, 125)

Schank points out that most people don't have a script for paying for expensive medical treatments. Yet such a situation is not unlike paying for college, making a down payment on a house, and so on—in a general sense, *raising a lot of money for an important family expense* (1984, 126).

But the problem is not solved by having *more* scripts: there will always be a new situation to which we can't apply an existing script. Rather than describing a stereotypical course of events such as riding a bus, this kind of discourse calls into play a set of *goals* and the *plans* required to achieve them. Some goals are far-reaching, requiring many sets of plans; others are quite simple—in Schank's example, "Fred couldn't get the jar lid off. He went down to the basement and got a pair of pliers." In applying world knowledge to texts, we bring to bear thousands of possible plans for achieving countless goals.

To program computers to work with natural language, AI researchers had to begin with simple goals achieved by simple plans. One goal, called CHANGE PROXIMITY, had several plans, such as USE PRIVATE VEHICLE, USE PUBLIC TRANSPORTATION, USE ANIMAL, USE SELF (Schank 1984, 127). Consider the example "Frank wanted to go to the Bahamas. He picked up a newspaper." On the surface, these two assertions are unrelated. It is only by inferring both a goal and a plan to realize it that the sentences can be related. In this case going to the Bahamas must involve changing proximity; changing proximity can be accomplished by using a private vehicle, using public transportation, and so on. In addition, a computer needs to know that not all the transportation plans available in its list will work to reach all goals of changing proximity. It needs to be able to fit action into a *model of the world*, to rule out, say, driving, kayaking, or riding a whale to the Bahamas, And then, using stored information, it needs to infer that there might be information in the newspaper about the remaining modes (boat, plane) that could create a plan to realize the goal (128).

This need for ongoing inferential processes becomes even more obvious when we add a third sentence to the text:

> Frank wanted to go to the Bahamas. He picked up a newspaper. He began reading the fashion section.

Any activated inferencing about transportation must be modified with the addition of the third sentence, since the goal cannot be accomplished by getting information from that part of the newspaper. Instead, perhaps Frank has the goal of obtaining light clothing for a warm climate (Schank 1984, 128), and an entirely new set of plans comes into play. The further textual information erases prior inferencing and replaces it with new inferencing—a new hypothetical goal and new hypothetical plans to reach it.

Other kinds of world knowledge essential for understanding text include "roles"—specific motives and actions assigned to people based on their positions. We interpret the sentence "The police officer held up his hand and stopped the car" not to mean that the police officer, Superman-like, pressed his hand against the oncoming car and held it from advancing, but that the driver applied the brakes in deference to the police officer's authority. Inferences about the plans, goals, and actions of people also derive from their roles: bank teller, pharmacist, teacher, politician, nurse, habitual child molester working as a gardener at a private middle school. Given that multiple themes, plans, goals, and scripts are at work in even relatively simple discourse, it is not difficult to imagine the complexity of "making sense" of broader, less constrained texts. Each inference can produce further inferences, a process that led the early AI programs to create what Schank calls "a combinatorial explosion of inferences," some "valid and sensible," others "ridiculous and irrelevant" (1984, 141).

An even more complex kind of inferencing involves applying knowledge of *themes* to natural texts. A theme consists of the background information that we need to interpret that a person wants to achieve a certain goal. A *role theme*, for example, allows us to interpret what might motivate a particular person or character in a text to do something. If we read that a wild West sheriff is told that someone's cattle has been stolen, we might infer that he has a goal of recovering them and/or bringing the thieves to justice. As Black, Wilkes-Gibbs, and Gibbs (1982) explain, "role goals are triggered by the actions of other 'players' when these actions become known to the character of the role. Once such a goal is successfully triggered, the character's plans are much more predictable than if a non-role person had the same goal" (335). For example, if the sheriff has the goal of catching the thieves, it's likely that he'll saddle up his horse, or enlist the help of a posse. If as readers we encounter, "Jack told the sheriff, 'My cattle are gone!' The sheriff went to the saloon to find his pals Slim, Ernie, Baldy and Pete . . . ," we assume the sheriff is rounding up a posse. But if we read the following line instead: "Jake told the chambermaid, 'My cattle are gone!' The chambermaid went to the saloon to find her pals Slim, Ernie, Baldy and Pete . . . ," we might be confused because the role member is acting in an unpredictable way (Black, Wilkes-Gibbs, and Gibbs 1982, 335). This violation of the role theme could be explained later, but notice that we do not *need* the action to be explained if is appropriate to the role member. Without this kind of information, a computer is unable to know whether certain information is redundant, necessary, predictable (and deleteable), and so on. When we consider presenting such an interpreting machine with a text far more complex than these sorts of simplistic, stereotypical examples—such as a the paper of a high school student who critiques the ideology of a talk-show commentator by analyzing the false assumptions and faulty logic of his claims—we can begin to see the problems associated with creating machines that can reach any sound conclusions about the nature and quality of writers' prose, including the inability to judge how much information they have included relative to the knowledge of their audience, what kinds of logical chains they create, how their lexical and stylistic choices relate to their persona or ethos, and how appropriate that relationship is to the text's genre and context, or what informational path they lead the reader down in exploring or supporting a point.

Other interpretation programs ran into further problems, but the difficulties were not—at least theoretically—insurmountable. Based on the limited success of these early trial-and-error experiments, it seemed possible to create a sort of "mini world" programmed to account for hundreds of causal chains, the application of various scripts and plans, and so on, as long as the domain was limited and the computer had been given sufficient knowledge. In many ways, this is how current AI-based programs now "read" texts and provide certain types of assessments and feedback. This kind of limited application has at least some pedagogical potential because it works within a fairly stable domain with pragmatic purposes—practicing the textual process of summarizing a longer text, for example, where the "scoring" program has enough information about the longer text and the permutations of summary that it can determine the effectiveness of the student's attempt. (See Brent and Townsend, chapter 13 in this volume, for this type of application.) But the problem of assuming that, if given all this ability, machines might be able to interpretively extract something similar to what humans can ignores an essential characteristic of texts: that they are subject to multiple interpretations. A person reading an informative passage about pit bulls, in the domain of "domesticated canines," might see the text through the lens of being mauled by a pit bull as a young child. The results would be experientially different if instead of having been attacked, the reader had helped the family to raise prize pit bulls. For some texts, such as driving directions, a single, desired interpretation may be useful; but for most of the sophisticated texts that we want students to read, interpret, and produce, there is no "right way" for them to be read—a point thoroughly explored in reader-response theories (see Rosenblatt 1978 for a good theoretical introduction and Beach 1993 for an overview). Although machine-scoring advocates might argue that reducing interpretive possibilities takes a step in the direction of more consistent, reliable assessments of writing, to do so is to strip writing of its relationship with readers—that is, to turn it from writing into mindless bits of linguistic code.

One final concern of AI experts is worth mentioning. Computer programs usually operate *on* text, but they must be programmed to *learn from* it as well. As Schank points out, the AI programs he and his colleagues created had one serious flaw: "They could each read the same story a hundred times and never get bored. They were not being *changed* by what they read. People are intolerant of such boredom because they hope to profit in some way from their reading efforts. . . . To [change], an understanding system must be capable of being reminded of something it has stored in its long-term memory. But memory mechanisms are not random . . . . if we see every experience we have as knowledge structures in its own right, then thousands of structures quickly become millions of structures" (1984, 168).

The aim of computer-based text understanding is to produce a single output or assessment of the text's content and features; the machine can't read and interpret the text in the productively various ways that we want students to read and interpret, drawing on and applying an almost limitless fund of information, experience, and memory. (See the introduction, McAllister and White's chapter 1, Ericsson's chapter 2, and Jones's chapter 6 in this volume for descriptions of what the most common essay-rating systems are capable of doing and the levels—mostly surface—at which they do them.) This problem of computerized language processing is described quite simply by Wagman (1998): "Language-processing systems are constituted of structures that manipulate representations of objects and events. The constituted structures *do not understand natural language*, and their manipulation of representations accord to them the proper appellation of information-processing automata" (2; emphasis added).

Machines, in other words, are only machines.

IN SERVITUDE TO KNOWLEDGE: THE PROMISE OF COMPUTERS FOR THE ANALYSIS OF WRITTEN TEXT

While I have argued that the capacities of computers is nowhere near that of humans for reading and understanding natural discourse, the early experiments in artificial intelligence that helped to support that argument also reveal the potential for computer technology to serve as an aid to research on language and writing development. Computers are far better suited to support advances in our understanding of human language processes than they are to relieve us of the need for human interaction so essential to people's learning and to the development of something as complex and socially determined as higher literacy. Computer analyses of text have yielded useful data that have furthered our understanding of many linguistic, textual, and even neurological processes. Machine analyses of style, for example, are well known, ranging from early studies of features in the work of specific writers such as Martin Luther King (Foster-Smith 1980) to documents such as the Declaration of Independence (Whissell 2002) to entire genres, especially for the purpose of document recognition and retrieval (see Kaufer et al. in press). In such increasingly sophisticated research, computers look for specific patterns in large quantities of prose and can correlate these patterns with other variables. In studies of the development of writing abilities, there is clearly much fruitful work to be done analyzing the prose of novice writers, especially longitudinally.

Correlational analysis facilitated by computers can also help us to understand the relationship between written language processes and other dimensions of human development, culture, psychology, and neurology. For example, in studies of women entering a convent in their twenties, Snowdon et al. (1996) found startling relationships in which "idea density" in the nuns' early writing, measured in part as a function of syntax, correlated with the results of cognitive test scores and the presence of Alzheimer's disease in the nuns' later lives, virtually *predicting* the development of the disease dozens of years before its onset. Content analyses also revealed that the nuns whose writing expressed more positive terms ended up living longer. Such new discoveries can be further tested on large numbers of texts using parsing, recognition, and content-analysis programs to identify specific features and variables, informing both neurobiology and language studies. Similarly, Campbell and Pennebaker (2003) have used Latent Semantic Analysis—a method commonly employed in machine-scoring systems—to relate stylistic features in subjects' personal writing to their overall health. In particular, they found that "flexibility in the use of common words—particularly personal pronouns . . . was related to positive health outcomes" (60). Changes in writing style across the subjects' texts were strongly related to wellness; the less the subjects' writing styles changed during a specific period, the more likely they were to visit a physician. The authors speculate that pronouns can be seen as "markers of psychological and physical health, and, indirectly, people's thinking about their social worlds over the course of their writing." Their study provides "compelling evidence that the 'junk' words that people use in writing and speech reveal a tremendous amount about how they are thinking" (64).

As these and countless other studies show, the main advantage of computer technology for the analysis of text is not that it can do things that human readers or coders can't do—after all, the programs must be created to look for things that humans already know how to look for (though, as we have seen, human readers far outpace computers in terms of the *sophistication* of our reading processes). It is that computers can work through a single text hundreds or thousands of times, creating feature matrices, or they can examine tens of thousands of pages of text at lightning speed and, when programmed well, identify features with 100 percent accuracy, without the chance of human error. Studies have also shown that human readers can effectively "look" for only a few features at a time when they read, meaning that they must make many passes through the same texts to identify multiple features when asked to do so. Not so with computers, which can complete many tasks simultaneously without slowing down significantly. In time, cost, and accuracy for some tasks, computers trump human readers, which is presumably why there is so much interest in programming them to rate student essays on the basis of quality.

When used with large corpora of student texts, computers might provide us with information about student writing that has important implications for teaching and learning. Computer analyses could also yield relationships between such features and other aspects of students' education, such as their learning styles or attitudes. For example, in a study of approximately a thousand first-year engineering students' learning styles, preferences, study habits, and performance, several colleagues and I used sophisticated text-mining software developed by the SAS Institute to look for specific features in the students' weekly journal writing (Anson et al. 2003). As part of a one-credit Introduction to Engineering module, the students were required to write brief reflective electronic journal entries at a Web site. The entries focused on their learning and study experiences during their first semester of university life. Programmed to search for hundreds of potential relationships within and across twenty-seven thousand journal entries at lightning speed, the data-mining software allowed us to look for simple features such as word length or the use of punctuation as well as more sophisticated relationships between the students' texts and their learning preferences as measured by the Learning Type Measure, a Myers-Briggs-type indicator. (Other work, notably Maid 1996 and Carrell and Monroe 1993, has also found relationships between learning style and features of student writing). Although it is not my purpose to report on the journal study here, it is interesting to note that among the simple measures, there was a relatively strong relationship between the average number of syllables in students' words (a crude measure of their lexical knowledge) and their grade point averages at the end of their first year of college. Female students used a statistically higher percentage of inclusive pronouns (*we, us*) than men, suggesting a profitable area for the continued study of gender variables in writing and learning. Other findings, such as the extremely low incidence of punctuation other than commas and periods across the twenty-seven thousand texts, remind us of the importance and determining influences of context and purpose: brief low-stakes journal entries instead of formal academic essays. Among the more sophisticated correlations generated by the SAS software, we found that the single most powerful textual predictor of first-year performance was the presence or absence of a single word: *physics*. Students who wrote about physics in their journal entries were much more likely to be in the high-GPA group than those who did not. This odd result reminds us as well that the results of computer analyses mean nothing until or unless humans can make sense of them in relation to other variables and aspects of the context in which the data have been gathered.

As computer programs further develop with insights from AI, linguistic theory, and areas such as computational semantics, there will be many opportunities to learn about written text and aspects of human physical, emotional, and cognitive development. Early proposals in the field of composition studies to use the insights of text analysis (such as cohesion, coherence, lexis, propositional structure, given-new information, and the like—see Cooper 1983) bore little fruit mainly because of the difficulty for human readers or coders to do the painstaking work of mapping such features across even small corpuses of texts. Technology now provides us with increasingly helpful ways to conduct such analysis, reopening abandoned pathways to new discoveries about the human capacity to write.

IN SERVITUDE TO LEARNING: FORMATIVE RESPONSE

The promise of digital technology to analyze human prose is not limited to research. To the extent that it can provide information to writers about their prose, it has some instructional potential. In this regard, it is helpful to borrow a distinction from the field of assessment between *formative* and *summative* evaluation. Formative evaluation refers to information used in the service of improving performance, without any possible negative consequences for the person being evaluated; it is meant to bring about positive changes (Centra 1993). In contrast, summative evaluation refers to the assessment of performance after a period of time in which new knowledge, structures, or activities have been put into place; it is used to "make judgments about . . . quality or worth compared to previously defined standards for performance" (Palomba and Banta 1999, 8).

Computer-assisted formative evaluation of writing has not gained widespread acceptance or use, partly because the information it provides can be unreliable and one-dimensional and partly because the most sophisticated programs are not available for general pedagogical use. Simple feedback programs such as the sentential analyses provided by popular word-processing programs operate on text uniformly, without regard for the discursive community in which it is located, the intentions of its author, or the conventions expected by its readers. Indices such as sentence length or the use of passive constructions may have some limited use educationally in calling students' attention to certain linguistic features, but they fail to describe or respond to the relationship between such features and their appropriateness in certain kinds of discourse or the norms and expectations of certain communities or activities. More sophisticated programs, however, may be useful pedagogically to help students recognize textual or stylistic patterns in their writing and develop metacognition and metalinguistic ability in the improvement of their writing.

Pearson Technology's program Summary Street, for example, is a tool that purports to help young writers to learn how to summarize text more clearly and effectively. Students read passages and then try to capture the basic concepts, or the "gist," of the passages in a written summary. The computer then reads the student's summary, assigns it a score, and provides some boilerplate responses as well as comments on specific problems, such as misspelled words. Further attempts—for example, added information, clarified sentences, and the like—can show improvements in the score.

Any learner's earnest attempts to use such a system cannot be critiqued as intellectually bankrupt or of no pedagogical use. Many of the passages are interesting and well written, and the attempt to learn from them and summarize their contents requires rigorous intellectual and literate work. And, given the often horrendous workloads under which many teachers of writing labor, especially in the schools, machine-aided practice and feedback for selected writing activities might provide some welcome relief. However, it takes only a little experimenting to reveal the limitations of such programs when compared with human readers and responders. After reading a passage about the ancient Aztec civilization that focused on their sacrificial practices, I wrote a summary designed to deviate from the original in noticeable ways. I located the sacrificial altar not at the top of the pyramid but inside a cave. Priests, not captives, were sacrificed in my summary, the purpose not to please the gods but pay homage to the peasants:

> The Aztecs believed that the peasants needed to be appeased constantly. As a result, they often sacrificed high priests to the peasants. They would take a captive into a dark and cavernous area they had hollowed out of the earth. There, to the sounds of beating drums and dancing, they would spear the priest with flaming swords.

In spite of the major differences in content between my summary and the original text about the Aztecs, Summary Street was unable to provide me with useful feedback. It questioned the line "A female peasant was then summoned from above," presumably because no females were mentioned in the original text (a relatively easy parameter to include in an assessment program). It flagged two misspellings (lower-case *aztec* and *disembowled*). In its final assessment, it assigned a high score to the summary, praising me for including so much extra information. Its canned response ended with the encouraging, "Good work, guest student!" Although the result took perhaps a millisecond to generate, the spurious response was in no way justified by its speed. A human reader, in contrast, would take a few minutes to read the summary but would offer a far more accurate assessment together with, if necessary, suggestions of far greater pedagogical value. (See McGee's chapter 5 in this volume for a similar and more extensive experiment using the Intelligent Essay Assessor—built on the same software that Summary Street relies upon.)

Such limitations of machine evaluation and response, of course, can be seen in the context of ongoing development: in a few years, programs may be sophisticated enough to simulate a fuller range of responses and judgments in domain-limited contexts for formative purposes. Considering the instructional potential of machine analysis of student prose, then, why should we object to the use of a machine-scoring program to determine students' writing ability summatively, for purposes of accepting them to college, placing them in courses, or certifying their ability as they pass from grade to grade in the schools? If such applications can provide formative data to students, why shouldn't they provide to teachers, testers, and administrators some useful data about the student as product—like quality-control mechanisms on assembly lines? If all we really want to do with machines is look for a few simple measures, especially those measures that correlate with ability, even on a basic level, why not use them and avoid our own drudgery and human labor?

Although there is compelling enough evidence that computers can't read, interpret, and provide helpful feedback on a range of student texts in open domains, the answers to these questions take us beyond the potential for computers to enact those processes as effectively as humans and into the ethics of having machines read and rate students' writing to begin with. In the field of composition studies, scholars and educators have advocated purposeful, contextually and personally relevant occasions for writing, criticizing mindless, vacuous assignments and activities in a genre Britton and colleagues called "dummy runs" (1975). The rupture that machine scoring creates in the human activities of teaching and learning begins with the denial of a sentient audience for the students' work. Like Herrington and Moran (2001), whose experiments writing for a computer evaluator chronicled their disquietude with the rhetorical implications of not actually being "read" by anyone, I believe that this simple fact about machines as automata dooms them to failure in any contexts as politically, educationally, and ethically complex as testing students for their writing ability and using the results to make decisions about acceptance to, placement in, or exemption from a particular curriculum.

The point of writing in a course is for students to explore and reflect on ideas through language, convey their own interpretations and informational discoveries to others, and in the process intersubjectively create purpose and meaning. When they are aware of the subjugation of these human motives to an unthinking, unfeeling, insentient, interpersonally unresponsive, and coldly objective "reader"—even in a high-stakes testing situation admittedly already void of much intrinsic purpose—human communication is relegated to silence. This claim lies at the very foundation of the field of composition studies, traceable to its earliest commentary and theoretical work and infusing its scholarship ever since. In its genesis, research in the field showed that denying students purposeful contexts for writing had deleterious effects on their learning and on the texts they wrote, and that the construction of purpose and audience is related to ability. Cannon (1981), for example, found that only the most proficient writers in the group he studied had developed higher-level purposes and showed a sense of ownership of and engagement in their texts. Similar conclusions were reached by Anson (1984), Emig (1971), Gage (1978), Newkirk (1984), Pianko (1979), and Nystrand (1982), who pointed out that without a full social context, writing "is not really discourse; it is [a] bloodless, academic exercise" (5). The centrality of human purposes and readers to written communication and to the development of writing ability is perhaps nowhere more important than in high-stakes assessment, since these rhetorical and social dimensions of writing appear to be so closely linked to performance. Largely unexplored empirically but of much concern to educators are the effects that vacuous contexts have on the manifestation of ability—a concern that shifts our focus away from whether machines can score writing as well as humans and toward what happens to students when they know they are not writing for flesh-and-blood readers. Until we know more about the psychological and compositional effects on performance of writing to and for computer readers/graders, we must proceed cautiously with their use in something as important and presumably humanistic as deciding the worth and value of people's writing.

CODA

As a reader, you have reached the end of a contribution to collective speculation about the subject of machine scoring. You have judged the validity of various claims, connected assertions and examples to prior knowledge and experience, affirmed and doubted, alternated between reasoned thought and emotional response. I have claimed that the process you've undergone cannot now, and probably not in the next several generations, be replicated by a computer, and that even if such a thing were possible, there is little point in doing so except for limited formative uses by developing writers. This and other contributions to the present volume, and continued national and international forums, conferences and meetings, published research, listserv discussions, blogs, and countless other opportunities for human interaction, will continue to create knowledge concerning writing development and instruction. Those contributions will proceed entirely without the responses, reactions, or ratings of machines, which are useful only insofar as they help *us* to make sense of our world and the nature of learning within it. For now, computers work best in servitude to the rich and varied human interactions that motivate and captivate us. To substitute them for human work as important as the testing and judgment of other humans' literate abilities—grounded as they are in social relations and human purposes—is to assume that at least some dimensions of literacy are not worthy of our time.

And so to the machine, we do not risk affronting its sensibilities by telling it that *it* has nothing to offer this discussion, and that its rating is irrelevant. Or, more baldly:

School is in, sucker. And U can't touch this.

4

AUTOMATONS AND AUTOMATED SCORING
Drudges, Black Boxes, and Dei Ex Machina

Richard H. Haswell

Her name really is Nancy Drew. Like her fictional namesake, she is into saving people, although more as the author of a mystery than the hero of one. She teaches English at a high school in Corpus Christi, Texas, and according to the local newspaper (Beshur 2004), she has designed a software program that will grade student essays. The purpose is to help teachers save students from the Texas Essential Knowledge and Skills test, which must be passed for grade promotion and high school diploma. Her software will also save writing teachers from excessive labor, teachers who each have around two hundred students to protect (plus their jobs). "Teachers are going to be able to do more writing assignments, because they won't have to grade until all hours of the morning," says a school director of federal programs and curriculum from Presidio, across the state—"I'm looking to earmark our funds." That will be $799 for their campus license, according to Drew, who predicts that sales will reach half a million the first year alone.

What the administrator in the Presidio school district will be getting for his $799 is not clear, of course. Drew cannot reveal the criteria of the program—trade secret—although she allows that they include "capitalization and proper grammar among other standards." Nor does she reveal any validation of the program other than a "field study" she ran with her own students, for extra credit, in which the program "accurately graded students' work." The need for the program seems validation enough. Drew explains, "There's just not time to adequately read and grade the old fashioned way. That's what is going to make this software so popular. It's user friendly and teacher friendly." She calls her program "the Triplet Ticket" (Beshur 2004).

In the capitalistic oceans of automated essay scoring, where roam Educational Testing Service's e-rater, ACT's e-Write, and the College Board's WritePlacer, the Triplet Ticket is small fry. But in research, design, and marketing, Nancy Drew's coastal venture obeys the same evolutionary drives as the giants of the open sea. Demand for the commodity rises from educational working conditions and the prior existence of huge testing mandates legislated by state and union. The design relies on algorithms approximating writing criteria that address standards already fixed in the curriculum. The exact nature of the algorithms is kept secret to protect the commodity (proprietary interests) and sometimes to protect the testing (test security). The validation of the software is so perfunctory that the product is sold before its effectiveness is known. The benefits are advertised as improving teaching and teachers' working lives, especially the hard labor of reading and responding to student essays. Yet the product is not promoted through teachers and students, although it is through everybody else, from legislators to administrators to the newspaper-reading public. No wonder Nancy Drew thinks the Triple Ticket will be a hit. Given the rapid commercial success of the giants, she might well have asked herself, how can it fail?[1]

I have a different question. Probably this is because I'm a writing teacher who feels good about the way he responds to student essays and who doesn't have any particular yen to pay someone else to do it for him, much less someone doing it through a hidden prosthesis of computer algorithms. I'm also a writing teacher who understands the rudiments of evaluation and can't imagine using a writing test with no knowledge about its validity. I'm also human and not happy when someone changes the conditions of my job without telling me. As such, I guess I speak for the majority of writing teachers. Yet here we are watching, helpless, as automatons take over our skilled labor, as mechanical drones cull and sort the students who enter our classrooms. So my question is this: how did we get here?

To answer this question I am going to set aside certain issues. I'm setting aside the possible instructional value of essay-analysis programs in providing response to student writers—both the fact that some programs are highly insightful (e.g., Henry and Roseberry, 1999; Larkey and Croft, 2003; Kaufer et al. in press) and the fact that other programs (e.g., grammar- and style-checkers) generate a sizeable chunk of feedback that is incomplete, useless, or wrong. I'm setting aside the Janus face the testing firms put on, officially insisting that automated scoring should be used only for such instructional feedback yet advertising it for placement (the name "WritePlacer" is not that subtle). I'm setting aside the fact that, no matter what the manufacturers say, institutions of learning are stampeding to use machine scores in order to place their writing students, and they are doing it with virtually no evidence of its validity for that purpose. I'm setting aside the fact that in 2003 El Paso Community College, which serves one of the most poverty-stricken regions in the United States, itself set aside $140,000 to pay the College Board for ACCUPLACER and Maps. I'm setting aside other ethical issues, for instance the Panglossian, even Rumsfeldian way promoters talk about their products, as if their computer program lies somewhere between sliced bread and the brain chip (Scott Elliot, who helped develop IntelliMetric, the platform for WritePlacer, says that it "internalizes the pooled wisdom of many expert scorers" [2003, 71]). I'm setting all this aside, but not to leave it behind. At the end, I will return to these unpleasantries.

DRUDGES

> *We love [WritePlacer] and the students think we are the smartest people in the world for doing essays like that.*
> —Gary Greer, Director of Academic Counseling,
> University of Houston–Downtown

I will return to the issues I've set aside because they are implicated with the history of writing teachers and automated scoring. We writing teachers are not ethically free of these unsavory facts that we would so much like to bracket. We are complicit. We are where we are because for a long time now we have been asking for it.

Not a happy thought. Appropriately, let's begin with an unhappy piece of history. From the very beginning the approach that writing instruction has taken to computer language analysis has ranged from wary to hands off. It's true that programmed-learning packages, which started to catch on in the mid-1950s, were hot items for the next twenty years, often installed in college programs with government grants: PLATO at the University of Illinois, TICCIT at Brigham Young University, COMSKL at the University of Evansville, LPILOT at Dartmouth, and so on. But teachers—not to speak of students—soon got bored with the punctuation and grammar drill and the sentence-construction games, and found a pen and a hard-copy grade book easier to use than the clunky record-keeping functions. They read in-discipline reviews of the programs insisting that the machinery was not a "threat" to their livelihood, and eventually they sent the reels and the disks and the manuals to gather dust at the writing center (Byerly 1978; Lerner 1998).

Style-analysis programs suffered a similar rejection, albeit of a more reluctant kind. At first a few enthusiastic souls wrote their own. In 1971

James Joyce—really his name—had his composition students at Berkeley compose at an IBM 360 using WYLBUR (a line editor), and he wrote a program in PL/I (a programming language) that produced a word concordance of each essay, to be used for revisions. But ten years later he was recommending teachers use UNIX programs developed at Bell Laboratories in the late 1970s, because they were ready-made and could be knitted together to generate vocabulary lists, readability formulas, and frequency counts of features of style, all on a microcomputer (Joyce 1982). The commercial side had seen the salability of style-checkers and were using their greater resources to beat the independent and unfunded academics to the mark. The year 1982 marks the threshold of the microcomputer with affordable memory chips—the most profitable vehicle for style, spelling, and grammar-checkers—and IBM and Microsoft were ready with the software to incorporate into their word-processing programs. Long forgotten were Mary Koether and Esther Coke's style-analysis FORTRAN program (1973), arguably better because it calculated word frequency and token words, Jackson Webb's WORDS (1973), which tried to measure initial, medial, and final free modification, and Robert Bishop's JOURNALISM (1974), which reported sentence-length variance—forgotten along with WYLBUR and PL/I. Many of the homegrown programs, such as the Quintilian Analysis, were arguably worse, certainly worse than slick and powerful programs such as Prentice-Hall's RightWriter, AT&T's Writer's Workbench, and Reference Software's Grammatik.[2] To this takeover the composition teachers were happy to accede, so long as they could grumble now and then that the accuracy rate of the industry computer-analysis software did not improve (Dobrin 1985; Pedersen 1989; Pennington 1993; Kohut and Gorman 1995; Vernon 2000; McGee and Ericsson 2002).

The main complaint of writing teachers, however, was not the inaccuracy of the mastery-learning and style-analysis programs but their instruction of students in surface features teachers felt were unimportant. Yet the attempts of the teachers to write less trivial software, however laudable, turned into another foray into the field and then withdrawal from it, although a more protracted one. The interactive, heuristic programs written by writing teachers were intelligent and discipline based from the beginning: Susan Wittig's Dialogue (1978), Hugh Burns and George Culp's Invention (1979), Cynthia Selfe and Billie Walstrom's Wordsworth (1979), Helen Schwartz's SEEN (Seeing Eye Elephant Network, 1982), Valerie Arms's Create (1983), William Wresch's Essay Writer (1983), to name some of the earlier ones. In 1985 Ellen McDaniel listed forty-one of them. But where are they now? Again, industry's long arm secured a few, and the rest fell prey to our profession's restless search for a better way to teach. WANDAH morphed into the HBJ Writer about the same time, the mid-1980s, that CAI (computer-assisted instruction) morphed into CMC (computer-mediated communication). In part discouraged by research findings that computer analysis did not unequivocally help students to write better, and in part responding to the discipline-old creed that production is more noble than evaluation, composition teachers and scholars switched their attention to the siren songs of e-mail, chat rooms, and hypertext. And true to the discipline-old anxiety about the mercantile, they associated a mode of instruction they deemed passé with the ways of business. In 1989 Lillian Bridwell-Bowles quotes Geoffrey Sirc: "Whenever I read articles on the efficacy of word processing or text-checkers or networks, they always evoke the sleazy air of those people who hawk Kitchen Magicians at the State Fair" (86).

The discipline's resistance to computer analysis of student writing was epitomized early in the reaction to the first attempt at bona fide essay scoring, Ellis Page and Dieter Paulus's trial, realized in 1966 and published in 1968. Wresch (1993), Huot (1996), and McAllister and White in chapter 1 of this volume describe well the way the profession immediately characterized their work as misguided, trivial, and dead end. Eighteen years later, Nancarrow et al.'s synopsis of Page and Paulus's trial holds true to that first reaction: "Too old, technologically at least, and for many in terms of composition theory as well. Uses keypunch. Concentrates on automatic evaluation of final written product, not on using the computer to help teach writing skills" (1984, 87). In the twenty years since that judgment, Educational Testing Service's Criterion has already automatically evaluated some 2 million "final written products"—namely, their Graduate Management Admission Test essays.

If today Page and Paulus's trial seems like a Cassandra we resisted unwisely, to the ears of computer insiders in 1968 it might have sounded more a Johnny-come-lately. Composition teachers had come late to the analysis of language by computer. By 1968 even scholars in the humanities had already made large strides in text analysis. Concordances, grammar parsers, machine translators, analyses of literary style and authorship attribution, and machine-readable archives and corpora had been burgeoning for two decades. Conferences on computing in the humanities had been meeting annually since 1962, and *Computers and the Humanities: A Newsletter* was launched in 1966. It was nearly two decades later that the first conference on computers and composition teaching was held (sponsored by SWRL Educational Research and Development, in Los Alamitos, California, in 1982) and their first journals appeared (*Research in Word Processing Newsletter* and *Computers and Composition* in 1983, *Computer-Assisted Composition Journal* in 1986). By then text analysis elsewhere in the humanities had already reached such exotic lands as Mishnaic Hebrew sentences, Babylonian economic documents, and troubadour poetry in Old Occitan. Between 1968 and 1988, the only articles on computer analysis of student writing in the general college composition journals stuck to grammar-checkers, style-checkers, and readability formulas. Even summaries of research into computer evaluation typically executed a perfunctory bow to Page and Paulus and then focused on style analysis, with caveats about the inability of computers to judge the "main purposes" of writing, such as audience awareness and idea development, or even to evaluate anything since they are only a "tool" (Finn 1977; Burns 1987; Reising and Stewart 1984; Carlson and Bridgeman 1986).

I pick the year 1988 because that is when Thomas Landauer says he and colleagues first conceived of the basic statistical model for latent semantic analysis, the start of a path that led to the commercial success of Intelligent Essay Assessor. It's worth retracing this path, because it follows a road not taken—not taken by compositionists. Statistically, latent semantic analysis derives word/morpheme concordances between an ideal or target text and a trial text derivative of it. It compares not individual words but maps or clusters of words. Historically, this semantic enterprise carried on earlier attempts in electronic information retrieval to go beyond mere word matching (the "general inquirer" approach), attempts at tasks such as generating indexes or summaries. In fact, latent semantic analysis's first payoff was in indexing (Deerwester et al. 1990; Foltz 1990). In 1993, it extended its capabilities to a much-studied problem of machine analysis, text coherence. The program was first "trained" with encyclopedia articles on a topic, and after calculating and storing the semantic maps of nearly three thousand words, used the information to predict the degrees of cohesion between adjoining sentences of four concocted texts. It then correlated that prediction with the comprehension of readers (Foltz, Kintsch, and Landauer 1993). A year later, latent semantic analysis was calculating the word-map similarity between a target text and students' written recall of that text and correlating the machine's estimate with the rates of expert graders (Foltz, Britt, and Perfetti 1994). By 1996, Peter Foltz was using a prototype of what he and Thomas Landauer later called Intelligent Essay Assessor to grade essays written by students in his psychology classes at New Mexico State University. In 1998, Landauer and Foltz put Intelligent Essay Assessor online after incorporating as KAT, or Knowledge Analysis Technologies. In the next few years their essay-rating services were hired by Harcourt Achieve to score General Educational Development test practice essays, by Prentice-Hall to score assignments in textbooks, by Florida Gulf Coast University to score essays written by students in a visual and performing arts general-education course, by the U.S. Department of Education to develop "auto-tutors," and by a number of the U.S. armed services to assess examinations during officer training. In 2004, KAT was acquired by Pearson Education for an undisclosed amount of money.

I dwell on the history of Intelligent Essay Assessor because it is characteristic. We would find the same pattern with e-rater, developed during the same years by Jill Burstein and others at ETS and first used publicly to score GMAT essays in 2002, or with IntelliMetric, developed by Scott Elliott at Vantage Laboratories, put online in 1998, and making its first star public appearance as the platform for College Board's WritePlacer, the essay-grading component of ACCUPLACER, in 2003. The pattern is that automated scoring of essays emerged during the 1990s out of the kinds of computer linguistic analysis and information retrieval that writing teachers had showed little interest in or had flirted with and then abandoned: machine translation, automatic summary and index generation, corpora building, vocabulary and syntax and text analysis. Researchers and teachers in other disciplines filled the gap because the gap was there, unfilled by us researchers and teachers in writing. All the kinds of software we abandoned along our way is currently alive, well, and making profits for industry in foreign-language labs and ESL and job-training labs, officers' training schools, textbook and workbook publishing houses, test-preparation and distance-learning firms, online universities, Internet cheat busters, and the now ubiquitous computer classrooms of the schools.

During those years of the entrepreneurial race for the grading machine, 1988-2002, the official word from the composition field on automated scoring was barely audible. Hawisher et al.'s detailed *Computers and the Teaching of Writing in American Higher Education, 1979-1994* (1996) does not mention machine scoring. As late as 1993, William Wresch, as computer-knowledgeable as could be wished, summed up the "imminence of grading essays by computer" by saying there was no such prospect: "no high schools or colleges use computer essay grading . . . there is little interest in using computers in this way" (48). The first challenges to Wresch's pseudocleft "there is" came from people who had programs of their own to promote: Emil Roy and his Structured Decision System (Roy 1993), Ellis Page and his revamped Project Essay Grade (Page and Petersen 1995), and Hunter Breland and his WordMAP (Breland 1996). Not until Dennis Baron in 1998 and Anne Herrington and Charles Moran in 2001 did the ordinary run of college compositionists learn that grading essays by computer in fact was not imminent, it was here. Had they been so inclined they could have heard the Cassandra truth forty years earlier from Arthur Daigon who, in 1966, when only one program existed to rate student essays, got it precisely right: "In all probability, the first practical applications of essay grading by computer will be to tests of writing proficiency not returned to the writers, perhaps large scale testing of composition" (47).

Anyone who worked as a college writing teacher during the seventies, eighties, and nineties, as I did, will protest, saying that it is only right that our attention was directed at the use of computers for classroom instruction, not for housecleaning tasks such as placement. But it's too simple to say that composition was focused on instruction and not on evaluation, because we were focused on evaluation, too. Moreover, our traditional take on evaluation was very much in sympathy with automated scoring. The unpleasant truth is that the need the current machines fulfill is our need, and we had been trying to fulfill it in machinelike ways long before computers. So much so that when automated scoring actually arrived, it found us without an obvious defense. We've been hoist by our own machine.

The scoring machines promise three things for your money, all explicit in the home pages and the glossy brochures of industry automated-scoring packages: efficiency, objectivity, and freedom from drudgery. These three goals are precisely what writing teachers have been trying to achieve in their own practices by way of evaluation for a century. The goal of efficiency needs no brief. Our effort to reach the Shangri-la of fast response, quick return, and cheap cost can be seen in the discipline all the way from the periodic blue-ribbon studies of paper load and commenting time (average is about seven minutes a page) to the constant stream of articles proposing novel methods of response that will be quicker but still productive, such as my own "Minimal Marking" (Haswell 1983). Writing teachers feel work-efficiency in their muscles, but it also runs deep in our culture and has shaped not only industrialized systems of evaluation but our own ones as well (Williamson 1993, 2004). Objectivity also needs no brief, is also deeply cultural, and also shapes methods of writing evaluation from top to bottom. The student at the writing program administrator's door who wants a second reading brings an assumed right along with the essay and is not turned away. The few counterdisciplinary voices arguing that subjectivity in response to student writing is unavoidable and good (Dethier 1983; Markel 1991) are just that, few and counter to the disciplinary mainstream.

But drudgery is another matter. Surely writing teachers do not think of their work as drudgery. Do we think of ourselves as drudges?

Actually, we do. Long before computers we have used "drudgery" as a password allowing initiates to recognize each other. More literally, we often further a long tradition of college writing teachers separating off part of their work and labeling it as drudgery. In 1893, after only two years of teaching the new "Freshman English" course, professors at Stanford declared themselves "worn out with the drudgery of correcting Freshman themes" and abolished the course (Connors 1997, 186). My all-time favorite composition study title is nearly sixty years old: "A Practical Proposal to Take the Drudgery out of the Teaching of Freshman Composition and to Restore to the Teacher His Pristine Pleasure in Teaching" (Doris 1947). Forty-six years later, in *The Composition Teacher as Drudge: The Pitfalls and Perils of Linking across the Disciplines* (1993), Mary Anne Hutchinson finds new WAC systems turning writing teachers into nothing but copy editors, "Cinderellas who sit among the ashes while the content teachers go to the ball" (1). As these cites indicate (and scores in between), "drudgery" covers that menial part of our professional activity involved with marking papers. And it refers not to our true wishes but to lift-that-bale conditions imposed on us ("paper load"). When it comes to response, we are good-intentioned slaves. In 1983, with the first sentence to "Minimal Marking," I made the mistake of writing, in manuscript, that "many teachers still look toward the marking of a set of compositions with odium." When the piece appeared in print, I was surprised, though I should not have been, to find that the editor of *College English* had secretly changed "with odium" to "with distaste and discouragement." We really want to mark papers but want to do so with more efficiency, more objectivity, and less labor. As William Marling put it the next year, in explaining the motivation for his computerized paper-marking software while defending the continued need for teacher response, "The human presence is required. It is the repetitive drudgery I wanted to eliminate" (1984, 797; quoted by Huot 1996, which provides more evidence of the discipline's vision of computers as "a reliever of the drudgery of teaching writing," 236).

But long before computers, the drudgery we had been complaining about we had been trying to solve with machinelike or servantlike devices: labor-saving contraptions such as (in rough historical order) correction symbols, checklists, overhead projectors, rubber stamps, audiotapes; and cheap labor such as lay readers and student peer evaluators and teaching assistants ("the common experience for adjunct faculty remains drudgery," Soldofsky 1982, 865). So when the computer came along, we immediately saw it as the mechanical slave that could do our drudgery for us. Even as early as 1962, when cumbersome mainframe line editors were the only means of computer-aided response, decades before spell-checkers, word-processing AutoCorrect, and hypertext frames, Walter Reitman saw computers in this light: "Just as technology has helped to relieve the worker of much physical drudgery, so computer technology thus may free the teacher of much of his clerical drudgery, allowing him to utilize more of his energies and abilities in direct and creative contact with the individual student" (1962, 106). With a computer there would be no issue of odium, or even discouragement and distaste. The computer is an "unresentful drudge," as Henry W. Kucera put it five years later—Kucera, who had just programmed his machine to order 1,014,232 words by alphabet and frequency as it trudged through a digitized corpus of romance and western novels, government documents, religious tracts, and other mind-numbing genres (1967).

It was the discipline's special condition of drudgery that early visions of machine grading hoped, explicitly, to solve. Arthur Daigon, extolling Ellis Page's Project Essay Grade two years before the findings were published, said that it would serve "not as a teacher replacement but ultimately as an aid to teachers struggling with an overwhelming mass of paperwork" (1966, 47). Page himself wrote that it would "equalize the load of the English teacher with his colleagues in other subjects" (Page and Paulus 1968, 3). And three years later, Slotnick and Knapp imagined a computer-lab scenario where students would use a typewriter whose typeface could be handled with a "character reader" (scanner) so the computer could then grace their essays with automated commentary, thus relieving teachers "burdened with those ubiquitous sets of themes waiting to be graded" (1971, 75), unresentful commentary that, as Daigon hoped, would ignore "the halo effect from personal characteristics which are uncorrelated with the programmed measurements" (52). Later, in the 1980s, when the personal computer had materialized rather than the impersonal grader, interactive "auto-tutor" programs were praised because they never tired of student questions, spell-checkers and grammar-checkers were praised because they "relieved instructors of such onerous, time-consuming tasks as error-catching and proofreading" (Roy 1990, 85), autotext features of word-processing programs were praised because they could produce "boilerplate comments" for teachers "who face the sometimes soul-deadening prospect of processing yet another stack of student papers" (Morgan 1984, 6), and when research couldn't exactly prove that computers helped students write better essays at least the teacher could be sure that word-processing saved them from the "detested drudgery of copying and recopying multiple drafts" (Maik and Maik 1987, 11).

So when automated grading suddenly returned to the composition scene in the late 1990s, we should not have been entirely caught standing in innocence and awe. Didn't we get the drudge we were wishing for? For decades, on the one computing hand, we had been resisting automated rating in the name of mission and instruction, but on the other computing hand, we had been rationalizing it in the name of workload and evaluation. What right do we have to protest today when Nancy Drew's Web site argues that her Triplet Ticket software will turn "rote drudgery" into a "chance for quality learning" for both student and teacher (2004)?

BLACK BOXES

> *That [computers] are black boxes with mysterious workings inside needn't worry us more than it did the Athenian watchers of the planetarium of the Tower of Winds in the first century B.C. or the congregation that stood with Robert Boyle and wondered at the great clock at Strassburg. We need only be concerned with what goes on outside the box.*
> —Derek J. de Solla Price (at the 1965 Yale conference on Computers for the Humanities)

There is another machinelike method with which our profession has long handled the onus of evaluating student essays. That method is the system of formal assessment we use to admit and place students. There, often we have managed efficiency, objectivity, and drudgery in a very forthright way, by turning the task over to commercial testing firms such as the Educational Testing Service, ACT, and the College Board. In turn they have managed *their* issues of efficiency, objectivity, and drudgery largely by turning the task of rating essays over to the scoring apparatus called holistic rating. The holistic, of course, has long been holy writ among composition teachers, even when they didn't practice it themselves.

In this section I want to argue that with our decades-long trust in holistic scoring, we have again already bought into machine scoring.

The word *trust* (or should I say *ignorance?*) ushers in a complicating factor, in need of explication. Enter the black box.

In the parlance of cybernetics a "black box" is any construction, hardware or software, that one can operate knowing input and output but not knowing what happens in between. For most of us, the entire operation that takes place after we hit the "print" key and before we pick up the printout is a black box—we cannot explain what happens in between. But even expert computer scientists function—manage input and output—via many black boxes. For instance, they can handle computer glitches whose source they don't know with diagnostic tools whose operation they cannot explain. I want to argue the obvious point that for writing teachers commercial machine scoring is largely a black box and the less obvious point that for writing teachers, even for those who participate in it, even for those who help construct and administer it, holistic scoring is also largely a black box. Finally, I want to argue the conspiracy of the two. Even more so than machine scoring and teacher aids such as undergraduate peer graders and criteria check sheets, machine scoring and holistic scoring enjoy a relationship that is historically complementary, even mutually supportive, maybe even symbiotic. Investigating the black boxes of both will make this relationship clear.

What does it take to investigate a black box? I turn to Bruno Latour (1987), who applies the computer scientist's concept of the black box to the way all scientists practice their research. In so doing Latour offers some surprising and useful insights into black boxes in general. In the science laboratory and in science literature, a black box can be many things—a standard research procedure, a genetic strain or background used to study a particular phenomenon, a quality-control cutoff, the purity of a commercially available chemical, an unsupported but attractive theory. In essence, it is anything scientists take on faith. Latour's first insight is counterintuitive, that normal scientific advance does not result in gain but in loss of understanding of what happens between input and output, that is, in more rather than fewer black boxes. How can that be? Take the instance of a laboratory of scientists who genetically engineer a variant of the mustard plant *Arabidopsis thaliana* by modifying a certain gene sequence in its DNA. They know the procedure by which they modified the sequence. Later scientists obtain the seeds and use the resulting plants in their own studies, understanding that the gene structure is modified but quite likely unable to explain the exact procedure that altered it, though they will cite the original work in their own studies. Latour would point out that as the *Arabidopsis* variant is used by more and more secondhand experimenters, the obscurity of the original procedure will grow. Indeed, the more the original study is cited, the less chance that anyone will be inclined to open up that particular black box again. Familiarity breeds opacity.[3]

Latour's insight throws a startling light on scientific practices, which most people assume proceed from darkness to light, not the other way around. Ready support of Latour, though, lies right at hand for us: commercial machine scoring. The input is a student essay and the output is a rate stamped on the essay, and as the chapters in this volume demonstrate over and over, students, teachers, and administrators are accepting and using this output with the scantiest knowledge of how it got there. Proprietary rights, of course, close off much of that black box from outside scrutiny. A cat can look at a king, however, and we can mentally question or dispute the black boxes. What will happen? Latour predicts our request for enlightenment will be answered with more darkness: every time we try to "reopen" one black box, we will be presented with "a new and seemingly incontrovertible black box" (1987, 80). As we'll see, Latour's prediction proves right. But although our inquiry will end up with a Russian-doll riddle wrapped in a mystery inside an enigma, the direction in which one black box preconditions another is insightful. With current-day machine scoring, the black boxes always lead back to the holistic.

Start with an easy mystery, what counts as an "agreement" when a computer program matches its rate on an essay with the rate of a human scorer on the same essay. By custom, counted is either an "exact agreement," two scores that directly match, or an "adjacent agreement," two scores within one point of each other. But why should adjacent scores be counted as "agreement"? The answer is not hard to find. Whatever is counted as a "disagreement" or discrepancy will have to be read a third time. On Graduate Management Admission Test essays since 1999, using a 6-point scale, Educational Testing Service's e-rater has averaged exact matches about 52 percent of the time and adjacent agreements about 44 percent of the time (Chodorow and Burstein 2004). That adds up to an impressive "agreement" of 96 percent, with only 4 percent requiring a third reading. But only if adjacent hits are counted as agreement. If only exact agreement is counted there would have been 48 percent of the essays requiring a third reading. And that would lower interrater reliability below the acceptable rate.[4]

But the notion of reliability leaves us with a new black box (we'll set aside the issue of the cost of third readings). Why is high concordance among raters a goal rather than low concordance? Isn't multiplicity of perspectives good, as in other judgments on human performance with the complexity of essay writing? The answer is that the goal of the scoring is not trait analysis but a unitary rate. The machine is "trained" on the same traits that the human raters are, and both arrive at a single-number score, the machine through multiple regression and the humans through training in holistic scoring, where only five or six traits can be managed with efficiency. With e-rater, these traits include surface error, development and organization of ideas, and prompt-specific vocabulary (Attali & Burstein 2004).

More black boxes. We'll set aside the mystery of why the separate traits aren't scored, compared, adjusted, and reported separately (more cost?) and ask why these few particular traits were chosen out of the plentiful supply good writers utilize, such as wit, humor, surprise, originality, logical reasoning, and so on. Here there are a number of answers, all leading to new enigmas. Algorithms have not been developed for these traits—but why not? A trait such as "originality" is difficult to program—but any more difficult than "prompt-specific vocabulary," which requires "training" the program in a corpus of essays written on each prompt and judged by human raters? One answer, however, makes the most intuitive sense. The traits e-rater uses have a long history with essay assessment, and in particular with holistic scoring at Educational Testing Service. History is the trial that shows us these traits are especially important to writing teachers.

History may be a trial, but as Latour makes clear, it is also the quickest and most compulsive maker of black boxes. How much of that essay-evaluation trial was really just unthinking acceptance of tradition? Does anybody know who first determined that these traits are important, someone equivalent to our biological engineers who first created the genetic variant of *Arabidopsis*? Actually, it seems this black box can still be opened. We can trace the history of traits like "organization" and "mechanics" and show that at one time Paul B. Diederich understood what goes into them. It was 1958, to be precise, when he elicited grades and marginal comments from readers of student homework, statistically factored the comments, and derived these two traits along with four others, a factoring that was passed along, largely unchanged, through generations of holistic rubrics at the Educational Testing Services, where Diederich worked (Diederich 1974, 5–10). It's true that even in his original study, Diederich was trusting black boxes right and left. When one of the lawyers he used to read and comment on student writing wrote in the margin, "Confusing," Diederich could not enter into the lawyer's head to find out what exactly he meant before he categorized the comment as "organization" or "mechanics" (or even "language use" or "vocabulary") in order to enter another tally into his factoring formula. The human head is the final black box that, as good empirical engineers of the creature *Homo sapiens*, we can never enter, can know only through input and output. (For more about the influence of Diederich's study on later holistic rubrics, see Broad 2003; Haswell 2002)

Surely there is another enigma here that can be entered, however. Why does machine essay scoring have to feed off the history of human essay scoring? Why does ETS's e-rater (along with all the rest of the current programs) validate itself by drawing comparison with human raters? Why establish rater reliability with *human* scores? Why not correlate one program's rates with another program's, or one part of the software's analysis with another part's? If machine scoring is better than human scoring—more consistent, more objective—then why validate it with something worse? The answer is that, historically, the machine rater had to be designed to fit into an already existing scoring procedure using humans. Right from the start machine scoring was conceived, eventually, as a *replacement* for human raters, but it would have to be eased in and for a while work hand in hand with the human raters within Educational Testing Service's sprawling and profitable essay-rating operation. The Educational Testing Service, of course, was not the only company to splice machine scoring onto holistic scoring. Ellis Page reminds us that in 1965 his initial efforts to create computer essay scoring was funded by the College Board, and "The College Board," he writes, "was manually grading hundreds of thousands of essays each year and was looking for ways to make the process more efficient" (2003, 43). The machine had to learn the human system because the human system was already implemented. It is no accident that the criteria that essay-rater designers say their software covers are essentially Diederich's original holistic criteria (e.g., Elliott 2003, 72). Nor is it any accident that developers of machine graders talk about "training" the program with model essays—the language has been borrowed from human scoring procedures. (Is human rating now altering to agree with the machine corater? There's a black box worth investigating!)

Obviously at this point we have reached a nest of black boxes that would take a book to search and enlighten, a book that would need to study economic, cultural, and political motives as well as strictly psychometric ones. We've supported Latour's startling contention that "the more technical and specialized a literature is, the more 'social' it becomes" (1987, 62). Our inquiry has not led only into blind alleys, though, and we can now see one thing clearly about machine scoring. From the start it has been designed to emulate a method of human scoring, but not any old sort of method. It is of a very particular and I would say peculiar sort. That method is the holistic as practiced in commercial large-scale ventures, where a scorer has about two to three minutes and a four- to six-part rubric to put a single number between 0 and 4 or 0 and 6 on an essay usually composed unrehearsed and impromptu within less than forty minutes. Let's be honest about this. The case *for* machine scoring is not that machine decisions are equal or better than human decisions. The case *against* machine scoring is not that machine decisions are worse than human decisions. These are red-herring arguments. The fact is that so far machines have been developed to imitate a human judgment about writing that borders on the silly. The machine-human interrater reliability figures reported by the industry are something to be proud of only if you can be proud of computer software that can substitute one gimcrack trick for another. Ninety-six percent "agreement" is just one lame method of performance testing closely simulating another lame method. The situation is known by another cybernetic term, GIGO, where it little matters that we don't know what's in the black box because we do know the input, and the input (and therefore the output) is garbage.[5]

The crucial black box, the one that writing teachers should want most to open, is the meaning of the final holistic rate—cranked out by human or machine. In fact, in terms of placement into writing courses, we know pretty much the rate's meaning, because it has been studied over and over, by Educational Testing Service among others, and the answer is always the same, it means something not far from garbage. On the kind of short, impromptu essays levered out of students by ACT, Advanced Placement, and now the SAT exams, holistic scores have a predictive power that is pitiful. Regardless of the criterion target—pass rate for first-year composition, grades in first-year writing courses, retention from first to second year—holistic scores *at best* leaves unexplained about nine-tenths of the information needed to predict the outcome accurately.[6] No writing teacher wants students put into a basic writing course on this kind of dingbat, black-box prediction. But we walk into our classes and there they are, and this has been our predicament for decades, back when the score was produced by humans imitating machines and now when the score is produced by machines imitating humans.

So how complicit are we? For every writing teacher who counts surface features for a grade, assigns mastery-learning modules, or takes testing-firm scores on faith or in ignorance, there are many who respond to essays with the student's future improvement in mind, hold individual conferences, and spend hours reading and conferring over the department's own placement-exam portfolios. Across the discipline, however, there is an unacknowledged bent—one of our own particular black boxes—that especially allies us with the testing firms' method by which they validate grading software, if practice can be taken as a form of alliance. This bent consists of warranting one inferior method of writing evaluation by equating it with another inferior method. One accepts directed student self-placement decisions because they are at least as valid as the "inadequate data of a single writing sample" (Royer and Gilles 1998, 59), or informed self-placement because it replaces teachers who don't have enough time to sort records (Hackman and Johnson 1981), or inaccurate computer grammar-check programs because the marking of teachers is inconsistent, or boring auto-tutors because human tutors are subjective, or the invalidity of Page's machine scoring because of "the notorious unreliability of composition graders" (Daigon 1966, 47). One of the earliest instances of this bent is one of the most blatant (Dorough, Shapiro, and Morgan 1963?). In the fall of 1962 at the University of Houston, 149 basic-writing students received grammar and mechanics instruction in large "lecture" classes all semester, while 71 received the same instruction through a Dukane Redi-Tutor teaching machine (a frame-controlled film projector). At the end of the semester neither group of students performed better than the other on a correction test over grammar and mechanics: "the lecture and program instruction methods employed were equally effective" (8). Yet three pages later the authors conclude, "It is clear that . . . the programmed instruction was superior to the traditional lecture instruction." The tiebreaker, of course, is efficiency: "The programmed instruction sections handled more students more efficiently in terms of financial cost per student" (11). In the world of writing evaluation, two wrong ways of teaching writing can make a right way.[7]

DEI EX MACHINA

Sólo la difícil es estimulante

—José Lezama Lima

I began with an image of college writing teachers watching, helpless, as automated essay scoring invades higher education. I end with an agenda to release us from this deer-in-the-headlights stance.

First, we should not blame the commercial testing firms. They have filled a vacuum we abandoned, they have gravitated toward the profits, they have sunk their own R&D money into creation and testing of the programs, they have safeguarded their algorithms and prompts, they have marketed by the marketing rules, and they are reaping their well-earned payoffs—this is all in their entrepreneurial nature.

Second, that doesn't mean we should necessarily follow the path they have blazed. Nor does *that* mean that we should necessarily follow our own paths. With the assessment and evaluation of writing, probably the best rule is to be cautious about any route that has been tried in the past, and doubly cautious about programs that swear they have seen the Grail. Pick up again the forty-year history of writing evaluation at the University of Houston. I don't know how long they stuck with their 1961 "superior" Redi-Tutors, but in 1977 they saw student "illiteracy" as such a problem that they classified *all* their entering students as "remedial" writers and placed them into one of two categories, NP or BC. NP stood for "needs practice" and BC for "basket case." So they introduced an exit writing examination. In the first trial, 41 percent of African Americans and 40 percent of Hispanics failed. Despite these results and an ever-growing enrollment, they remained upbeat: "Writing can actually be taught in a lecture hall with 200 or more students. We are doing it" (Rice 1977, 190). In 1984 they installed a junior writing exam to catch "illiterate" AA transfers. They judged it a success: "The foreign students who used to blithely present their composition credits from the junior college across town are deeply troubled" (Dressman 1986-87, 15). But all this assessment consumed faculty and counseling time. So in 2003 they turned all their testing for first-year placement and rising-junior proficiency "exclusively" over to ACT's WritePlacer. They claim their problems are now solved. "WritePlacer Plus Online helps ensure that every University of Houston graduate enters the business world with solid writing skills," and "it also makes the university itself look even more professional"

(University of Houston 2003, 32). Other universities, I am suggesting, may want to postpone looking professional until they have looked professionally at Houston's model, its history, and its claims.

Third, not only do we need to challenge such claims, we need to avoid treating evaluation of writing in general as a black box, need to keep exploring every evaluative procedure until it becomes as much of a white box as we can make it. I say keep exploring because our discipline has a long history of Nancy Drew investigation into writing evaluation, longer than that of the testing firms. Our findings do not always concur with those of the College Board and Educational Testing Service, even when we are investigating the same box, such as holistic scoring. That is because our social motives are different, as Latour would be the first to point out. In fact, our findings often severely question commercial evaluation tactics. Stormzand and O'Shea (1924) found nonacademic adult writers (including newspaper editors and women letter writers) using the passive voice much more frequently than did college student writers, far above the rate red-flagged years later by commercial grammar-check programs; Freedman (1984) found teachers devaluing professional writing when they thought it was student authored; Barritt, Stock, and Clark (1986) found readers of placement essays forming mental pictures of the writer when decisions became difficult; my own analysis (Haswell 2002) snooped into the ways writing teachers categorized a piece of writing in terms of first-year writing-program objectives, and detected them ranking the traits in the same order with a nonnative writer and a native writer but assigning the traits less central value with the nonnative; Broad (2003) discovered not five or six criteria being used by teachers in evaluating first-year writing portfolios but forty-six textual criteria, twenty-two contextual criteria, and twenty-one other factors. This kind of investigation is not easy. It's detailed and time-consuming, a multiround wrestling match with large numbers of texts, criteria, and variables. Drudgery, if you wish a less agonistic metaphor. And dear Latour points out that as you challenge the black boxes further and further within, the investigation costs more and more money. To fully sound out the *Arabidopsis* variant may require building your own genetics lab. To bring e-rater construction completely to light may require suing the Educational Testing Service. "Arguing," says Latour, "is costly" (1987, 69). But without black-box investigations, we lack the grounds to resist machine scoring, or any kind of scoring. I second the strong call of Williamson (2004) for the discipline "to study automated assessment in order to explicate the potential value for teaching and learning, as well as the potential harm" (100).

Fourth, we need to insist that our institutions stop making students buy tests that do not generate the kind of outcomes right for our purposes. Here I am not saying anything new. For a quarter of a century now, researchers in composition have been showing that holistic scoring is not the best way to diagnose or record potential in student writing, yet potential is what placement in writing courses is all about. What I have been saying that may be new—at least the way it is disregarded suggests that it is new to quite a few people—is that from the start current machine scoring has been designed to be counterproductive for our needs. As I have said, the closer the programs get to traditional large-scale holistic rating—to this particular, peculiar method by which humans rate student essays—the less valid the programs are for placement.

Fifth, we need to find not only grounds and reasons but also concrete ways to resist misused machine scoring. Usually we can't just tell our administration (or state) to stop buying or requiring WritePlacer. Usually we can't just tell our administration we do not accept the scores that it has made our students purchase, even when we are willing to conduct a more valid procedure. For many of the powers that be, machine scoring is a deus ex machina rescuing all of us—students, teachers, and institution—from writing placement that has turned out to be a highly complicated entanglement without any clear denouement. The new scoring machines may have a charlatan look, with groaning beams and squeaking pulleys, but they work—that is, the input and the output don't create waves for management. So composition teachers and researchers need to fight fire with fire, or rather machine with machine. We need to enter the fray. First, we should demand that the new testing be tested. No administration can forbid that. Find some money, pay students just placed in basic writing via a commercial machine to retest via the same machine. My guess is that most of them will improve their placement. Or randomly pick a significant chunk of the students placed by machine into basic writing and mainstream them instead into regular composition, to see how they do. If nine-tenths of them pass (and they will), what does that say about the validity of the machine scores?

To these two modest proposals allow me to add an immodest one. We need to construct our own dei ex machina, our own golems, our own essay-analysis software programs. They would not be machine scorers but machine placers. They would come as close as machinely possible to predict from a pre-course-placement essay whether the student would benefit from our courses. Let's remember that the algorithms underlying a machine's essay-scoring protocol are not inevitable. Just as human readers, a machine reader can be "trained" in any number of different ways. Our machine placer would take as its target criterion not holistic rates of a student's placement essay but end-of-course teacher appraisals of the student's writing improvement during the actual courses into which the student had been placed. All the current methods of counting, tagging, and parsing—the proxes, as Page calls them—could be tried: rate of new words, fourth root of essay length, number of words devoted to trite phrases, percentage of content words that are found in model essays on the placement topics, as well as other, different proxes that are associated with situational writing growth rather than decontextualized writing quality. This machine placer would get better and better at identifying which traits of precourse writing lead to subsequent writing gain in courses. This is not science fiction. This can be done now. Then, in the tradition of true scholarship, let's give the programs free to any college that wants to install them on its servers and use them in place of commercial testing at $29 a head or $799 a site license. That will be easier even than hawking Kitchen Magicians. And then, in the tradition of good teaching, let's treat the scores not as single, final fiats from on high but embed them in local placement systems, systems that employ multiple predictor variables, retesting, course switching, early course exit, credit enhancement, informed self-placement, mainstreaming with ancillary tutoring—systems that recognize student variability, teacher capability, and machine fallibility.

Sixth, whatever our strategy, whatever the resistance we choose against the forces outside our profession to keep them from wresting another of our professional skills from out of our control, we have to make sure that in our resistance we are not thereby further debilitating those skills. We need to fight our own internal forces that work against good evaluation. Above all, we have to resist the notion of diagnostic response as rote drudgery, recognize it for what it is, a skill indeed—a difficult, complex, and rewarding skill requiring elastic intelligence and long experience. Good diagnosis of student writing should not be construed as easy, for the simple reason that it is never easy.

Here are few lines from a student placement essay that e-Write judged as promising (score of 6 out of possible 8) and that writing faculty members judged as not promising (they decided the student should have been placed in a course below regular composition). The prompt asks for an argument supporting the construction of either a new youth center or a larger public library.

I tell you from my heart, I really would love to see our little library become a place of comfort and space for all those who love to read and relax, where we would have a plethora of information and rows upon rows of books and even a small media center. I have always loved our library and I have been one of those citizens always complaining about how we need more space, how we need more room to sit and read, how we need a bigger building for our fellow people of this community.

But, I thought long and hard about both proposals, I really did, how nice would it be for young teens to meet at a local place in town, where they would be able to come and feel welcome, in a safe environment, where there would be alot less of a chance for a young adult of our community to get into serious trouble?

What is relevant here in terms of potential and curriculum? The careful distinctions ("comfort and space")? The sophisticated phrase "plethora of information"? The accumulation of topical points within series? The sequencing of rhetorical emphasis within series ("even")? The generous elaboration of the opposing position? The unstated antimony between "fellow people" and "young adult"? The fluid euphony of sound and syntactic rhythm? All I am saying is that in terms of curricular potential there is more here than the computer algorithms of sentence length and topic token-word maps, and also more than faculty alarm over spelling ("alot") and comma splices. Writing faculty, as well as machines, need the skill to diagnose such subtleties and complexities.

In all honesty, the art of getting inside the black box of the student essay is hard work. In the reading of student writing, everyone needs to be reengaged and stimulated with the difficult, which is the only path to the good, as that most hieratic of poets José Lezama Lima once said. If we do not embrace difficulty in this part of our job, easy evaluation will drive out good evaluation every time.

5

TAKING A SPIN ON THE INTELLIGENT ESSAY ASSESSOR

Tim McGee

The following narrative recounts an experiment I performed upon a particular essay-scoring machine, the Intelligent Essay Assessor (IEA), that was first brought to my attention by Anne Herrington and Charles Moran's 2001 *College English* essay "What Happens When Machines Read Our Students' Writing?" As a writing program administrator, I was experienced in the progressive waves of writing assessment historically performed by human readers and well versed in many aspects of computer-assisted instruction. At the time of my experiment, however, I was still a neophyte in the area of automated essay scoring. Nevertheless, despite serious misgivings about my qualifications in the arcane realm of artificial intelligence, I took to heart Herrington and Moran's call to learn about these programs "so that we can participate in their evaluation and can help frame the debate about the wisdom of their use in our own institutions" (484–85).

This account of my experiment with IEA and how it helped me frame the debate about machine scoring, first to local colleagues and later at the NCTE conference in Baltimore, represents both a report of my research and a story about how English teachers (and other mere humanists) might respond to corporate vendors of increasingly sophisticated programs in the technically bewildering arena of automated essay scoring. Consequently, in addition to recounting my method, results, and conclusions, I have included certain historical and biographical material to help the reader understand how my practice was informed by theory (of both textual analysis and writing assessment) and motivated by site-specific relationships of knowledge and power.

NOT YOUR FATHER'S SCORING MACHINE

Unlike the scoring machines that are aimed specifically at the needs of large-scale placement assessment, IEA is pitched as a "new learning tool, useful in almost any subject" that promises to ease the burden of assigning writing across the curriculum and purports to measure the "factual knowledge" displayed in student essays. IEA is just one of several products marketed by Knowledge Analysis Technologies, whose Web site included the tagline "Putting Knowledge to the Test" and promised "[m]achine learning technology that understands the meaning of text."[1] Compared to the average academic sites, many of which had yet to exploit the graphical possibilities of the Web, Knowledge Analysis Technologies' home page was as visually enticing as the most polished commercial and entertainment Web sites. At the same time, the easily navigated site provided the scholarly apparatus one normally associates with academic research, including impressive lists of publications by the company's principals and full-text access to several white papers. (The home page has since been toned down visually, the heavily Photoshopped montage of learners—including smiling children, a female soldier, and a U.S. flag—now replaced by a file-folder navigation bar and a color scheme to match that of the new corporate parent, Pearson Education.) The rhetorical sophistication of the original site was equally impressive, as the content and tone of the promotional copy aimed at military clients contrasted noticeably with those portions of the Web site where the implied audience was college professors. However, most stunning of all were Knowledge Analysis Technologies' invitations to "[i]magine intelligent Internet technology . . . that understands the meaning of written essays, evaluates them and provides feedback as accurately as a professional educator or trainer." Particularly amazing were the following claims:

> IEA is the only essay evaluation system in which meaning is dominant. It measures factual knowledge based on semantic content, not on superficial factors such as word counts, punctuation, grammar or keywords. IEA also provides tutorial commentary, plagiarism detection, and extensive validity self-checks. And it does it right now—not in days or weeks. (Knowledge Analysis Technologies 2001)

What made these claims stand out were the bold assertions about understanding meaning, both in light of conventional wisdom among compositionists and in comparison to the far more cautious claims of competing vendors. The conventional wisdom had been succinctly stated ten years earlier by Fred Kemp when he wrote that "computers can process text in only the most superficial of senses; computers cannot grasp the meaning in the text" (1992, 14). While it was possible that great leaps in natural language processing had been made in the intervening decade, Knowledge Analysis Technologies' claims still sounded outlandish when compared to ETS pronouncements about e-rater, the scoring engine behind Criterion and other products, which scrupulously avoided even claiming that e-rater "read" essays, much less "understood" them. As a potential adopter of products that seemed likely to help teachers and students with the important work of assessing writing, I was interested in interrogating Knowledge Analysis Technologies' claims.

INSTITUTIONAL SETTING

I was interested not just in the sense of piqued curiosity but, as an administrator cum teacher/scholar, I was an interested party in the shifting interrelationships among teaching, research, and commerce now found in several areas of computer-mediated communication. That interest was complicated by an accident of geography that put my institution in a particularly cozy relationship with ETS; while not in the vanguard of embracing instructional technology, the college was poised to adopt, or at least try, machine scoring of some student essays.

Located fifteen minutes from the national headquarters of ETS, the college had numerous faculty members who regularly worked as evaluators and consultants in several content areas, while the school generated considerable income every year by renting out blocks of classrooms for mass scoring of various tests. The impacts were not strictly financial, as the employment opportunities also yielded a familiarity with holistic essay scoring that extended well beyond the disciplinary borders of English and composition. For example, when the School of Business requested a workshop to help its faculty integrate writing into their curricula, I learned that some business professors were already using holistic scoring guides lifted from a Graduate Management Admissions Test essay-scoring session by one of their colleagues.

The college's interest in investigating machine scoring had already found expression from various corners, including the dean of Academic Support, the director of the Economic Opportunity Fund Program, and the Writing Assessment Committee of the School of Business. It was the last group (formed as part of the pursuit of Association to Advance Collegiate Schools of Business accreditation) that actively pursued machine scoring, as the business faculty sought a mechanism for implementing a value-added assessment of their students' writing skills that would meet their own quantitative notions of reliability and validity while also appearing objective to outside evaluators.[2] This led to the purchase of enough access to Criterion for a pilot study in which a portion of incoming business majors wrote to a GMAT-style "issue" prompt.

As a result, I had some firsthand experience with a scoring engine that relied, as Knowledge Analysis Technologies dismissively put it, upon "superficial factors such as word counts, punctuation, grammar or keywords," and I held the quaint notion that an evaluation system that claimed to get at "meaning" might not want to abandon punctuation, much less grammar. In other words, I was willing to grant limited possibilities for machines that performed automated essay scoring the old-fashioned way: counting, measuring, and using keywords and parsers for recursive syntactical analysis to compare a new sample essay to a large batch of essays previously scored holistically by trained human readers.

Admittedly, that willingness bespeaks a certain unreconstructed New Critical approach to textual analysis that many (myself included) now find theoretically problematic when talking about serious analyses of texts, including student texts. However, the assembly-line analyses of timed impromptu essays written to a "general knowledge" prompt by students under duress, with no recourse to the usual parts of their composing process (much less such aids as dictionaries or peer critics) is already such a constrained response to a rather inauthentic text-production event that the analytical approaches designed to remedy the severe limitations of New Criticism need not be invoked. In other words, given the severe limitations of what a short impromptu essay test allows students to display,[3] an analytical approach that assumes the meaning and value of a piece of discourse is discernible by an examination of the text itself is not theoretically inappropriate. While fully agreeing with Herrington and Moran's (2001) conclusions about other harms that machine scoring does to the entire project of rhetorical education, I believed that the latest generation of scoring engines could, in fact, replicate the scores given by humans in the relatively restricted domain of large-scale placement assessments.[4]

But that is a far cry from accepting the claim that a scoring engine "understands the meaning of written essays." And given that humans would be hard pressed to understand an essay without relying, to some degree, on "punctuation, grammar or keywords," I was thoroughly mystified about how IEA could possibly do so. Neither the promotional copy of the Knowledge Analysis Technologies site nor the teacher-friendly account provided by Herrington and Moran did much to demystify how the artificial intelligence behind IEA actually worked. Here is what the promotional portions of Knowledge Analysis Technologies' site said about IEA's approach:

> The Intelligent Essay Assessor uses Latent Semantic Analysis, a machine-learning algorithm that accurately mimics human understanding of language. This patented and proprietary technology is based on over 10 years of corporate and university research and development. IEA analyzes the body of text from which people learn to derive an understanding of essays on that topic. The algorithm is highly computer intensive, requiring over a gigabyte of RAM, which is why IEA is offered as a web-based service. (2001)

Herrington and Moran call IEA "quite an interesting product" and provide two pages of eminently readable explanation that begins as follows:

> IEA derives from Thomas Landauer's work on what he termed "latent semantic analysis." Latent semantic analysis (LSA) is, briefly and for our purposes, based on the assumption that there is a close relationship between the meaning of a text and the words in that text: both what these words are and how these words are related to one another in the space of the text. Landauer and his group are not talking here about lexical or grammatical relationships but about spatial relationships: what words the text includes and in what spatial relationship to one another. For their purposes, lexical and grammatical relationships are irrelevant. (2001, 491)

They go on to explain that Landauer and company posited the existence of "vast numbers of weak interrelations" in some domains of knowledge and the ability to describe them mathematically. This, in turn, allows a machine "to measure whether someone has learned something or not by looking at the text that person produces and seeing whether this text contains some of the 'vast number of interrelations' that are characteristic of the material that was to have been learned" (491). The focus on learning content is peculiar to IEA because, unlike the machines marketed primarily as aids to placement assessment, IEA promises to help teachers and learners by evaluating essays based on what their authors appear to know about a topic.

METHOD

Intrigued by the prospects of this seemingly revolutionary approach to machine scoring, I wanted to design an experiment that would give me a better sense of how IEA actually worked. I modeled my method upon that of Herrington and Moran, who had submitted multiple drafts to the machines, watched the scores change, and then asked what the ratings seemed to indicate about how the machines "read" the essays and what criteria were operating (2001, 490). In the end, I wanted to compare IEA's notion of "meaning" with my own. That led me to consider what I meant by "meaning," not in a broad philosophical sense, but in the relatively restricted domain of student essays written to specific prompts.

Rarely, when reading impromptu essays, had I felt compelled to decode ironies, ponder obscure cultural references, or interpret subtle uses of symbolism. The textual ambiguities I regularly encountered in impromptu essays rarely seemed intentional, productive, or fodder for deconstructive performance; rather, they usually appeared to be the results of imprecise word choice and careless syntax. I concluded that making face-value meaning out of impromptu essays is an interpretive process that relies primarily upon lexicon, syntax, propositional content, and the arrangement of ideas. In effect, I had no reservations about granting the machines ample ground on which to perform admirably in the analysis of multiple textual features that, in my estimation, contribute heavily to face-value meaning. Furthermore, having taught composition mostly to well-prepared first-year college students, I held the view that most were able to compose legal sentences in decent paragraphs but not yet skilled in global text arrangement, especially when writing arguments (as opposed to narratives, reports, or expositions of processes). As a result, I was of the opinion that arrangement exerts considerable influence as a higher-order source of meaning, especially in student essays.

Consequently, when I began my experiment, I had some positive expectations about the potential for an analytical approach that depended in part upon how "words are related to one another in the space of the text." My intention was not to trick the machine into awarding high scores to meaningless gibberish, but rather to make some calculated revisions to texts that the machine purportedly scored well so I might consider what the changed scores told me about how IEA was "reading" these essays and what criteria were operating for determining meaning.

While Knowledge Analysis Technologies' claims about IEA understanding meaning might seem to have invited something like a Turing test,[5] my aims were considerably more modest. Holding no illusions about IEA deserving to be deemed intelligent based upon any dialogue with a user, I was simply attempting to get a fix on Knowledge Analysis Technologies' definition of and criteria for meaning. I proposed to accomplish this by analyzing what features of a text appeared to affect the evaluations produced by a "system in which meaning is dominant." I also had a desire to operate upon something like the principle of charity, submitting only essays that might meet the criteria for what the some of the test vendors call a "good faith effort."

In a panel session at CCCC 2001 titled "Challenging 'E-rater': Efforts to Refine Computerized Essay Scoring," Mary Fowles of ETS recounted how their researchers used various tactics to trick their scoring machine and then used those results to refine the program. While she and other representatives of ETS have admitted that it is possible to design essays specifically aimed at tricking the machines into awarding top scores to texts that no human would rate highly, they contend that a fair assessment of the machine's reliability and validity depends upon the submission of essays that are like ones that real students would actually submit, what they refer to as "good faith efforts."[6] However, any requirement to limit the revisions of their sample texts to ones that possessed some degree of verisimilitude to actual student texts would represent a substantial restriction upon my efforts to quickly ascertain what features contributed to meaning. Furthermore, such a restriction would seem to turn my experiment back in the direction of a sort of reverse Turing test, as if I were attempting to ascertain when IEA knew that the submission was not from a real student. So, I opted to look at the sample essays IEA offered and try to determine what specific characteristics of each essay seemed most integral to its meaning.

RESULTS OF THREE SPINS ON THE MACHINE

The Knowledge Analysis Technologies Web site provided unfettered access to the "Intelligent Essay Assessor™ Demonstration Page," which included five different "content-based essays" that visitors could experiment with. Each of the five was identified by subject, topic, and grade level. These were the choices:

- Biology: Function of Heart and Circulatory System (College Freshman)
- Psychology 1: Attachment in Children (College Freshman)
- Psychology 2: Types of Aphasia (College Freshman)
- Psychology 3: Operant Conditioning (College Freshman)
- History: The Great Depression (11th Grade High School) (KAT 2004a)

The instructions give the visitor the choice to "compose your own essay or use one of the sample essays provided" and include, for each essay, a prompt that requests (with varying degrees of specificity) a certain response from the writer. The prompt for the "Function of the Heart" essay makes the following request:

> Please write down what you know about the human heart and circulatory system. Your essay should be approximately 250 words. We would like for you to be as specific as possible in discussing the anatomy, function, and purpose of the heart and circulatory system.

The IEA demonstration page included three different essays in response to the "Function of the Heart" topic, each one scored on a 1 to 5 scale in four categories: overall, content, style, and mechanics. The best of their three sample essays (biology sample 1) scored 4 overall, receiving 4 for content and 3 each for both style and mechanics. This sample starts with a functional definition ("The heart is the main pump in the body that supplies the rest of the body with oxygenated blood by way of the arteries") and then proceeds through an orderly exposition that includes the replacement of oxygen in the blood by CO_2, traces the path of the blood through the veins to the heart and lungs, and concludes "now the blood will be pumped to the rest of the body and the cycle begins again." As I attempted to determine how I made meaning of this particular essay that explained a biological process, I decided that I was relying heavily upon a combination of lexicon, syntax, and sequence, especially in terms of the various techniques used to foster cohesion from one sentence to the next.[7]

Experiment 1

I was struck by the highly sequential nature of the exposition and imagined that the aptness of the particular sequence the author had chosen had considerable bearing on both the correctness of the content and the global coherence of the essay. I wondered what effect changing the sequence of the sentences might have on the essay's score. I assumed that such a change would have no effect on the essay's mechanics score, but should have some effect on its style score, and wondered just how large an effect changing the sequence of the sentences might have on the essay's content score. So, I took biology sample 1 and, leaving each individual sentence unchanged, reversed the order of its thirteen constituent sentences, so the first sentence becomes the last and vice versa. The result is a rather peculiar text that doesn't actually describe the heart and lungs working opposite of the way they really do. Rather, the effect is more like that of the movie *Memento*, in which each individual section of narrative runs chronologically but the narrative as whole runs backward.

Hence, the revised essay begins as follows:

> The left ventricle is the most muscular of the heart because now the blood will be pumped to the rest of the body and the cycle begins again. The blood is then pumped into the left ventricle through the left atrioventricular valve. The blood, now oxygenated, goes back to the heart by way of the pulmonary vein and then into the left atrium.

The meaning of the individual sentences is unchanged, but the assembled whole has suffered a substantial reduction in both cohesion and coherence, not to mention factual accuracy. I was surprised (and disappointed) when IEA awarded the exact same score to the fully reversed essay as it had awarded sample 1. Someone with a better understanding of latent semantic analysis might have guessed that the reversed sample 1 would receive a score identical to the original sample 1 because, to the Intelligent Essay Assessor, the two are the same essay. However, to mere mortals who rely upon cohesion, coherence, sequence, and arrangement as ways to make meaning of written discourse, sample 1 and reversed sample 1 are radically different essays, with reversed sample 1 providing a substantially less meaningful exposition of the function of the heart and circulatory system. I therefore concluded that global arrangement is not part of IEA's notion of "meaning." Even more disconcerting was the realization that neither cohesion nor coherence (in the senses used by Joseph Williams in *Style* [2000]) had any impact on "meaning" as that term is used by the producers of IEA.

Experiment 2

Based upon Knowledge Analysis Technologies' claim that IEA "measures factual content," I attempted to see how a change to the factual content of an essay might alter its score. Of the various samples available on the IEA demonstration page (2004a) the history essays on the Great Depression seemed the ones most chock-full of factual content. The prompt for the history essay is not nearly as specific as the one for biology, asking simply, "Please write a structured essay on the 'Great Depression' and the 'New Deal.'"

Again, history sample 1 received the highest score, getting a 5 overall, with 5 for content and 4s for both style and mechanics. At 564 words, it was the longest essay in the IEA demonstration page and seemed the best candidate for attempting to determine how IEA's measurement of factual content affected its analysis of meaning. The most straightforward way I could imagine altering the factual content of the essay was to simply reverse the truth value of many of its propositions. Where the original essay wrote "was," I substituted "was not." "Biggest" became "smallest," "before" became "after," and "start" became "end." For example, here is the beginning of original history sample 1:

> There were many problems facing the nation in 1938, following the stock market crash in 1929 and in the midst of Franklin D. Roosevelt's New Deal. Roosevelt, a moderate, attempted to combat the system of rising tariffs, expand opportunity in business for the independent man, reestablish foreign markets for America's surplus production, meet the problem of under consumption, distribute the nation's wealth and instigate a level playing field in America.

The revised history sample 1 begins as follows:

> There were few problems facing the nation in 1929, following the stock market crash in 1938 and at the end of Franklin D. Roosevelt's New Deal. Roosevelt, a radical, attempted to promote the system of rising tariffs, diminish opportunity in business for the independent man, end foreign markets for America's surplus production, meet the problem of over consumption, centralize the nation's wealth and instigate a tilted playing field in America.

This process was continued throughout all twenty-four sentences of the original sample. Clearly, the factual content in the revised sample 1 is markedly different from that in the original sample 1. A machine that somehow "measures factual content" ought, it would seem, to come up with a different measurement, unless, of course, it measured only the amount of factual content, in which case, the revised sample 1 might measure up to the original. But surely, the meaning has changed substantially. To "diminish opportunity in business for the independent man" means the opposite of to "expand opportunity in business for the independent man."

Frighteningly, IEA awarded the same high score of 5 (with all the same subscores) to the revised sample 1, despite the fact that it is as factually inaccurate as could be while still being an essay on the topic of the Great Depression and the New Deal.[8] So, unlike this humanist's definition of meaning, on which such pedestrian notions as the logical denotation of a phrase have considerable bearing, IEA's notion of meaning appears to exist quite independent of any relationship to factual accuracy. And yet, amazingly, Knowledge Analysis Technologies claims that IEA "measures factual content."

Experiment 3

Having acted in what I considered to be good faith on my first two efforts and beginning to feel like a bit of a chump for having believed that this machine could, in fact, isolate something in a text that bore some relationship to what normal people consider to be the text's meaning, I was now ready to submit something outlandish, but perhaps not quite as outlandish as Knowledge Analysis Technologies' claims about IEA understanding meaning and measuring factual content.

I chose "Psychology 2:Types of Aphasia" and endeavored to find out if there was, in fact, anything that IEA did not find meaningful. I was looking to see if there was a bottom discourse that IEA would not accept as a meaningful text. The actual prompt for "Types of Aphasia" I considered to be one of the best and most interesting on the IEA demonstration" page, because of its high specificity and potential for eliciting somewhat authentic displays of knowledge and understanding. Here is the prompt:

> After a mild stroke, Mr. McGeorge showed some signs of aphasia. What pattern of symptoms would lead you to believe he had suffered damage primarily in: (a) Broca's area, (b) Wernicke's area, (c) the angular gyrus? (2004a)

This collection of samples was scored on a 10-point scale, with sample 1 receiving a 7 overall, with 7s for content and style and a 6 for mechanics. On this sample revision, I preserved much of the original vocabulary and maintained most of the sequence, while turning the diagnosis itself into nonsense, complete with multiple cases of mangled syntax. Here is the entire original sample 1:

> To detect the effects that Mr. McGeorge's stroke had I would conduct several experiments testing his ability to communicate. If he had trouble verbalizing words I would be alerted that his Broca's area of the left frontal lobe was damaged. However, if he could not even comprehend the meaning of a word that would indicate damage to his Wernicke's area of the left temporal lobe. Finally, if Mr. McGeorge could not even "see" the words in his head, or understand writing, I would conclude he had damaged his angular gyrus located in the occipital lobe. (It is assumed that Mr. McGeorge is right-handed with his speech center being the left hemisphere).

And here is the revised sample 1 that I submitted to IEA:

To effect the detects that Mr.stroke McGeorge had I would several conduct experiments testing ability his communicate to. If he had trouble verbalizing the left frontal lobe I would alert Tom Broca that his communicate was damaged. However, if he could not even meaning the comprehend of a word that would indicate damage his to area Wernicke's the of left lobe temporarily. Finally, if Mr. McGeorge could not even "pronounce" the words in his mouth, or understand the meaning of finally, I would fasten his angular gyrus to his occipital lobe. (It is assumed that Mr. McGeorge is even-handed with his speech center being on the far left wing).

I was pleased to discover that IEA did not award this gibberish the same score as the original, and did, in fact, reduce its content score. That indicated to me that the machine really did process submitted texts in some fashion—apparently the lights were on and somebody was home. Unfortunately (or fortunately for my purposes, which had undergone some revision in the course of the experiment), IEA awarded the revised sample 1 the same overall score, because the one content point it lost (slipping from a 7 down to a 6) was balanced by the one point it gained in the area of mechanics (rising from a 6 to a 7). This caused me to wonder what the makers of IEA could possibly mean by "mechanics" if the revised sample 1 was mechanically superior to the original.

However, by that time I had seen enough to draw two conclusions: the meaning of "meaning" that Knowledge Analysis Technologies was using in its claims about IEA was nothing like the conventional meaning of that word as used by laypeople, humanists, compositionists, or even such esoteric groups as philosophers of language. The meaning of a text that latent semantic analysis actually gets at, if in fact it gets at any, is so far removed from any notion of meaning that anyone assigning writing to students would be employing that it appears to render the claims that Knowledge Analysis Technologies was making about IEA's analytical abilities patently false. Latent semantic analysis does appear to do something, but whatever it does appears to be wildly unsuited to the scoring of student essays. Whatever subtle information latent semantic analysis may yield, the Intelligent Essay Assessor's performance on the three sample essays was seriously at odds with and far inferior to the results of blatant semantic analysis, or the meaning that a mere mortal might make from those sample texts.

PRESENTATION OF FINDINGS

Shocked as I was by the inadequacies of IEA for evaluating student essays, and appalled as I was at the thought that this product was being marketed to high school and college faculty as an appropriate tool to aid in the integration of writing "in almost any subject," I felt compelled to share my views with my colleagues, first at a collegewide Teaching and Learning with Technology workshop and later at the 2001 NCTE conference. At both venues, the reenactment of my experiment was met by a mixture of dropped jaws and howling laughter. So, for two audiences, with a total number of perhaps fifty souls, I was able to demonstrate that one particular approach to automated essay scoring was unlikely to be as useful as the vendor's promotional copy would lead potential adopters to believe. Meanwhile, stories about IEA kept appearing in the mainstream media, telling millions of people what Knowledge Analysis Technologies said their product promised to do.

At my own institution, there was never any likelihood that IEA was going to be adopted widely, and even the pilot use of Criterion turned out unsuccessfully, as too many of the first-year students at that selective college scored near the top of the 6-point scale for ETS's machine to serve the value-added purposes that the School of Business had hoped to use it for. But I shudder to think how many high school and college students have already had their rhetorical education impacted by the introduction of Knowledge Analysis Technologies' IEA into the curriculum.

As I mentioned, since being purchased by Pearson Education, Knowledge Analysis Technologies' Web site has been toned down considerably, both visually and in terms of its claims about understanding meaning. However, four years after my original experiment, IEA still works as abysmally as it did in 2001; the scores it awards to the three revised samples are unchanged from those it coughed up four years ago. But now it has the corporate backing of Pearson Education, a company that many educators associate with an outstanding collection of composition and rhetoric titles from what used to be the publishers Addison-Wesley, Longman, and Allyn & Bacon, but are now Pearson "brands." The combination of deep corporate pockets, the credibility that attaches to Pearson's stable of authors, and the marketing ploy of bundling ancillary Web resources with textbook adoptions seems likely to spell huge increases in the deployment of IEA upon unsuspecting students hoping for meaningful responses to drafts and polished essays, a prospect I find both frightening and depressing.

MORAL OF THE STORY

My experience with IEA began with Herrington and Moran's essay in *College English* (2001) and their call to learn about the scoring machines and to participate in the debate surrounding them. I quickly learned that despite my inability to engage in an informed debate about the merits of the artificial intelligence behind IEA, it was really quite easy to demonstrate that latent semantic analysis, at least as it is embodied in IEA, cannot be trusted to score student essays well. In effect, it may have been my innocence in the realm of artificial intelligence that led me to this emperor's new clothes sort of revelation. I concluded that IEA represents a form of automated essay scoring that no conscientious educator would unleash upon students wanting meaningful evaluation of their writing. In the end, my experience did help me frame the debate in my own institution, and I hope that the presentations of my findings can help others to do the same.

6

ACCUPLACER'S ESSAY-SCORING TECHNOLOGY
When Reliability Does Not Equal Validity

Edmund Jones

Placement of students in first-year writing courses is generally seen as a time-consuming but necessary exercise at most colleges and universities in the United States. Administrators have been concerned about both the expense and inconvenience of testing, about the validity of the tests, and about the reliability of the scorers. Over the past decade, computer technology has developed to the point that a company like ACCUPLACER, under the auspices of the College Board, can plausibly offer computer programs that score student essays with the same reliability as expert scorers (Vantage Learning 2000). Under this system, schools need hire no faculty members to score essays, and students can arrange to be proctored off-site; thus placement testing becomes far more convenient without increasing costs. In fact, for these very reasons, Seton Hall University currently uses ACCUPLACER to aid in placing students in College English I and basic skills courses. On the middle school and high school level as well, classroom teachers appear willing to use computer ratings to help rate students or to supplement their feedback on students' writing (Jones 1999).

However, for reasons both theoretical and pedagogical, some in the discipline of composition have questioned the appropriateness of using computers to score writing. In a critical discussion of machine scoring in *College English* in 2001, Herrington and Moran raise several concerns. They wonder about the effect that writing for a computer instead of a human being will have on composing an essay. And they believe that "an institution that adopts the machine-reading of student writing sends its students two messages: human readers are unreliable, quirky, expensive, and finally irrelevant; and students' writing matters only in a very narrow range: its length, its vocabulary, its correctness," or its ability to conform to what a computer can measure (497).

Perhaps living with less theoretical concerns, professional testing administrators at New Jersey colleges have generally embraced

ACCUPLACER (Kozinski 2003). And they are happy about WritePlacer *Plus*, the direct writing-assessment component of ACCUPLACER, precisely because it *is* reliable. Reliability refers to the ability of a scorer, whether human or machine, to give the same score consistently to essays of similar quality and for one scorer to give the same scores as another scorer. When two humans score an essay, there is always the possibility that they will have somewhat different criteria and, consequently, score the essay differently—unless, of course, they are carefully trained under controlled circumstances. This training takes time and money. If a computer can be trained to score essays, on the other hand, reliability problems should disappear. IntelliMetric, the proprietary electronic essay-scoring technology developed by Vantage Technologies, always scores the same way. As for human-computer interreliability ratings, according to ACCUPLACER its computers agree with human scorers within one point between 97 percent and 99 percent of the time (Vantage Learning 2000).

But the directors in the writing program at Seton Hall wondered if, despite high marks on reliability, IntelliMetric lives up to Vantage Learning's claims for construct validity.[1] That is, we wondered if the computer evaluates what we think it is evaluating. In this concern about validity over reliability we are not alone. Powers et al. (2002) explain that computers will always agree with each other, thus being reliable, but that they may be programmed to focus on a restricted number of criteria for evaluating essays (409). While Herrington and Moran (2001) raise questions about the validity of writing for a nonhuman audience, they also wonder whether the computer can be trusted to evaluate some of the nuances of writing. On the local level, Nancy Enright and I, both directors in the English department at Seton Hall University, had informally come to the conclusion that WritePlacer *Plus* rewards essay length out of proportion to its value. Like Herrington and Moran, however, we couldn't go beyond developing hunches about the validity of the scoring itself because we hadn't systematically analyzed data from student placement essays. We could only suspect that length and mechanical correctness matter to IntelliMetric. One might wonder, though, why not just write to Vantage Learning to ask how the computer goes about scoring the essays? The answer: proprietary information is not divulged by companies that have created software to evaluate writing. As a result, we needed to work with the only evidence we had about how the computers worked: computer-generated essay scores.

Herrington submitted an essay and two revisions—one to improve the original and one to weaken it—to investigate IntelliMetric's powers of discrimination. This approach is logical enough, but Vantage Learning might argue that she wasn't writing the way students actually write essays. After all, IntelliMetric "learns" how to score essays by digesting actual students' essays along with scores given by expert human scorers. In order to address this potential criticism, I thought it important to identify anomalies in actual placement-test essay scores before performing any experiments. Two other instructors at Seton Hall University and I reviewed 149 essays submitted by incoming freshmen Seton Hall students from the summers of 2002 and 2004. We grouped essays by score and then read them, thus deliberately norming ourselves against WritePlacer *Plus*'s holistic scoring system. (Although it would be possible to critique holistic scoring in general, I wanted to examine ACCUPLACER on its own terms—to critique machine scoring in a way that would speak most effectively to the majority of institutions which, for better or worse, accept holistic scoring.) Our method allowed us to readily identify those essays that seemed significantly worse than or better than others in that score group. From this collection of anomalously scored essays, we searched for patterns: which types of essays posed problems for WritePlacer *Plus*? In a preliminary study (Jones 2002), I was able to find a pattern among essays that scored high but seemed weak: they tended to be long. I found a second pattern among essays that were mechanically correct and well developed but seemed weak: they had awkward phrasings that didn't look like English. I expected these patterns to enable me to identify hidden criteria and to identify problems that are invisible to the computer.

Once these hidden criteria were identified, I planned to enter doctored essays, always starting from actual student originals. For example, after Nancy and I suspected that essay length was overvalued, I chose two essays that were each awarded a 6 (out of 12) by WritePlacer *Plus*, appended one to the other, and resubmitted them as one essay. The resultant score? A 9. The computer did not seem to recognize the incoherence that must result from such an operation but apparently rewarded length as a value by itself. Others have used the method of identifying anomalous scorings (Roy 1993), but none, as far as I know, have systematically investigated the ability of the computer to discriminate according to specific criteria by submitting doctored essays.

THE ANOMALOUS ESSAY

WritePlacer *Plus* scores essays based upon five criteria: focus, development, organization, sentence structure, and conventions. I will not challenge the writing construct behind these criteria, though it would be
possible to do so. Similar criteria are used in many holistic assessment
rubrics. Certainly a somewhat different construct lies behind the WPA
Outcomes Statement for First-Year Composition (Council of Writing
Program Administrators 2000), which focuses on rhetorical knowledge,
critical thinking and reading, writing processes, and conventions. The
WritePlacer *Plus* criteria are, perhaps, appropriately narrow because
of the decontextualized nature of the writing assignment students
face when taking a placement test. How can any reader—human or
machine—really consider audience, for example, or consider what students know about multiple drafts? My interest is to take on WritePlacer
Plus on its own terms. If it doesn't work on its own terms, it cannot meet
the minimum standards for validity.

WritePlacer Plus scores range from 2 to 12, though in practice, at least
at our institution, there are no 2s or 3s. The great majority of institutions
use 8 or 9 as a cutoff point for their college English courses, according
to Suzanne Murphy (2004), an associate director at ACCUPLACER.
Certainly, an essay that WritePlacer *Plus* scores as a 9 should be an
acceptable one. Here is a typical example, in response to a prompt
about the advisability of working a second job or overtime:

> I believe working full time or having a second job is too stressful for a per-
> son. Many people who are in this position never have time for themselves
> and their families. Their social life always revolves around their employees
> and their is no change in their lives. The overwork can also disturb a per-
> son academically and physically due to the lack of exercise.
>
> To become better people, many of us need to relax and to take time
> out for ourselves and with our families. It is very important to spend qual-
> ity time with the people we are closest to because they are the ones who
> will help us with all your problems. People with two jobs, and who work
> overtime have that type of companionship but can not take advantage of it
> because of their jobs. This can result in many negative effects like depres-
> sion and not a very good social life.
>
> Having the same, overworked routine everyday is not the ideal life.
> People who are in this position are very bored of their lives due to the
> same working habits everyday with the same people. Many overworked
> people also become cranky and moody because of their jobs and are not

polite to the customers. This can make matters worse because they do not work with passion, they work because they have to. They also envy the people around them that are enjoying their lives and are partying on friday and saturday nights!

People who work full time, or have two jobs are never in shape because they never receive the excerise they need. They can not concentrate on their health as much due to all the work on their mind. They are also disturbed academically due to the small time frame they put into their education. I have seen many cases where overworked students have gotten failings grades when they were capable of higer scores. Jobs can really divert a persons attention from the important aspects in their lives, which is wrong.

As a student, I believe everyone should get an education and have one job that fullfills their life. This way, there will be time for a good personal and social life. It is important for a person to give time to everything and to live life to the fullest. Everyone is here in the world to enjoy, not just to work. In conclusion, I believe that jobs are important, however, to a certain extent because it is more important to enjoy life. (415 words)

There is a simple but recognizable organization to the essay: introduction, thesis with predictor statements, three body paragraphs, and conclusion. Sentences are generally well constructed and grammar errors don't interfere with understanding. The author implicitly acknowledges that examples can be a useful thing, even if there is no recognition of the value of multiple perspectives or of complexity. But then, given testing conditions and training in writing the five-paragraph theme, it is not surprising that virtually no student exhibits these latter qualities. In any case, I had no problem placing this student in the College English class at our school, where the average verbal SAT score that year was 531.

In 2002 we found an essay whose WritePlacer *Plus* score, also a 9, stunned us—so much so that we asked ACCUPLACER what might account for such an apparent error in scoring—but before going any further, please read the essay for yourself. The writing prompt asks students to judge which form of technology has had the greatest impact on our society.

Technological advances in the world today or in our daily lives have hit in the business world and the home itself. By bringing technology to high standards has in a way sped up the way of life of how it used to be lived. The most largest affect that anyone one man or woman has used in technology is the computer.

The computer itself has been the key or the base of this change in life. The usage of the computer has probably excess in millions from 1992 to the modern day we live. Kids these days of me asking how many computers they have in one household is brought to me that there families out there that carry more then one.

However, the computer is just the base like I said, because what the computer carries is more to push us up the technology ladder. Now there are the word processors that have take our typing machines and just toss them in the garbage. Then, the microsoft excel programs which have shaped charts then need to be graphed for business and school. There is also the new programs like adobe pagemaker which is the process of making cards and brochures and using scanned pictures, also, microsoft power point what is basically makign your own power point film, by using slides.

Although, these programs have consisted in the building of a high corporate ladder of technology, nothing evens out with the world of the internet. The internet has shaped everyone in the world into some type of character on the internet. The internet has been the faster things to catch on to by anyone one invention. Even the process has always been going on in the U.S. government but when given to the public it took off like a rocket. It's like faster then anyone other library in the world where tons and tons of information are being transfered back and forth. Even though there is the msn chattings and the aol chattings with just surfing the net there is this great monster coming at the internet at full speed.

That monster is the online gaming that is going on in the world and the leading forfront is the games of Quake and Counter-strike. From the United States to Turkey to England these games are being played. Of course I am one of them and from other experiences and my own it is addictive.

The feelings that I have to the new inventions that have come out in the past quarter of a century have no affect like the computer itself and the power of the net. I really can't think of anything else in the near future that could top this phenomenom that has been growing so fast. But if so by that time we should be living in the planet Mars and my grand kids learn about these computer and internets that we used. (486 words)

Although this student, Carl,[2] shows real enthusiasm for his subject, does generally focus on how computers have sped up our lives, and presents some evidence in support of the thesis that computers are the most important technological advance today, his prose is very tough to plow through. The first paragraph is not more egregious in its language than other paragraphs, but it provides significant insight into the magnitude of the sentence-level problems this student has. I will go into some depth to make the case that the language problems are not insignificant.

> Technological advances in the world today or in our daily lives have hit in the business world and the home itself. By bringing technology to high standards has in a way sped up the way of life of how it used to be lived. The most largest affect that anyone one man or woman has used in technology is the computer.

If you were to read this in Word, you might be surprised to discover that there is only one grammar error noted: the double superlative, "most largest." In fact, this is the least troublesome problem in simply getting through the prose. The word "hit" in the first sentence stopped me briefly. It seems an odd word to use; we might expect "occurred." However, the word "hit" might have been more easily negotiated if there weren't redundant phrases signifying where the technological advances are occurring. The sentence would be clearer if it read as follows: "Technological advances have hit the business world and the home itself." The syntax confusion in the second sentence is profound. It begins with a prepositional phrase used as a subject and ends with the strange interjection of the phrase "of how it" that mars what would have been more comprehensible if left out: "sped up the way life used to be lived." The last sentence has, in addition to the double superlative, the following nonsensical kernel sentence: "Any one man or woman has used the most largest affect in technology." A possible revision of this paragraph, applying principles of syntax, concision, and correctness, would look like this:

> Technological advances affect us daily in the business world and in the home itself. Bringing high standards to technology has sped up our way of life. The largest effects that technology has had on men and women have come through the computer.

To say that this student struggles mightily with the English language is an understatement. No teacher in our program would rank the above two essays as equivalent, both scored 9—and thus passing—by WritePlacer *Plus.* The first student belongs in College English; the second belongs in our intensive, six-credit version of College English. I don't believe that this student simply needed more time to proofread his essay. There are far too many problems—and problems that indicate major syntax and usage problems—to believe that this student will quickly adapt himself to the relatively fast pace of College English. He will need the kind of one-on-one help that is both available and required in the intensive course. He needs someone who can help him understand the assumptions that he makes about how to communicate in writing.

If you don't buy my argument that the two essays above are of markedly different quality, there is no point in reading further. The chief reader at ACCUPLACER did not, for example; he concurred with the machine (Rickert 2002). However, if you do buy my argument, then the remainder of this chapter will focus on teasing out the kinds of problems that WritePlacer *Plus* seems blind to and the kinds of criteria it values instead.

It may be surprising that I must, at this juncture, admit that I believe WritePlacer *Plus* is a generally reliable placer of student essays. I am prepared to believe, as Vantage Learning (2000) asserts, that "the results [of their study] confirm earlier findings that IntelliMetric scores written responses to essay-type questions at levels consistent with industry standards and traditional expert scoring" (3). Timothy Z. Keith (2003), of the University of Texas at Austin, examines the validity studies of several automated essay-scoring systems and states that "IntelliMetric indeed produces valid estimates of writing skill" (158). (I would question Keith's use of the word "valid" here, but I will agree to the extent that reliability is one component of validity.) On 138 more or less randomly selected[3] essays, the average score assigned by my two readers and me agreed exactly with WritePlacer *Plus*'s score in 103 cases, agreed within one point in 33 cases, and agreed within two points in 2 cases. This is well within the reliability figure of 97 percent to 99 percent.[4]

How can I claim that IntelliMetric is both reliable and invalid at the same time? The focus of the remainder of this essay will be to point out the problems in validity that will cause some reliability problems *only when certain types of writing errors or problems occur.* Two of these errors were forecast by the paired essays above: the exaggerated value placed upon sheer length and the undervaluing of problems that have to do with readability.

THE PLACE OF LENGTH IN WRITEPLACER *PLUS*'S SCORING

As I mentioned earlier, we at Seton Hall University had developed the hunch that length seemed to be a disproportionally large factor in scoring. Faculty evaluating WritePlacer *Plus* at Middlesex County College have developed a similar intuition, that ACCUPLACER overvalues length in scoring student essays (Lugo 2005). To test such a hypothesis, a standard statistical method called regression analysis can easily be applied. Regression analysis calculates the variance in the WritePlacer *Plus* score that is accounted for by length, in this case, number of words per essay. An analysis of 221 randomly selected essays from 2002 through 2004 showed that fully 85 percent of the variance in essay scores was due to length.[5] This is a figure far higher than my intuition had led me to believe, and the implications are substantial. First, it means that length is valued far more than any teacher of writing would value it. It's true that, at the level of a first draft, length is an important indicator of fluency. In a way, it's a pleasant surprise to see that a testing company would value sheer length, as opposed to correctness, since length is related to fluency and idea development. However, 85 percent seems too high.[6]

The hypothesis that WritePlacer *Plus* valued length over all other variables was confirmed when I appended one essay to another—simply copying and pasting two essays together and submitting the combination as a single essay—to see how the score would change. In the first case, I appended two essays that each scored a 7, but each component essay had a position that contradicted the other. The first argued that taking two jobs or working overtime was a fine choice to make, while the second argued that making such a decision would ultimately be destructive. The result? An essay that scored a 10. In the second case, I appended two essays that also scored 7s, but in this case the two essays were on two entirely different topics, one on the most significant technology and the other on the advisability of working two jobs. The result? An essay that scored a 9, including a 9 on the focus subscore.

Of course, students don't naturally append essays of opposite points of view or of different topics altogether, but they do have problems recognizing when they have contradicted themselves and when they have gone off topic. These experiments provide some indication of how unlikely WritePlacer *Plus* is to "notice" the difference between essays that are well focused and essays that aren't. Or, at the least, WritePlacer *Plus* will value length so greatly that differences in focus may not show up even when they're egregious. It is hard to imagine a human reader so taken by the sheer verbiage in a piece of writing that he or she wasn't far more put off than was the computer by a complete and inexplicable switch in point of view or topic. Focus is one of five subcriteria upon which WritePlacer *Plus* scores the essays, yet my experiments suggest that focus takes a distant second place to the criterion of length.

Another experiment shows that WritePlacer *Plus* cannot judge the difference between concise and bloated language. An essay can be more confusing because of redundancy and superfluity and still score higher, because of length, than a concisely written essay. The first of the following two excerpts is the original introductory paragraph from a concisely written essay that scored a 6 (176 words). The second excerpt is the same paragraph that I loaded with bloat; the entire essay, filled throughout with such verbiage to reach 276 words, scored an 8.

> Many technological changes have occured since the formation of this country. The invention of the automobile has had a larger effect on the United States than any other invention.

> Many technological changes have occured since the formation of this country. Lots of changes have happened ever since our country first started. The invention of the automobile has had a larger effect on the United States than any other invention, even though there are indeed lots of inventions worth talking about.

One of the attributes of writing that English teachers prize is clarity. Generally, this means weeding out the extraneous words and phrases that do not contribute directly and powerfully to the idea at hand. If 85 percent of what WritePlacer *Plus* values is length, it's impossible for it to value concision as well. In the experiment above, I carefully padded the sentences to add absolutely nothing useful to the original phrasing, often merely rephrasing a sentence to create pure redundancy. The inability to detect the difference between spare and bloated writing explains why Nancy and I both passed some essays that received a 7, a failing score, from WritePlacer *Plus*.

The message for any high school seniors reading this essay is clear: write more and you'll pass. Specifically, write at least 400 words, if your institution has a cutoff of 8, to be placed in College English. Of the 208 essays that I examined myself, no essay of more than 373 words received less than an 8. This is hardly a large number of words, considering that the directions for writing the essay stipulate that the essay should be between 300 and 600 words.

CORRECTNESS

Herrington and Moran (2001) suspected that computers evaluated essays for length and correctness. They were certainly right about length. I believe they are partially right about correctness.

The following is the first paragraph from Andy's essay, perhaps the most error-filled non-ESL essay of the batch we reviewed.

> With all the different types of technological advancements that has changed the face of the world as we no it, the most influencial thing to be the cumputer. the reason that i say the cumputer is because the cumputer has the ability to organize, meanig file, alphabitized, and even manage. the cumputer in my opinion is the saving grace of the twenty first century.

Andy's essay received a 6 overall, with 5s for both the sentence structure and conventions subscores. I edited his essay to eliminate all the mechanical and grammatical problems (though not other, less obvious, word-choice problems, like "influential thing"), yielding a first paragraph that looks like this:

> With all the different types of technological advancements that have changed the face of the world as we know it, the most influential thing has to be the computer. The reason that I say the computer is that the computer has the ability to organize, meaning file, alphabetize, and even manage. The computer, in my opinion, is the saving grace of the twenty-first century.

The revised essay received an 8 overall, with 8s for the sentence-level subscores. This dramatic improvement suggests that WritePlacer *Plus* does indeed pay attention to correctness.

However, correctness is fairly narrowly conceived in WritePlacer *Plus*. The changes in spelling, subject-verb agreement, punctuation, sentence structure, and capitalization do make a difference in how this essay reads. But all these changes do not make as much difference as the editing to the anomalous essay cited in full at the beginning of this chapter. In its original form, Carl's essay received a 9, with subscores of 9 for sentence structure and 8 for conventions—a passing score at the vast majority of colleges that use ACCUPLACER. My revision, which involved drastic editing, resulted only in a 10, with subscores of 10 for both sentence structure and conventions. The readability problems for Carl's essay are at least as great as for Andy's—and require far more substantive editing. I changed 52 percent of the words from the original in Carl's essay, in contrast with only 21 percent of the original in Andy's essay. Yet the score went up only one point; WritePlacer *Plus* appears to have had a harder time "noticing" errors in Carl's essay. This may be due to the type of error. Of the 65 words I changed in Andy's essay, 40 were spelling or capitalization errors.

To learn whether WritePlacer *Plus* has problems "noticing" the types of errors in Carl's essay, I edited it only for the relatively few spelling and mechanical errors it has. When I finished editing, Word showed no green or red underlining, hence no spelling errors and no obvious grammatical errors, and yet a great number of syntactic and word-choice problems remained. Nevertheless, the new *limited* revision scored a 10, albeit with slightly lower subscores (10, 8, 8, 9, 9 vs. 10, 9, 8, 10, 10). The new revision had all the old readability problems but scored just as high as the far more thorough revision I had submitted earlier. WritePlacer *Plus* appears to value the combination of length plus mechanical correctness over concision and clarity.

Unless an essay has sentence-level problems of a certain type—generally mechanical—WritePlacer *Plus* has a hard time noticing them. Carl's essay required so much revision that only 231 words of the original 486 (or 48 percent) remained. By comparison, Andy's essay included 240 words of the original 305 (or 79 percent). The difference was that the 65 words that were changed were the kind that WritePlacer *Plus* "noticed."

Analysis of another essay confirms this finding. Gail's essay has a different sort of error—not as mechanical as in Andy's essay and not as subtle and pervasive as in Carl's essay. This excerpt reveals the kind of error this student is prone to:

> First of all when you apply for applications, jobs ask you to list your computers skills. Reason being most office work deals with online communications or some other type of knowledge of software. So if you have no experience in the field than you won't be able to get the job done. Then this person is left mad and disappointed because when he/she was growing up computers weren't used. Now that can be hard on a person who needs work to provide for their family. Computers being fatal to the workforce can be hard for a non computer literate person to get a job.

Table 1 (next page) indicates the types and number of errors in her essay. (The labels may be disputed in some cases, and the significance of Gail's use of "you" may be debated, but the overall number and significance should not be in question.)

I edited out 46 errors. The result? Absolutely no change in score, not even in the subscores, despite changing 114 of 398 words in the original essay (29 percent), more than I changed in Andy's essay. Gail's essay received a 9 overall, with subscores of 9, 8, 8, 9, and 9. Her errors, perhaps not coincidentally, do not all appear in Word. There are only four green underlined phrases, and only one in the excerpted passage above. Perhaps WritePlacer *Plus* has as much difficulty noticing these types of problems as Word does. In the above passage, no one would

TABLE 1

Errors in Gail's essay

Type of error	Number of errors
Subject/verb agreement	1
Fragment	4
Inappropriate informality (you)	8
Spelling/typo	7
Word choice	9
Wordy language	7
Switching persons	2
Faulty antecedent	2
Sentence structure	1
Comma splice	2
Verb form	1
Missing word	1
Misplaced modifier	1
Total	46

question the logic problem in the sentence "jobs ask you to list your computers skills." And the change between "you" and "this person" represents a confusing switch in person. The great majority of errors in Andy's essay that I changed were purely mechanical—mostly spelling—yet changing those relatively few errors had far more impact on the score than changing the wide variety of largely nonmechanical errors in Gail's essay.

In conclusion, WritePlacer *Plus* "values" correctness narrowly conceived. It certainly picks up spelling and other obvious grammatical problems, but it does not pick up more subtle differences having to do with word choice and syntax, differences that often make a greater difference in the readability of an essay. Especially when the values of concision and length are at odds—and they often are—WritePlacer *Plus* does not make meaningful distinctions.

Finally, the astute reader may notice that I have used no ESL essays to make my argument in this section. Some of the errors may sound like ESL errors—and it's true that Gail is an African-heritage student, possibly explaining why her writing has certain errors, like subject-verb agreement, in common with ESL writers—but the problems are not confined to ESL errors. Nevertheless, the most egregious scoring of essays occurs with ESL student essays. Here is an excerpt from Juan's essay, which received an 8:

Technology across the countries,is and will the fist thing to discovery more important idead and permit to grow in many aspecs of the humanlife The general purpose technologies is to have much succesful improvement and eventually comes to be used for many people aroud the word, to have many uses, and to have many technological complementarities. The most cited examples include electricity, computers tv, E.T.C. Second, because thechnological changes give to as big information to undestand was happened in the word, thought the media, but also our technology can destroy many beuty things include human life.

On the one hand, I cringe to place an excerpt from Juan's essay here because his writing seems more thoughtful and engaged than many students', but on the other hand, he would not have been well served in a College English I classroom.

SENTENCE-SKILLS SCORE AS CORRECTIVE?

Although WritePlacer *Plus* clearly does not take into account the full extent of sentence problems in scoring placement essays, its sentence-skills test often provides useful information to alert the administrator to potential writing problems. Of twenty anomalous essays in which my readers and I all agreed that the frequency of errors made the WritePlacer *Plus* score unlikely, in thirteen cases the writers had sentence-skills scores that were more than 10 points below the average for their essay score. In three cases the sentences-skills scores were 7 or 8 points below. In only four cases were the sentences-skills scores the same or higher than we would have expected. In Table 2 (next page), note that the sentences-skills score (out of 120) is usually far below the average sentence-skills score for a given essay score. Notice also that in a few cases, the essay score is anomalously *higher*, and in these cases the sentence-skills score is significantly higher as well.

The differences between essay score and sentence-skill score are especially pronounced for those students who have English as a second language. Remember the excerpt from Juan's essay (essay F in table 2), for example, which received an 8—a passing score at Seton Hall—and compare it to this paragraph from Kim's essay (essay M in table 2), a more normal-quality 8:

These days, without a proper education and some luck, it is beyond impossible to receive a decent job. People need to work hard to support not only themselves but their families. That may mean getting a second job

TABLE 2

Anomalous essays with associated sentence-skill (SS) scores

Essay	WritePlacer Plus score	Readers score	Sentence-skills score	Average SS score for a given essay score	Sentence-structure subscore	Conventions subscore	ESL status
A (Gail)	9	7	86	97	9	9	No
B (Carl)	9	7	75	97	9	8	No
C	7	6	91	88	6	6	No*
D	7	6	80	88	7	6	No
E	5	4	29	67	5	4	Yes
F (Juan)	8	5/6	35	94	7	7	Yes
G	11	8	64	103	11	10	Yes
H	9	7	33	97	8	8	Yes
I	12	9	66	103	11	10	Yes
J	6	7	104	85	6	6	No
K	6	7	101	85	5	5	No
L	8	7	35	94	8	8	No
M (Kim)	8	7	104	94	8	7	No
N	8	9	110	94	8	8	No
O	9	7/8	76	97	8	8	Yes
P	9	8	96	97	9	9	No
Q	9	7/8	119	97	9	9	No
R	11	9/10	68	103	10	10	No
S	12	11	96	103	12	11	No
T	5	4	47	67	5	6	Yes
U	11	10	96	103	10	10	No
V	11	10	83	103	11	10	No
W	12	11	92	103	11	10	No

*Language other than English spoken at home

or working overtime. Although, working more then the average person may make one more tired and sleepy, it does not necessarily make them unhealthy or anti-social. If one can manage their time wisely, there is plenty of time in a day to work as much as needed and to find some time in between for your families and friends.

Fortunately, the sentence-skills score for each student helped clarify the placement. Juan received a 35; Kim received a 104.

Unfortunately, in many cases, a lower sentence-skills score does *not* accurately predict an anomalously lower-quality essay. And higher sentence-skills scores rarely predict anomalously higher-quality essays.

Understandably, when I added the sentence-skills score to the word count in the regression analysis, it accounted for only an additional 1 percent in the variance of the WritePlacer *Plus* grade. Still, the question remains, why would a computer-scoring system that includes sentence structure and conventions in its criteria appear to ignore the kinds of problems evinced by ESL students and even English speakers who have significant sentence-level problems? Note that the sentence-structure and conventions subscores for each of the students in the above table are either the same or just one lower than the overall score (with one exception).

ORDER AND COHERENCE

If WritePlacer *Plus* overvalues the most macro criterion, length, and the most micro criterion, mechanical correctness, how does it fare with the criteria that lie between these two: order and coherence? (See McGee's "Experiment 1" section in chapter 5 of this collection for a related analysis.) When we read the entire collection of essays, problems of organization and cohesiveness struck us less than complexity of thought, depth, and length. However, I was struck on numerous occasions by essays that seemed especially strong because they seemed more like an argument than a list of points.

Dan's essay was rated superior to the rest of the 8s we examined. Lengthwise, at 364 words, it ranked in the middle third of all the 8 essays. Its subscores were 8 for focus, sentence structure, and conventions; 7 for development and organization. Thus, it was rated an 8 but not a particularly strong 8. However, it had a quality that many other essays, even 9s, did not have: a sense of argument, a building of statements toward a conclusion, so that sentences and paragraphs had a uniquely possible position in the overall scheme of the essay. Sentences and paragraphs could not be randomly distributed and still make sense.

In contrast to Dan's essay, here is an example of a paragraph from Larry's essay, rated 9, that reads just as well (or not well) in a very different order. The original:

> (1) Basically everything in America is organized by computers. (2) Important places like banks rely heavily on computers for business. (3) Computers have contributed a great deal to criminal justice as well. (4) Computers are capable of storing massive amounts of information and scanning through information rapidly. (5) Solving crimes has been made easier because everyone's background and fingerprints can be saved and if a search of a person to a particular fingerprint is needed, it can be matched.

Here is a version with sentences in this order: 3-5-2-4-1.

(3) Computers have contributed a great deal to criminal justice as well. (5) Solving crimes has been made easier because everyone's background and fingerprints can be saved and if a search of a person to a particular fingerprint is needed, it can be matched. (2) Important places like banks rely heavily on computers for business. (4) Computers are capable of storing massive amounts of information and scanning through information rapidly. (1) Basically everything in America is organized by computers.

In fact, one might argue that this order is an improvement, but the point is that there is nothing compelling about the order in the original version.

Dan's essay, on the other hand, suffers a good deal if rearranged. Look, for example, at his second paragraph:

(1) Unfortunately, many people in the world have to work multiple jobs in order to survive. (2) As a result, their quality of life is harmed extremely. (3) Their relationship with their family suffers because they rarely see them. (4) Their marriage (if it lasts) suffers largely due to the lack of quality time that the person spends with their spouse. (5) As a result of their relationships suffering, the person may develop emotional or physical problems due to the stress. (6) All this happens just because of working too much.

The preceding paragraph in Dan's essay had set up the importance of achieving balance between work and relaxation. Thus the word "unfortunately" logically alerts us to the first sentence of the above paragraph. None of Dan's other paragraphs could logically go here. The second sentence, beginning with "As a result," does in fact logically follow "as a result" of the first proposition. Sentences 3 and 4 must follow sentence 2 because they both provide examples of how the quality of life can be harmed (even though sentences 3 and 4 themselves could be switched). Sentence 5 summarizes sentences 3 and 4 and identifies the consequence. Sentence 6 offers a conclusion that echoes the theme of the first sentence.

But Dan's essay received an 8, whereas Larry's essay, coming in at 298 words, received a 9. How could I test my hunch that sentence order doesn't "matter" to WritePlacer *Plus*? The solution seemed obvious: order the sentences randomly to see what effect there was on the scoring. I cut out pieces of paper, numbered them from 1 to 21, shuffled them, then created a new essay based on the new order. To give you an idea of how unsatisfying it would be to read this essay, I give you the first several sentences:

Too much work usually results in stress, and stress is harmful to one's quality of life. I belive that too much work is only harmful to one's life. Unfortunately, many people in the world have to work multiple jobs in order to survive. As a result of free time, one has a chance at a good life and therefor are less likely to undergo physical and emotional stress. All this happens just because of working too much. As a result of their relationships suffering, the person may develop emotional or physical problems due to the stress.

It's still possible to discern a topic and even a point of view, but there is certainly no clearly demarcated progression of ideas with evidence, as I saw in the original. Yet this piece of writing received the same score, an 8. In fact the subscores were the same, except that the randomly ordered essay received a 7 instead of an 8 for conventions. The results of this experiment appear to challenge Vantage Learning's claim that IntelliMetric examines "transitional fluidity and relationships among parts of the response" (Vantage Learning 2004a, 3).

Not content with one example, I took another essay, a 7, that was composed of very short paragraphs (mostly one sentence each) that had a definite structure to them. It might be synopsized as follows: "Technology has greatly impacted us, making our lives easier and more enjoyable. For example, consider instances A, B, C. However, instance D is the most important for reasons X, Y, and Z. Thus the impact of the Internet has been large and positive. As for those who opposed technology, they can't stop it but they can adapt to it." Not a brilliant essay, but one in which order actually counts. I reordered the essay deliberately to undo the rhetorical effectiveness of the order. WritePlacer *Plus* scored the original essay a 7 (7, 6, 6, 6, 6). It scored the reordered paragraphs a 7 (7, 6, 6, 7, 6). Notice that the score for organization, the third criterion, remains the same.

If randomly ordering the sentences of an essay that is reasonably effectively ordered results in no change of score, it's hard to understand what WritePlacer *Plus* counts as "organization."

RETHINKING THE PLACE OF LENGTH AS A CRITERION

What are we to make of WritePlacer *Plus*'s apparent inability to discriminate among texts that seem so different? One possibility is that the problem lies not in the computer but in the human scorers. After all, ACCUPLACER's "chief reader" read Carl's essay and agreed with WritePlacer *Plus* that it is "a very good writing sample that substantially communicates a whole message to a specified audience. . . . The writer competently handles mechanical conventions such as sentence structure, usage, spelling and punctuation, though very minor errors in the use of conventions may be present" (Rickert 2002). However, no one to whom I have shown this essay at Seton Hall or elsewhere would place the writer in College English. Certainly no one, even ACCUPLACER's chief reader, would give Juan, the ESL writer, an 8 for his essay or think that College English I was an appropriate course for him. But this doesn't eliminate the possibility that ACCUPLACER's essay readers have been normed to value development of idea (length) over sentence-level readability.

For those involved in the development of computer scoring over the past thirty-five years, my finding that length is so prominent a factor may come as no surprise, since early on length was identified as the most reliable measure of the quality of holistically scored essays (Huot 1996; Powers et al. 2002; Roy 1993). However, current technology promises to move beyond the use of mere length to evaluate essays. Vantage Learning (2004e) recently put out a press release extolling the virtues of its product, implying that we have entered a new era in machine scoring: "IntelliMetric is the world's most accurate essay scoring engine, using a rich blend of artificial intelligence (AI) and the digitization of human expertise to accurately score and assess examinee responses to open-ended essay questions in a range of subjects." Yet in fact IntelliMetric appears to have little ability to discriminate between essays that are bloated or concise, ordered well or chaotically, focused on the same topic or on entirely different topics, written in clear prose or marred throughout by nonsimple errors. It is unfortunate that, because Vantage Learning wants to keep proprietary information secret, it will not share the information that would help educators understand why there would appear to be such a gap between Vantage Learning's claims and the findings in this chapter.

In the final analysis, the experiments above offer strong evidence that IntelliMetric cannot really "read" for the criteria that ACCUPLACER says it can. They suggest, instead, that it discriminates according to length and a limited number of mechanical and grammatical errors. What is remarkable is that, in so doing, WritePlacer *Plus* is able to reliably place the great majority of students. As much as I'm concerned with WritePlacer *Plus*'s ability to evaluate essays where superior length is not matched by superior coherence, correctness, or concision, the discovery that length is a far more reliable predictor of quality than any-body—even ACCUPLACER—would have expected forces us to rethink the relationship between fluency, the ability to get words down on paper, and quality in writing. How is it possible that 85 percent of the variance in WritePlacer *Plus*'s scores is attributable to the length of the essay? It suggests that sheer fluency—even in an *untimed* test—is extraordinarily important. Sheer fluency correlates, in the great majority of cases in which WritePlacer *Plus* is reliable, with focus, organization, coherence, sentence structure, and grammatical and mechanical correctness. The implications of this discovery and the connections to composition theory lie beyond the scope of this essay, but it would seem to confirm the priority that the "process approach" places on freewriting and journaling and the emphasis that WAC gives to informal writing as a vehicle for helping students make sense of constructs within the disciplines. That is, there is much value in doing lots of writing—not, of course, without a meaningful context, but writing to explore, to make sense of, to make connections, to play around with words.

IMPLICATIONS FOR PRACTITIONERS

In practical terms, the concerned test or writing program administrator will not be able to accurately place all students based on the essay score alone. The sentence-skills score will be of some real help in alerting the placement administrator to potential problems. So will questions about whether the student's first language is English and whether other languages are spoken at home. Since we saw occasional 11s that were questionable and occasional 7s that we considered passes (at least in conjunction with the reading and sentence skills), we had to do a fair amount of spot-checking to feel comfortable with all the placements. We also encouraged retesting if students believed the tests did not accurately represent their abilities. Of course, none of the discussion here takes up larger validity questions related to one-shot placement tests, as opposed to portfolios or directed self-placement, for example.

Increasingly, computer scoring is making its way into the K–12 educational market. At the 2005 New Jersey Writing Alliance conference, about twenty instructors from both college and high school attended an interest group on machine scoring of essays. They wanted to know whether computers might be useful in helping them ease their monstrous teaching loads in some way. Other reports confirm the interest of teachers and entire school districts using AES in the classroom (Borja 2003; Manzo 2003). MY Access! is an online instructional writing program, based upon IntelliMetric, that Vantage Learning has offered for a few years now at all levels from elementary through high school.

A Vantage publicist explains that MY Access! "provides immediate diagnostic feedback to engage and motivate students to write more and improve their composition skills" (Vantage Learning, 2005b). Scott Elliot, COO of Vantage Learning, claims, "Teachers can focus on specific strengths and weaknesses, by domain" using MY Access!'s "highly prescriptive feedback" (Vantage Learning, 2005b). The findings in this chapter certainly raise questions about IntelliMetric's ability to give meaningful diagnostic feedback. Its holistic scoring and assessment of certain mechanical and grammatical problems may be trusted, but the evidence here suggests that IntelliMetric is unable to make judgments about order, word choice, certain grammatical errors, and focus. Using MY Access! as a way to accurately assess even a modest range of problems in a student's text would appear unwise.

The analysis in this chapter suggests that, as many English teachers would like to believe, the computer cannot really read—or even simulate reading—but it also suggests how reliability and validity can be separated to some degree. If most of the quality of an essay is directly attributable to length and some mechanical and grammar errors, then the great majority of essays will be scored reliably. Only a relatively few essays—those that are loaded with lack of coherence, loss of focus, and the more subtle syntax and word-choice problems that IntelliMetric cannot "see"—will reveal the validity problems that are always present but usually hidden, masked by the computer's ability to do a few simple tasks consistently.

ACKNOWLEDGMENTS

I want to thank Gita DasBender and Christy Guerra, both writing instructors at Seton Hall University, for their enthusiastic participation in this research, as well as acknowledge the support of the Seton Hall University Research Council.

7

WRITEPLACER *PLUS* IN PLACE
An Exploratory Case Study

Anne Herrington and Charles Moran

In 2001, we published an essay in *College English* entitled "What Happens When Machines Read Our Students' Writing?" In it, we discussed two computer programs, then relatively new to the market, that were designed to evaluate student writing automatically: WritePlacer *Plus*, developed by Vantage Technology, and Intelligent Essay Assessor, developed by three University of Colorado faculty who incorporated as Knowledge Analysis Technologies to market it. At this time, ETS had also developed its own program, e-rater, and was using it to score essays for the Graduate Management Admissions Test.

Flash forward to 2004, and a quick check of company Web sites shows that business is booming for these companies' automatic-scoring programs, with all marketing a range of products and listing a range of clients from educational institutions and state departments of education to publishing companies and the military.[1] In this chapter, we return to one of the programs we examined in 2001, WritePlacer *Plus*. If you Google WritePlacer, you come up with approximately three hundred hits, most of them testing-center Web pages at schools using WritePlacer *Plus*, many of them community colleges and most of them public institutions.

Our 2001 study was based on our own examination of WritePlacer *Plus*. In it, we raised concerns about the cost of computer-scored writing, of how computer-scored placement testing removes faculty from the placement process, and how writing to a computer distorts the nature of writing as a meaning-making and rhetorical activity. But these concerns, however deeply felt, were grounded in our own past experience. Were we simply resisting change, fearing for our own obsolescence? So we wanted to test these concerns against an actual case. How would WritePlacer *Plus* be experienced when used by a school for placement purposes? Why did schools choose to use WritePlacer *Plus*? How did administrators and faculty assess its impact? How did students perceive having their writing evaluated by a computer program?

Central to our inquiry is the question of validity. Is the test evaluating what it aims to evaluate? For us, *construct validity* remained a key concern for WritePlacer *Plus* because of our belief that it distorts the nature of the construct "writing." Would test administrators, faculty, and students see it this way too? We were concerned as well with what Samuel Messick (1989) terms the *consequential basis* for validity, specifically the "potential social consequences of test use" (85). Those consequences, for Messick, include both "unintended outcomes and side effects" (86). One of Messick's examples is "the curriculum enhancement function of such tests as those of the College Board's Advanced Placement Program, where the utility of the test resides partly in its effect on the quality of secondary school curricula" (85). This implied positive effect is realized only if the tests are valid, which is itself a question of values: for example, does the AP literature test construct the learning of literature in ways that match with the values of most teachers of literature? In considering the consequential basis for WritePlacer *Plus*, any potential effect on curriculum needs to be concerned with how the testing process constructs the activity of writing.

To begin to examine these questions, we conducted an exploratory case study at a community college that we'll call Valley College. At this college, the testing center had been using WritePlacer *Plus* for the past two years to place its incoming students in a three-course sequence of first-year writing classes, the first course being developmental. Before the institution of WritePlacer *Plus* as a placement vehicle, faculty had themselves been reading placement essays and scoring them holistically for some eighteen years.

To gather our information, we held one-hour interviews with the two administrators who brought the program to the college; forty-five-minute interviews with three English faculty who were involved in the change of placement systems; and twenty-minute interviews with ten students who had just completed the computer-scored placement test. The protocols for our interviews with students and faculty are included in appendix A. In addition, we visited and observed the testing site and talked with the staff that ran the Testing and Advising Center. All in all, we spent the best part of three days at the college. We felt entirely welcome. Both administrators and two of the three faculty we interviewed had read our 2001 article in *College English*. Despite that, we were warmly and openly received by the administration, faculty, and staff and given wide access to the placement process and its participants. One faculty member declined to be interviewed; the others agreed willingly.

What we found, in general, was a system that was functioning smoothly within its institution. The administrators were generally satisfied with the new placement program; the faculty were generally opposed to the new program; and the students were generally unaware that their writing was being read by a computer. When we told the students we had interviewed that this was the case, some of them were, in different degrees and in different ways, disturbed.

The administrators were on balance satisfied with the computer-scored placement system, though they acknowledged that with it came some gains and some losses. The dean of the college had been at Valley College for twenty-seven years, first as an English teacher for seven years and then as an academic administrator. He reviewed the history of the placement system: twenty-two years ago they had their faculty trained in holistic scoring for placement purposes—a system that he termed, in its time, "wonderful." Six hundred to eight hundred incoming students were tested in four to five groups; the placement essays were read by a team of four from the English department. The admissions process, including the placement process, was, as he described it, cumbersome for students: incoming students would come to the college, get a form, go home to fill it out, come back, pay a fee, sign up for a testing session and go home, come back for the testing session, go home, and then, after the placement results were in, come back again to register for fall courses.

Then, as he told us, the state moved to enrollment-driven budgeting. The college's president called together an Enrollment Management Team, telling its members, "We are going to have the finest registration process . . . one-stop registration." The English faculty and the dean wanted to keep the placement system as it was, but from the dean's perspective, it was hard to keep it going. They tried to accommodate to the mandate of "one-stop shopping" by having faculty available every day during the summer to read the essays, but that proved difficult, as "they were off in Maine or the Cape. It was their system, but they were not there to make it go. I did everything I could, but it fell apart." The dean hired a new director of the Testing and Advising Center, a person who had had experience with WritePlacer *Plus* at several other institutions, and in the spring of 2002 they brought WritePlacer *Plus* in; it was fully implemented as a placement tool in the summer of 2002. There were no faculty complaints about misplaced students, so the system seemed to be "working." In closing, the dean told us, "I prefer the old method, but the old system wasn't working—it became routine, sometimes we used old essays as range-finders, sometimes scanted on the norming process. The old system was not the golden age."

When we asked the administrator in charge of the testing program why they were using WritePlacer *Plus* to score incoming students' writing-placement test, she echoed the dean in saying that "the college had moved to a one-stop shopping type of placement," that with the holistically scored essay-placement system it was "difficult to find readers in a timely enough manner," and she added that the old system was "not cost-effective." Not only did the administration want one-stop shopping, "students didn't want to come back for a second day" in order to complete the admission and registration processes. She described the institution's initial testing of the computer-scoring system: faculty scored student writing against the same rubric as the computer, and there was a correlation of .79. When we asked her whether she was "satisfied" with the new system, she said, "as satisfied as you're going to be with an instrument." It is "as valid as any type of placement is." Interestingly, she argued that even with computer-scored placement "you need to do that intake essay in the first class . . . because the day you wrote for the computer might have been a bad day. . . . The greatest thing about WritePlacer is that it takes out bias. . . . It is a very fair test. . . . Administratively, it is a thousand times easier." On the other hand, she was candid about what was lost under the new placement system. "The faculty should have input as to who gets into their classes," and "If the faculty saw all of these essays, they'd have a better sense of all the students—to make them better teachers, they need to see that full spectrum." And, in thinking about the old system in which the faculty read placement essays, she remembered that the faculty readers picked up on suicidal students. "You'd miss that with the computer."

The first faculty member we interviewed (whom we'll call A) had taught at Valley for many years. When WritePlacer was first suggested, A told us, "I kind of backed off the entire controversy about three years ago. I really didn't want to get involved. People got very heated about WritePlacer versus the old method. Quite frankly, I did not want to step into that swamp. . . . I decided that I would not make a big deal about it. It was an administrator's decision apparently to do it, and I didn't want to lose energy over it. . . . It is the enemy. When I hear about Web pages and Blackboard, I reach for my gun." When we asked A about the use of WritePlacer as an exit test—something we'd heard about in talking with other faculty—A said, "I give my students grades, and I have faith in the grades, and I don't feel that I should have to be second-guessed by a machine."

The second faculty member we interviewed (whom we'll call B) had been at the college for just a few years. B had also worked with the faculty-scored placement system. B loved the old placement system, because when faculty read the placement tests "it was good to do things together with faculty and we'd be able to talk about writing. . . . I thought that was good for us." B saw the computer-scored test as under-placing ESL students and thought that the computer gave too much weight to mechanical errors in generating its scores. If offered the choice, B would go back to the old system "[b]ecause it is so easy for us to blame the machines. And we don't have to take responsibility. And also I think that just for the discussions that would go on during and after the meetings—these were really help-ful. Otherwise, there are so few opportunities to talk about what we do in the classroom." B was eloquent about the "disaster" of using WritePlacer *Plus* as an exit test for Composition 101, a writing course, and Composition 102, a course in responding to literature. B saw WritePlacer *Plus* as inevi-table as a placement-testing tool, given the "one-stop shopping" approach to registration, but was not sure that students could not use a little time in thinking about their academic program as they approached their first year at the college. But B was absolutely opposed to extending WritePlacer *Plus* to the tutoring center, to be used by students for feedback on their writing. "Oh, my God. That would be the worst thing."

The third faculty member we interviewed (whom we'll call C) had tenure at the college and had been teaching there for more than ten years. In 2001 C and a colleague had volunteered to come in every day during the summer to score essays "because we sort of knew what was coming." C liked the old system because in reading the essays "[w]e did also spot problems, issues. It felt appropriate for the faculty to know ahead of time about students' work, what we needed to think about. I liked it for that reason." C, who was on the college's Outcomes Committee, described their opposition to using any sentence-skills test, but particularly WritePlacer *Plus*, as an outcomes test for Composition 102, a course in responding to literature. After concerted opposition, the use of WritePlacer *Plus* as an exit test has been abandoned but, C thinks, chiefly because of its cost, not because of its evident lack of fit with the curriculum being taught. C objected to using WritePlacer *Plus* even for placement purposes because, as C said, "It undermines the philosophy I have inherited about the nature of writing—that you write to people. That's what is important to me. So I just feel that it sets up a false premise. I am not very eloquent here—but in very human terms, it is just not right."

And C went on to give an example of a case in which one of her students had produced writing that, if it were read by human beings, might bring about social change.

> Just the other day a student said to me, "Is this really important?" He's an American Indian, writing about different images that still persist about Native Americans—he's gotten involved in the Nipmunk Nation—there's a lot going on in his essay—he's a very eloquent writer. He asked me, "Does this really matter? You write all this stuff, and will it change anything?" I said, "Of course, . . . because you will be affecting other human beings." He's going to be assessed by computer? That's going to turn him off to the idea that you can actually connect to a human audience.

In addition to the interviews with faculty and administrators, we observed two test sessions and interviewed ten students immediately after they finished the placement testing. The test sessions were held in the Testing and Advising Center, the office in charge of all testing. At the test sessions, students were taking arithmetic, elementary algebra, reading comprehension, and the writing-sample tests, all on computers. Students had preregistered for the session, with each session open to twenty-three students. The room in which they took their exams was quiet and well lit, with the computers arranged around the exterior of the room, with two rows facing each other up the middle. On the walls hung motivational posters.

The Testing and Advising Center employee who explained the testing to students was friendly and took care both to explain the testing and to encourage students to do their best and trust in their abilities. She stressed that the tests were for placement, not admissions, and that there was no such thing as a good or bad score. The purpose was to select the right class for each of them. The writing test was explained as a forty-five-minute timed essay to test such writing skills as "spelling, grammar, and how to organize your thoughts. . . . The more you write the better. You want to make a really good argument" (see figure 1 for the prompt that was used).

Although students were writing on computers, no mention was made of who or what would evaluate their essays. The center employees were also very accommodating: so for instance, if students had difficulty with typing, they had the option of writing their essay by hand and having it typed in by someone else.

We also introduced ourselves to the students, explaining that with their consent, we would like to interview a few of them briefly. We stated our purpose as studying the use of the computer writing-placement

FIGURE 1

Placement Question for which Students Were to Write Their Essay

Some schools are considering a move to year-round schooling. This would change the current school schedule from a nine month to a twelve month academic school year. The current school calendar that includes a break for the entire summer would be replaced by a schedule of attendance year round, with several two to three week breaks for students during the year.

Some people argue that year-round schooling benefits students and improves student learning. Others argue that having students attend school all year can have a negative effect on students and their lives outside of school.

Write an essay for a classroom instructor in which you take a position on whether or not schools should move to a year round schedule. Be sure to defend your position with logical arguments and appropriate examples. (cpts.accuplacer. com/writeplacer/writerplacer.options.jsp)

system, with our "primary interest being understanding your experiences with writing the essay. . . . Our hope is that the findings will be helpful to academic testing people and teachers as they plan and implement writing tests." We made clear that their decision whether to be interviewed or not would in no way affect their essay rating. When students completed their tests, one of the center employees asked if they would be willing to do the interview. If they said yes, they were brought to us. The center graciously provided coffee mugs to those who completed the interviews.

When we interviewed the students, then, they had just completed their testing and received their results but had not yet spoken with their advisors. As an overview, here's what they said:

- Seven of the ten were used to using computers. Three were not, and two of these wrote their placement essays by hand and had the center's staff type them in to the computer to be computer scored.
- Two of the ten realized that their writing was going to be scored by computer; eight did not.
- One wrote to a specific audience (his mother); eight named a general audience ("someone smart," "the college," "the instructors"); and one, who said that she knew the computer was scoring her essay, said that she imagined her English teacher was reading the piece anyhow.
- Four felt that the computer would be more fair than a human reader; the rest did not know or said that it depended on the programming. Six would have preferred that their essay be read by people; two preferred the computer; and two were unsure.

- All ten believed that a teacher would be reading their writing in their college courses, and all ten preferred that.
- Most believed that the computer can tally only surface features, although three, when shown the descriptors for a "7," thought that the computer could judge how well the writing responded to aspects of the rhetorical situation: audience and purpose. The other seven did not (see figure 2).

In the following excerpts from the interviews, the students speak to important issues. Do they write differently to machines? Do they prefer to write to people or machines? Do they see the computer as a "fair" reader of their writing? Do they expect that computers will be reading their writing in college? And if so, what do they have to say about this possibility?

One student, who volunteered that he preferred the computer to a teacher as an evaluator of his writing, elaborated on this statement, giving his reasons for his preference: "I have nothing wrong with a computer grading my paper. I don't have any problems with it. Then you don't have to worry about, like, your teacher and that idea, you know—sometimes a reader . . . what if he really didn't like you? If a computer does it, it would be fair to everybody?" Asked whether he expected teachers or computers to be reading his writing at the college, this student responded, "I have no idea. To tell you the truth, this was one of the first times I've been in a classroom and seen nothing but computers. I mean, when I went to school, it was like one or maybe two computers in a room. . . . I was like, excited—wait until my kids go to school! Jeez, they might not even have teachers!" He laughed. Later in the same interview he elaborated: "I prefer a teacher, but I know my kids are probably going to say, 'We want a computer,' you know. I don't know. We'll see."

When asked if the computer-scoring program would be "fair," he responded, "I don't know what to say on that, because I don't know. . . . I guess it would be the person who programmed it. There's got to be someone who programs it; maybe it should be a male and a female come to an idea to grade that or make the program. . . . The way I look at it, if somebody's got to make a program, if it's just one person, say it was a male, I think that it may be gendered slightly, but if it was a male and female working together, I think you get more . . . the best of both worlds."

A second student, when asked, "Does it matter to you whether your writing will be read by teachers or computers?" responded, "It might. I don't know. Depends on my grades. If they come out fine, I'm not

FIGURE 2

WritePlacer Plus Score Descriptor for a Rating of 7 on a Scale of 2 to 12

A restricted writing sample that only partially communicates a message to the specified audience. The purpose may be evident but only partially formed. Focus on the main idea is only partially evident. The main idea is only partially developed with limited supporting details. While there is some evidence of control in the use of mechanical conventions such as sentence structure, usage, spelling and punctuation, some distracting errors may be present. (cpts.accuplacer.com/writeplacer/writeplacer.options.jsp)

going to argue about it. But if they are low, then of course I will bring it to their attention."

Interviewer: Which you could do with teachers but not the computer?

Student: You'd have to bring it up with the teacher and have them override the grade. You'd have to force the interaction back on the teacher. . . .I don't see how the computer could grade you on a paper you write from scratch, with no predefined guidelines, about a subject.

Interviewer: But what if it was in chemistry?

Student: If they gave you a subject, then they could create these conditions they could test you against. But if they just say "Write whatever you want, about whatever" and give it to you, how can they test that?

Told that her writing was going to be computer scored, a third student was surprised—"That's really odd—I had no idea—my goodness, I suppose if I had known this before I'd written it things might have been—my thought process might have been different."

Interviewer: What do you think the difference might have been?

Student: I don't know. I just know that deep down somewhere in my brain I would have been thinking, "I'm writing this to a computer, I'm not writing this to a teacher" or—that's strange, that's really odd.

Interviewer: Would you feel different or better if a faculty person read this?

Student: Is it going to give you feedback? When I get the scores, am I going to have some feedback? No. I don't know. I just think that if I'd known this ahead of time, just knowing this might have created some different—in the way I'm doing it—just different.

Interviewer: When you took the math test did you imagine that a computer was going to read that?

Student: No. Just because it's multiple choice.

Interviewer: But when you sat down to write an essay, that felt different?

Student: Yes, I'm assuming that someone is going to be reading this thoroughly and, you know, thinking about what you wrote, and not really—I mean I know the computer is smart, but I'm not thinking of them as thinking about what I'm writing as the way a human would think about what I'm writing.

One final excerpt. A fourth student, when asked, "Would you be okay about having a computer score your writing in college?" responded: "I think it would be something I'd have to get used to. After a while, I don't think it would bother me any more."

Interviewer: Could you expand on that at all? What would it mean "to get used to"?

Student: I mean, I've never had a computer grade any of my writings before. Obviously multiple-choice tests—I can understand that because there's only one answer. But writing is just—there is no boundaries for it, and a computer kind of puts limits to that. But I think that if that is the way it was, I would get used to a new style of writing, not just to please the computer, but just to start off with—if that's all that there was there.

CLOSING REFLECTIONS

So where does this leave us? Given this study of an institution that has adopted WritePlacer *Plus* as a placement tool, what has happened to our original concerns, voiced in our *College English* article in 2001? At that time, as you remember, we were concerned about the cost of computer-scored writing, of how computer-scored placement testing removes faculty from the placement process, and how writing to a computer changes, even cancels, the inherent nature of writing as a meaning-making and rhetorical activity.

First, our initial concern about cost seems not to be a factor at Valley College, although we know that the people-scored placement process at our home institution is cheaper than WritePlacer *Plus* would be for us. According to the testing program administrator at Valley College, the Testing and Advising Center generates enough money from such fee-based tests as CLEP to cover the costs of WritePlacer *Plus*. At Valley College, it appears that WritePlacer *Plus* meets the school's need for a time- and cost-efficient means of evaluating a writing sample and placing students, a means that administrators believe to be as accurate as using faculty readers. Viewing placement as a relatively low-stakes assessment, the test administrator said, "Placement is just a quick screening," and of WritePlacer *Plus*, "as a filter, it's a great filter." Interestingly, she recognizes the limits of most all placement testing. Reflecting on self-placement as an alternative to testing, she commented, "I personally am all for it. . . . I don't know where this huge concern for placement came from. Driven by test companies looking for a market or faculty saying students are not college ready."

Second, our initial concern about removing faculty from the placement process is supported by our study. Administrators and faculty at Valley College agree that having faculty read placement essays gives faculty a sense of their students and their writing. In the view of two of the faculty and one of the administrators, this reading of placement essays has had an important impact on curriculum, in that it gives the faculty an early indication of the issues and skills that their students bring with them to the college. Two of the faculty also spoke to the professional development value of sessions in which they came together to develop scoring rubrics and to discuss how they apply those rubrics to specific essays. In these meetings there was informal talk about the teaching of writing, something that faculty valued and felt the loss of under the new dispensation.

Third, our concern about the ways in which computer scoring of writing constructs the act of writing was supported by the study. The dean and two of the faculty—all graduate-trained experts in English and experienced teachers of writing—expressed reservations about how automated essay scoring constructs writing. Because of this new construction of writing, they were not in favor of extending the use of automated essay scoring to tutoring or instruction. Reflecting on the nature of automated essay scoring, the dean said, "[Y]our mind, the way in which it organizes language, is evaluated by a machine." He explained that he wants "experienced human beings, with full cognitive faculties, to see the essay." Still, he continued, while he does not like the idea that "some machine is counting words, paragraphs—for this task, gross placement, it works! It asks the question, 'Is this student in the weakest 30 percent?'" Given his reservations, though, it is not surprising that he says he would not support using an automated essay program for tutoring purposes. Echoing the dean's concerns about the incompatibility of automated essay scoring with writing, one of the faculty explained, "It undermines the philosophy I have inherited about the nature of writing—that you write to people."

That philosophy or belief is not just artificial school-taught theory; it is fundamental to the nature of writing, as all ten of the students also sensed in stating their preference for having teachers evaluate their writing in their courses at the college. Recall that one of them said that if she had known that a computer was "reading" her writing, "I just know that deep down somewhere in my brain, I would have been thinking, 'I'm writing this to a computer, I'm not writing this to a teacher' or—that's strange, that's really odd." Another: "I know that a computer is smart, but I'm not thinking of them as thinking about what I'm writing as the way a human would think about what I'm writing." And that is precisely the problem when automated essay scoring moves from assessment to instruction.

We bring up these concerns about instruction because the companies marketing automated essay-scoring programs are making the move into instructional settings. In marketing IntelliMetric, the engine for WritePlacer *Plus*, Vantage claims that it provides "high quality, accurate electronic essay scoring" and "authentic assessment" (2004a). As a field, we would be hard pressed to argue that mass placement testing, even with human readers, is "authentic," but we should be very concerned with the move into instructional settings. Programs like MY Access!, Elements of Language, and Criterion promise to assist teachers with the "burdens" of providing feedback to student writing, of assessing in relation to externally established norms, and of record keeping. But what are we teaching students if a computer rubric is their initial target when writing, a target that will evaluate formal criteria but not respond to what a student is saying or the purpose he or she is trying to accomplish, that will not be able to answer the Native American student's question, "Does this really matter?" In an insightful critique of Criterion and automated scoring in general, Julie Cheville (2004) writes: "Ultimately, automated scoring technologies scan to count and humans beings write to make meaning. To be effective, writers need the opportunity to share their purposes and plans with readers, who, in turn, assume an appropriate stance and read critically. The possibilities available to writers depend on the capacity of readers to perceive what works and to imagine what might work better. Writers are only as sophisticated as the readers they have encountered in their literate lives" (51).

Here Cheville is pointing to the consequential basis of validity, arguing that if one writes to computers, a consequence will be that one will be less prepared to write to people. Students in our study anticipated this consequence as well. As one commented, "I would get used to a new style of writing, not just to please the computer, but just to start off with—if that's all that there was there." This student also raises, for us, the issue of class and access to education. Will it be the case for this student that "that's all that there was there"? The site of our study was a two-year college, whose students are largely part-time, seeking job-related credentialing. From our review of the Web sites advertising these products, it appears that our research site is characteristic of the institutions that have adopted computer-scored placement services. On the list of institutions using WritePlacer *Plus* or Criterion there is no Harvard or Princeton, no Williams or Oberlin or Amherst. There is, however, Truckee Meadows Community College, Camden County Community College, University College of the Cariboo, the University of South Florida, Northern Arizona University, and Valley College. The distribution of this product suggests to us an extension of the social and economic stratification that has been such a feature of the past decade: the wealthy and connected learn to write to make meaning and to achieve their rhetorical purposes; the poor and unconnected learn to write to scoring engines.

We don't think that this two-class system is the conscious aim of our institutions or of the people who administer and teach in them. But it may be the result of incremental decisions—to use computers to score placement essays, and then to give feedback to writers in writing centers, and then to use them to read exit exams for "value added," and then to grade papers in a large lecture course—each decision not made in a vacuum but in an atmosphere created by heavy teaching loads, under-funded public institutions, heavy marketing, and claims of "efficiency" and "authenticity."

Placement essays, as we have said, may already be an a-rhetorical, somewhat mechanical writing situation. William L. Smith (1993) has described a placement-testing system that draws on teachers' expertise of the courses in the curriculum, but most often placement essays are read in holistic reading sessions by readers who have been "normed" against scoring rubrics and made, arguably, into something like reading machines. So we may want to grant that placement by machine is not that much worse—more a-rhetorical, more impersonal—than place-ment by readers normed by a holistic scoring training session. But even as we grant this, we need to listen to the faculty and administrators at Valley College, who, in different degrees, felt that the "washback" from the faculty placement readings into the curriculum was educationally valuable. Certainly we need to resist the extension of computer-scored writing beyond placement and into teaching situations. Our study leads us to support the CCCC "Position Statement on Teaching, Learning, and Assessing Writing in Digital Environments" (Conference on College

Composition and Communication Committee 2004): "Because all writing is social, all writing should have human readers, regardless of the purpose of the writing" (789).

ACKNOWLEDGMENTS

We wish to thank Valley College for allowing us to conduct this study at their school. In particular, we thank the students, administrators, and faculty who participated in the interviews and those who helped make the arrangements for those interviews. They were gracious in granting us their time and thoughtful in their interview responses.

Appendix A

INTERVIEW PROTOCOL FOR STUDENTS

Background Information

1. Female_____ or Male_____
2. Age: 18–22____   23–35_____   over 35_____
3. When were you last in school?
4. When did you last take an English class?

WritePlacer *Plus*

5. What was it like to write your placement essay online?
6. Who did you think you were writing to when you wrote this essay? (Did you feel that you were writing to a person or a computer?)
7. Do you think that the computer program will be fair to you in evaluating your essay for placement? (Do you think a person would be fairer?) (If given a choice, would you prefer to have a person or the computer program evaluate your writing, or doesn't it matter? Why?)
8. Do you expect that here at school your writing will generally be read by your teachers or a computer program? (Does it matter to you whether your teacher or a program reads your writing? Why?)
9. What do you think the computer program is reading for when it evaluates your writing? That is, what aspects of your writing do you think it's considering when evaluating it? (Do you think a computer looks for different things when evaluating your writing for placement than a person would?)

INTERVIEW PROTOCOL FOR FACULTY

(Note: we used substantially the same questions for the interviews with the two administrators.)

Background Information

1. How many years have you been teaching at this school?
2. Have you read placement essays here in the past? If not here, elsewhere?
3. Why did this school decide to shift to using a computer program to evaluate students' placement essays? (Probe to get a sense of the history of this decision.)

WritePlacer *Plus*

4. Have you tried WritePlacer *Plus* yourself? If so, what was it like to write an essay online to be evaluated by a computer program?

5. If yes to #4: who did you think you were writing to when you wrote this essay? (Did you feel that you were writing to a person or a computer?)

6. Are you generally satisfied with the writing-placement process that includes WritePlacer *Plus*? (Do you think it is a fair way of evaluating students' writing for placement?) (If given a choice, would you prefer to have a person or the computer program evaluate students' placement essays, or doesn't it matter? Why?)

7. What do you think the computer program is reading for when it evaluates your writing? That is, what aspects of your writing do you think it's considering when evaluating it? (Do you think a computer looks for different things when evaluating your writing for placement than a person would?)

8. What's the best thing about WritePlacer *Plus*?

9. What's the worst thing about it?

10. Do you feel there's a connection between the placement system with WritePlacer *Plus* and the curriculum? If yes, what is it? If no, why not? (Probe to get a sense of the nature of this connection or lack thereof and the import of that.)

8

E-WRITE AS A MEANS FOR PLACEMENT INTO THREE COMPOSITION COURSES
A Pilot Study

Richard N. Matzen Jr. and Colleen Sorensen

In the fall of 2002 Utah Valley State College (UVSC) began institutional research into placement tests for first-year composition courses: two basic writing courses and a freshman composition course. UVSC researchers had previously presented evidence in the article "Basic Writing Placement with Holistically Scored Essays: Research Evidence" (Matzen and Hoyt 2004) that suggested the college's multiple-choice tests—ACT, ACT COMPASS, and DRP (Degrees of Reading Power)—often misplaced UVSC students in composition courses. As an alternative to placement by these tests, a research team including people from the Department of Basic Composition, the Institutional Research and Management Studies Office, and Testing Services suggested to colleagues and administrators that placement might be more accurately accomplished by timed-essay scores alone or by combining timed-essay scores with reading test scores.

This chapter represents an extension of previous research and is a description of a pilot study regarding the following questions that are relevant to a WPA: will ACT e-Write, an automated essay-scoring program, accurately score UVSC students' timed essays? Will e-Write be a practical technology when used? Will e-Write scores be reported in a timely manner?

PLACEMENT AT UVSC: AN ISSUE OF FAIRNESS AND RETENTION

We saw that a bridge was needed between the current placement system and a possible new placement system.

- Current placement system: placement by composite ACT scores or combined scores of the reading (ACT COMPASS) and editing (DRP) tests.
- Possible new placement system: placement by timed-essay scores alone or by combining timed-essay scores with reading test scores.

Fairness was a significant issue when considering changing the placement system. On the one hand, we thought that the current placement system was unfair to students who were misplaced, but on the other hand, we did not want to replace that system with another system containing unfairness, too. Consequently, the pilot study was not only a dress rehearsal for a new placement system but also a test of e-Write's validity and reliability. In any case, the students in the pilot study had already been placed into composition courses by the current placement system. The bridge to a new placement system was still being formed.

Fairness is a larger issue, too, because of the number of students affected by the current placement system. Each fall semester, the system—based on multiple-choice tests that are not direct measures of writing—affects over seven hundred students who enroll in a basic writing course (ENGH 0890 or ENGH 0990) and affects over nineteen hundred students who enroll in the freshman composition course (ENGL 1010). According to one study, the editing and reading tests at UVSC may accurately place about 62 percent to 65 percent of students into ENGH 0990, while accurate placement into ENGH 0890 is worse (Matzen and Hoyt 2004, 4, 6). At UVSC, consequently, significant numbers of students would be more accurately placed into composition courses if the placement system included timed-essay scores. More UVSC students, in other words, would enroll in and pay for a composition course more aligned with their writing skills as they exist at the beginning of a semester. Another part of defining fairness in this context is that the two basic writing courses do not bear academic credit that can be transferred or applied toward earning a degree, whereas the freshman composition course bears transferable credit as well as credit applicable toward a UVSC degree.

Besides fairness, placement tests for composition courses have implications for retention at UVSC, where retention is a significant problem. Statements such as the following are not unusual to find in institutional research reports about retention at UVSC: "In general, the college has very low retention rates for students. Over half the students drop out of college failing to earn a degree or transfer. The college generally loses 30% to 35% of its students from fall to spring and nearly 60% of its students by the following fall" (Hoyt 1998, 4). Meanwhile, accurate placement into basic composition courses has been linked to improved student retention (Baker and Jolly 1999; Boylan 1999; Cunningham 1983; Glau 1996; Kiefer 1983; McGregor and Attinasi 1996; White 1995). In short, placement by timed essay might improve retention and fairness for each freshman cohort at UVSC.

AN OVERVIEW OF THE PILOT STUDY INTO ACT'S E-WRITE PROGRAM

In the spring of 2003, we wrote and submitted a grant to UVSC Foundation's Exceptional Merit Grants Program. The grant, entitled "ENGH 0890 and 0990 Placement," was approved, funding the e-Write pilot study. We hoped that the grant and e-Write would be the first steps toward having a cost-effective, accurate placement system based on timed-essay scores for three of the courses in the composition sequence: ENGH 0890, ENGH 0990, and ENGL 1010. We had read the ACT marketing pamphlet that announced, *COMPASS e-Write Direct Writing Assessment from ACT*. The pamphlet's first line was this: "COMPASS e-Write™, ACT's exciting new direct writing assessment, can evaluate a student writing sample, score it as reliably as two trained raters, and cost-effectively deliver a score report in seconds" (ACT 2001). This promotional material led us to believe that the program might have promise for UVSC.

Grant funds were spent in two ways. First, prior to the beginning of the fall semester of 2003, Testing Services at UVSC bought three hundred e-Write units (or tests) and installed the e-Write program on thirty computers in a classroom in the testing center. According the all reports, ACT's directions for the installation were thorough and easy to follow.

Thereafter, UVSC students completed the e-Write tests during the first week of classes that fall semester. However, because completion of the tests was like a dress rehearsal for a new placement system, we explained to teachers and students another, more immediate benefit of their participation in the pilot study. Students heard, as the proctor's instructions were read to them, that their teacher would read the e-Write essays to determine the rhetorical and grammatical needs or strengths of individual writers and the entire class. In other words, teachers would read the e-Write essays as diagnostic writing samples. As such, the essays might trigger more or less grammar instruction during the semester or identify students who might be particularly weak or strong writers. In total, approximately three hundred students completed e-Write tests, approximately one hundred from each of the three courses: ENGH 0890, ENGH 0990, and ENGL 1010.

Besides buying e-Write units, grant funds paid human raters for scoring the e-Write essays. The essays were written in response to two of eight possible e-Write prompts. Only two prompts were used because we doubted that an acceptable level of interrater reliability would be achieved in this sampling of three hundred e-Write essays if there were more than two essay topics. We had previously organized successful norming sessions in which two essay topics defined the anchor and range-finder essays. At the same time, we hoped that better-written timed e-Write essays might result if students were allowed to choose between two prompts.

Interrater reliability was important because a part of the research design was to test another claim in the ACT pamphlet: "A key factor, of course, is how the results of electronic scoring compare to those of trained raters. Our research shows very strong agreement: 100 percent of COMPASS e-Write scores are within one point of each other; approximately 76 percent of scores match exactly" (2001). We understood this statement as a minimum and reliable claim of accuracy and assumed that ACT would not exaggerate its claims, knowing that e-Write administrators might independently test e-Write's accuracy. Moreover, the ACT statement suggested to us that no splits existed when e-Write rated timed essays.

THE DIFFICULTIES OF RECEIVING AND RETRIEVING E-WRITE SCORES AND ESSAYS

Typically, a UVSC student finished his or her e-Write test and saw his or her score on the computer screen while the score sheet was also printing at the testing center's printer. But, immediately after some students completed their e-Write tests, we noticed that some scores were missing. Students with missing scores received this e-Write message on their computer screens: "The response was judged to be unscoreable (e.g., blank response, illegible response, or a response written in a language other than English)." This message confused us because we had watched the students who received it type e-Write essays. In addition, none of us were sure that these *e*-Write essays were preserved in the database.

On the third day of testing, another negative unanticipated event occurred. The first class arrived at the testing center as scheduled at 8:00 a.m., received the proctor's instructions, and began typing timed essays in e-Write. As students finished and submitted their essays, the normal sequence of e-Write messages or screens "froze." Similarly, if a student was word processing, when he or she clicked the "save" button, the computer immediately froze, without any indication whether the document had been saved or not. As each student in the 8:00 a.m. class submitted his or her e-Write essay, a similar event occurred. We directed the students not to give their computers any more commands and called ACT Technical Support for help. The ACT personnel told us that the server, where all the e-Write tests were sent, was down. An ACT

Technical Support person also said that this was the first time such an event had occurred.

We wondered what to do next. ACT Technical Support personnel would not indicate when the e-Write server would be restored and would not answer these questions: were the class's e-Write tests received by the server? If the testing center computers were shut down and restarted, would that mean that the e-Write tests would be permanently lost? At that time, too, the larger problem was whether to administer e-Write tests to the 9:00 and 10:00 classes. We decided to have students in the 8:00 class finish their essays and submit them—only to have the computers, predictably, freeze. After all the e-Write tests were finished and the 8:00 class had left, we shut down and restarted the frozen computers. For the 9:00 and 10:00 classes, we decided to provide students with a paper copy of the two e-Write prompts and to have the students type their timed essays as Word documents to be later typed into the e-Write program by staff. The 9:00 and 10:00 classes received the same proctor's instructions as the previous class but, unlike that class, some students used spell- and grammar-check programs when writing their timed essays.

In general, the freezing incident added to the problem of missing scores and complicated the pilot study. The central problem of the missing scores was that if placement had actually depended on e-Write scores, a significant number of students would not have been able to register for their first composition course at college. Each student would have had to wait for his or her ACT score report and then register for a composition course the following semester.

ACT personnel eventually provided us with explanations as to why some e-Write scores were missing. Apparently, e-Write does not score one of every fifteen essays automatically; some selected e-Write essays are sent to ACT human raters for scoring as a "quality-control measure." Also, according to ACT personnel, some e-Write essays are too short for scoring except by ACT human raters.

Regarding our missing e-Write scores, however, communications with ACT were problematic, and their communications to us were not always received when needed. For example, at least several weeks after the e-Write testing, ACT Technical Support personnel informed us that we had been receiving encoded e-mails regarding the missing scores and missing e-Write essays. Testing center staff did not notice these e-mails because they were not expected and were sent to a generic e-mail address for the testing center. Learning of this, we asked ACT Technical Support personnel to resend them. In response, we were told to look for the encoded e-mails again. When we failed to find them, ACT Technical

Support personnel agreed to resend them. Later we learned that the ACT instructions for decoding the e-mails were incomplete.

By January of 2004, about four months after the e-Write essays had been written, communications between ACT Technical Support personnel and the testing center's technical staff had still failed to resolve the issue of missing test scores and missing e-Write tests. This caused us to contact a representative in the research component of ACT Placement Programs. As a result, by mid-February, or approximately six months after the testing, we had finally received most of the missing e-Write scores. Until then, approximately 17 percent of e-Write scores had been missing. If the college had actually been using e-Write for placement purposes in the fall of 2003, would that have meant that an alternative placement assessment would have had to be devised for at least 17 percent of students?

Other aspects of the situation were relevant when considering the desirability of using e-Write for placement purposes. The exact number of missing scores was subject to interpretation, because during the e-Write testing, some students typed two essays, one or both having a missing score. Sometimes, but not always, students with missing scores experienced this sequence of events: first, they typed their e-Write essays and submitted them for scoring but then received the message, "The response was judged to be unscoreable. . . ." Responding to that message, some students reentered e-Write and typed a second essay which, like the first, may or may not have been scored. After this situation had occurred about twenty times, we realized what was happening and modified the proctor's instructions to lessen the occurrence of the problem. Regarding other practical glitches, we found instances of a student submitting two e-Write essays or exiting the program without finishing one essay. This meant that the testing center paid for more e-Write units than planned. Incidentally, early in 2004, we received the frozen e-Write essays and scores, meaning that the ACT server had received them. Reception was delayed because of encrypted files as well as ACT Technical Support not knowing where the scores and essays were for a time.

ENGLISH TEACHERS SCORE THE E-WRITE ESSAYS

Although paper copies of e-Write essays were normally not available to the testing center administrator, much less an e-Write user, prior to the testing sessions, we received information from ACT Technical Support personnel about how to obtain paper copies of the e-Write essays. With those in hand, we worked with two other English professors to identify anchor and range-finder e-Write essays. In December of 2003, we led a norming session for nine English teachers or raters to ensure the reliable application of an adapted ACT 8-point scale to rate e-Write essays. To make that scale more meaningful to raters, we also suggested that a score below 4 placed students into ENGH 0890, below 6 into ENGH 0990, and below 8 into ENGL 1010. A score of 8 would exempt students from an entry-level English course. The raters had taught all of these courses and established their interrater reliability as 83 percent, which meant that the two raters' scores agreed for 83 percent of the e-Write essays. A third reader read the 17 percent of e-Write essays that received split scores and assigned a final score to them.

Besides the adapted ACT 8-point scale, shared curricular knowledge helped the raters score the e-Write essays. The ENGH 0890 curriculum is designed for basic writers whose writing suggests written-down speech, the lack of a reading history, or significant problems with common orthographic conventions or with controlling sentences and writing paragraphs. The ENGH 0990 curriculum, which serves about 75 percent of UVSC basic writers, is designed for students who are ready to read academic texts, possess a general knowledge of an essay, and control most of their sentences and paragraphs in terms of rhetorical and mechanical structures. ENGL 1010, Freshman Composition, is designed for high school graduates who are ready to begin writing at a college level.

COMPARING MULTIPLE-CHOICE TEST SCORES, E-WRITE SCORES, AND HUMAN RATERS' SCORES

The office of Institutional Research and Management Studies analyzed multiple-choice test scores, e-Write scores, and human rater scores. Table 1 (next page) suggests that the rater scores have a moderately strong correlation with the student scores on multiple-choice tests.

In contrast, table 2 (next page) suggests that e-Write scores have a much weaker correlation with the same multiple-choice test scores.

In other words, e-Write's validity is weak in terms of its correlations with multiple-choices tests cited in table 2. The correlation between e-Write scores and raters' scores, moreover, is .56, which is below expectations created by ACT. These results mean, first, that the rater scores have greater criterion-related validity, and second, the e-Write scores would have resulted in a substantial misplacement of students.

PLACEMENT AND E-WRITE AT UVSC

Based on this limited experience with e-Write, the Department of Basic Composition and the Department of English and Literature foresee two significant difficulties with e-Write. First, e-Write scores are *not* received

TABLE 1
Correlations between human rater scores and other test scores

Correlation	Test	Correlation	Test
.430	DRP (Degrees of Reading Power)	.431	ACT COMPASS (editing test)
.559	ACT English	.421	ACT Reading
.512	ACT Composite		

TABLE 2
Correlations between e-Write scores and other test scores

Correlation	Test	Correlation	Test
.180	DRP (Degrees of Reading Power)	.267	ACT COMPASS (editing test)
.290	ACT English	.192	ACT Reading
.209	ACT Composite		

in a timely fashion and second, the validity of the e-Write scores is questionable. If the e-Write scores had been used for placement purposes, for example, apparently only 4 of 298 students would have enrolled in the lower-level basic writing course, an outcome that experienced basic writing teachers at UVSC believe is inaccurate.

That said, the e-Write study has had some positive outcomes. Whereas the publication of "Basic Writing Placement with Holistically Scored Essays: Research Evidence" (Matzen and Hoyt 2004) seemed to suggest that only the Department of Basic Composition was concerned about accurate placement, the Exceptional Merit Grant that funded the e-Write pilot study signaled that an active concern for accurate placement is shared by the Department of English and Literature. English faculty in both English departments have agreed to trust human raters and to advocate that timed essays become a part of a placement system for first-year composition courses.

9

COMPUTERIZED WRITING ASSESSMENT
Community College Faculty Find Reasons to Say "Not Yet"

William W. Ziegler

Community colleges exist to provide educational opportunities to a fluid population, many of whom encounter sudden changes in their work, family lives, and financial situations. For this reason, community colleges often admit, place, and register a student for classes all within a little more than twenty-four hours. This need to respond promptly explains why Virginia's community college administrators took notice when the computerized COMPASS placement test appeared in 1995. The test, published by ACT Inc., promised to gather demographic data as well as provide nearly instant placement recommendations in mathematics, reading, and writing. Several colleges piloted the test independently, and by 2000 the Virginia Community College System required all its colleges to use the test, with system-developed cutoff scores, unless they could show that other measures were superior. The Virginia Community College System now had a test that not only reported scores quickly and recorded data for easy manipulation but could be used uniformly at each college, unlike the previous patchwork of commercially published and homegrown tests used by the system's twenty-three member institutions.

Faculty had little difficulty accepting COMPASS/ESL (renamed when English as a second language tests were added in 2000) as a test for mathematics and reading once pilots had shown that it produced valid placements. Writing was a different case. The COMPASS/ESL writing-placement test is a multiple-choice editing test, requiring students to detect errors and evaluate coherence and organization within short passages. However, for most English faculty, the only valid test of writing competence is writing. Pilot testing led faculty at J. Sargeant Reynolds Community College and elsewhere in the Virginia Community College System to conclude that the COMPASS/ESL writing-placement test could not identify underprepared writers as accurately as trained faculty could by evaluating impromptu writing samples. Therefore, several colleges continued to use writing samples for placement in composition, exempting only students with high standardized test scores, which had proven to correlate strongly with the ability to produce satisfactory writing.

Unfortunately, trained faculty raters need time to read, so students and counselors facing registration deadlines still fidgeted daily while waiting for faculty to evaluate dozens of writing samples. Faculty did not always enjoy the process, but they disliked even more the idea of giving up a direct writing measure in favor of a grammar test alone.

So, when ACT Inc. introduced e-Write as a component of the COMPASS/ESL test, faculty and administrators again took notice. The e-Write test elicits writing samples using a set of argumentative prompts. Each prompt describes a simple rhetorical context, such as a letter intended to influence government or educational leaders to make a policy decision. The college can designate a time limit or allow untimed testing. Test takers type their samples in a bare-bones word processor—not much more than a message window—and submit it via the Internet to ACT for electronic evaluation by the IntelliMetric Essay Scoring Engine, which returns an overall placement score on an 8-point scale as well as five analytic scores, each on a 4-point scale. The placement score, while not as prompt as the multiple-choice writing test, arrives in a few minutes. For those thinking of placement as a customer-service function, here was the answer: analysis and direct assessment, plus the advantages that had attracted them to COMPASS/ESL at the beginning—speed, accessible data, and uniform placement practices across the state system.

Most English faculty in Virginia's community colleges would probably agree with Joanne Drechsel's (1999) objections to computerized evaluation of writing: it dehumanizes the writing situation, discounts the complexity of written communication, and tells student writers that their voice does not deserve a human audience. However, faculty at the two colleges conducting pilot studies of e-Write (Tidewater Community College and J. Sargeant Reynolds Community College) did not object to the trial. Some may have been mollified by the prospect of serving students more quickly, others by the wish to be rid of a burden. And others may have reasoned cynically that for students used to receiving a reductive, algorithmic response to their writing (put exactly five sentences in each paragraph; never use *I*), one more such experience would not be fatal.

As it turned out, composition faculty never had to fight a battle for humanistic values on theoretical grounds because the pilot studies showed e-Write could not produce valid writing placements. Among the findings:

- Both the overall scores and the five analytic scores tended to cluster in a midrange. Few samples received scores other than 2 or 3 in the five 4-point analytic scales, while 82 percent received overall scores of 5 or 6 on the 8-point scale. No scores (other than the few at the extremes of the scales) corresponded closely with instructors' ratings of the samples.
- A follow-up survey of students' grades showed that e-Write scores did no better at predicting success in the college composition course than faculty reader scores.
- The IntelliMetric Essay Scoring Engine was at a loss more often than hoped. When the artificial-intelligence engine cannot score a sample, the writing is evaluated by human raters at ACT at a higher cost and after a longer time—a day rather than minutes. More than 25 percent of the pilot samples stumped the scoring engine and required human assessment.

THE E-WRITE PILOT AT J. SARGEANT REYNOLDS COMMUNITY COLLEGE

For one week in July 2003 the college suspended its normal writing-placement process, in which students complete the COMPASS/ESL writing (grammar) test followed by a writing sample for those whose grammar scores fall below the 65th percentile. Instead, students were asked to complete the COMPASS/ESL e-Write test. Those who preferred not to use the computer were offered the regular placement writing sample, which students write by hand. Forty-six students chose the e-Write option.

The e-Write pilot used three of the five prompts provided; two would not have been suitable because their fictional contexts presented situations that would arise only at a residential college. Full-time faculty members evaluated the e-Write essays, judging the writers as either developmental (assigned to ENG 01, Preparation for College Writing I) or ready for first-semester college composition (ENG 111, College Composition I). Three faculty readers took part at first. One of these evaluated all forty-six essays, a second evaluated thirty-seven, and a third evaluated twelve. Because the e-Write prompts were rhetorically similar to our own placement prompts and because we did not want to require more time from students for additional testing, we decided to use the resulting samples for actual placement if we found them suitable. However, we would rely on our own evaluations rather than the e-Write scores.

A few months later, when all English faculty had returned for fall semester, six more readers evaluated the same samples, each reading a set of twelve. Eventually, all samples had evaluations from at least two readers. Twenty-seven essays received evaluations from three readers, and ten essays had evaluations from four readers. All readers examined only the writing samples, which included the names of the student authors. Other information, such as COMPASS/ESL reading-placement scores, time spent on the test, students' first language, and demographic data, were withheld.

All faculty readers teach primarily first-year composition. In addition, four teach at least one section of developmental writing each academic year, and three are qualified to teach developmental reading, although only one does so regularly. The readers included the English program chairperson, the coordinator of developmental English, and the head of the academic division of arts, humanities, and social sciences.

Time

E-Write provides a choice of time limits; however, the Reynolds pilot used the untimed mode. We reasoned that most students would probably not exceed the one-hour limit we place on our current writing sample. In addition, an untimed mode accommodates students with special needs recognized under the Americans with Disabilities Act.

We were correct about how much time students would use to write. E-Write data showed that the mean average time spent on the test was 31.6 minutes (excluding two sessions with recorded times of over four hours, likely the result of machine error). Only five students took more than 50 minutes; times ranged from 5 to 79 minutes.

E-Write Test Scores

One limitation we observed in e-Write was its tendency to assign mid-range scores to nearly all the samples. Only three samples received over-all ratings of 7 or 8; only five received ratings of 3 or 4. E-Write awarded scores of 6 to eighteen (39.1 percent) of the samples and scores of 5 to twenty samples (43.5 percent). The five analytic scores also grouped in the midrange. Out of 230 analytic scores (five scores for each of the forty-six samples), only eight scores were 1 or 4. No essay received the highest score of 4 in conventions, organization, or style; no essay received the lowest score of 1 in conventions or style. E-Write awarded a score of 3 for focus to 69.6 percent of the samples and a score of 3 in content to 56.6 percent. Ratings for style and organization were split evenly: 50 percent each for style scores of 2 and 3; 47.8 percent each for organization scores of 2 and 3. E-Write awarded a score of 2 in conventions to 63 percent of samples.

An uneven distribution of scores is not fatal if a test needs only to facilitate a two-level placement decision. Writing instructors might not object to a test that gives scores of only 5 or 6 if they perceived consistent, relevant distinctions between each group of samples. However, we found that e-Write's overall and analytic scales could not do this to the satisfaction of our faculty.

Time and E-Write Test Scores

The samples receiving overall scores of 5 and 6, the two largest contingents, differed little in average time spent on the test: 33.2 minutes for samples scored 6 versus 32.6 minutes for samples scored 5. Not surprisingly, the few essays rated below 5 recorded a shorter average time (21.4 minutes), but two of these spent 31 and 35 minutes on the test, not much different from those with higher scores. Likewise, the few essays receiving top scores (one with overall 8, two with overall 7) were written in 36, 35, and 48 minutes—not drastically different from average times for the midrange scores.

In the analytic measures, writers who took more time enjoyed an advantage in only two areas: content and style. Samples rated 3 in content averaged 34.4 minutes, while samples rated 2 averaged 26.5 minutes. On the style scale, samples rated 3 averaged 33.8 minutes, compared to 29.4 minutes for samples rated 2. On the other scales (focus, organization, and conventions), the average time for samples receiving scores of 3 was slightly lower than for those scored 2; the largest difference was only 2.2 minutes.

The time difference between higher and lower content scores is unsurprising; presumably quantity affects the content score, although the ACT COMPASS scoring guide (2003) states distinctions in both quantitative (number of supporting reasons offered) and qualitative terms (elaboration, selection of examples, and clarity) (61). It is unclear why those receiving scores of 3 for focus, organization, and conventions required slightly less time than those receiving 2.

Reading Scores and E-Write Test Scores

The higher a student's overall e-Write score, the higher the score in the COMPASS/ESL reading-placement test was likely to be. All three students with e-Write overall scores of 7 or 8 scored in the 85th to 99th percentile in reading (relative to all students tested at Virginia's two-year colleges). Students with overall e-Write scores of 6 averaged 86.1 (54th percentile) in reading; those with e-Write scores of 5 averaged 76.8 (28th percentile). The five writers who received 3 or 4 in e-Write averaged 64.4 (12th percentile), none scoring higher than 79 (34th percentile).

The same was true for analytic scores. The largest difference was in the focus scale, where students whose samples received 3 averaged 86.1 in reading, compared to 65.4 (13th percentile) for students with 2-rated samples. Differences were smaller in the ratings for content, organization, style, and conventions, where students with 3-rated samples averaged from 84.7 to 87.6 (47th to 57th percentile) in reading, compared to students with 2-rated samples, whose reading scores averaged from 74.8 to 77.6 (25th to 30th percentile).

Faculty Evaluations

Faculty readers were unanimous in their ratings for twenty-two of the forty-six samples, judging nineteen as composition-ready and three as developmental. Of the remaining samples, thirteen were rated composition-ready and three developmental by a split vote. Four samples received a 50-50 split vote from an even number of readers. The votes of the three July readers determined the students' formal placements. By this method, thirty-six students were placed in ENG 111 and ten in ENG 01.

To examine interrater agreement, we examined paired readers. (For example, three readers for an essay amounted to three pairs: readers A and B, readers A and C, and readers B and C.) By this method, there were 136 pairs of readers, with 64.6 percent agreeing on either an ENG 111 or an ENG 01 placement.

Faculty Evaluations and E-Write Test Score.

Faculty tended to favor samples with higher e-Write scores, but not to a degree that justified setting an e-Write criterion for placement. Nine of the eighteen samples receiving e-Write overall ratings of 6 elicited unanimous recommendations for ENG 111, and another six elicited split decisions, with ENG 111 votes predominating. Only one sample with an e-Write score of 6 received a split ENG 01 recommendation. Five of the twenty samples receiving overall scores of 5 elicited unanimous ENG 111 recommendations, and six received ENG 111 recommendations on a split vote. Four of the 5-rated samples received unanimous ENG 01 recommendations, with another three receiving ENG 01 recommendations on a split decision.

The same pattern showed in the analytic scores: a 3 score nearly always coincided with unanimous or split decisions in favor of ENG 111, whereas scores of 2 coincided with an array of outcomes, leaning more toward ENG 01 decisions. One of the most curious outcomes involved the conventions scale, where twenty-seven students received e-Write ratings of 2; of these, eight received unanimous ENG 111 ratings from faculty, while nine received unanimous ENG 01 recommendations.

Clearly, e-Write scores did not coincide closely enough with faculty judgments to persuade instructors to turn their placement function over to the test. However, what if e-Write knew better than we did whether a writing sample showed readiness for a college composition course? To answer this question, we recorded the pilot students' final grades in ENG 111 classes during the subsequent academic year.

Faculty Judgments, E-Write Test Scores, and Success in College Composition

Typically, a large but unknown number of students who take placement tests at Reynolds do not enroll in classes during the subsequent semester. Of the forty-six students who wrote e-Write samples, six did not enroll in any class at the college during the following academic year, and another nine did not enroll in ENG 111 or ENG 01 classes, although one enrolled in an ESL composition class, one completed first-semester college composition at another community college, and one transferred credit for first-semester composition from a four-year college.

Subtracting noncompleters from the pilot group leaves a sample too small to bear up under statistical scrutiny, but these students' success rates in ENG 111 are distressingly and uncharacteristically low. During the last several years, the success rate in ENG 111 at Reynolds (the proportion of students earning grades of A, B, or C) has ranged from 65 to 69 percent. The balance includes students who withdraw or earn incomplete grades as well as those who earn D or F. But in the e-Write pilot group, just under half of students who enrolled in ENG 111 completed it with grades of C or better. The two largest groups by overall score (6 and 5) differed little from each other. Six of the thirteen students whose samples were rated 6 and who enrolled in the course completed it successfully, while five of the eleven enrolling students with samples rated 5 did so. However, composition grades for students scoring 6 included more As and Bs, while C was the most common grade for those scoring 5. No students scoring at the extremes of the overall e-Write scale—3, 4, 7, and 8—enrolled in ENG 111 at Reynolds, although one (with a 7 score) completed the course elsewhere.

In only one of the five analytic scales—content—did a relatively high score tend to mark successful composition students. Thirteen of the eighteen students with content scores of 3 received grades of C or better, with As and Bs predominating. The analytic score for conventions did the poorest job of picking out successful students: three of the ten enrolled students scoring 3 on this scale completed the course successfully, compared to eight of the eleven enrolled students scoring 2.

Faculty proved no more prescient than e-Write. Half of the students whose samples drew either unanimous of split-decision ENG 111 recommendations from faculty readers completed the course successfully. Successful students receiving unanimous recommendations earned mostly A and B grades, while those receiving split decisions received mostly Cs, but the proportion of unsuccessful students was the same—about 50 percent—for each group.

Scoring Engine at a Loss—Humans to the Rescue

One feature of e-Write is the human backup. As explained in the COMPASS/ESL technical manual, "COMPASS e-Write does not score responses that deviate significantly from the patterns observed in the original training papers" (ACT 2003, 62). The choice of modal verb—*does* not rather than *can*not—suggests disdain, similar to distaste toward washing windows, but the manual explains that the rating engine has trouble with samples that are "off topic" or too brief. If the scoring engine cannot determine a rating for a sample, ACT's human readers take over, evaluating the sample on the same scoring scales and returning the results in two days. The scoring engine needed human backup in twelve of the forty-six samples (26 percent). In a typical semester, when Reynolds tests more than two thousand students, this projects to more than five hundred students for whom one advantage of e-Write—speedy response—would vanish.

E-WRITE AND THE FUTURE OF WRITING PLACEMENT IN THE VCCS

The speed and convenience of the e-Write test fulfills certain needs in a customer-service model of placement. However, the e-Write version tested here tended to pile samples into barely distinguishable masses at a few points in the rating scale—an insurmountable practical barrier to its acceptance at Reynolds for the time being. ACT is developing a version of e-Write using a 12-point overall scale that may answer that objection. If it succeeds, faculty can expect renewed pressure to adopt a single test that makes student transitions easier through a uniform placement measure.

However, writing faculty see placement through a lens that finds usefulness in the work of creating and maintaining a placement instrument. In addition to the honoring of humanistic values Drechsel (1999) identifies, conducting writing placement forces faculty to revisit vital questions: what are the basic skills of writing? What traits do we agree to recognize as demonstrating competence in these skills? Are argumentative contexts the best or only ones for eliciting the best examples of students' performance? For faculty, the work of placement may be a pearl-producing irritant; the answer to computerized testing may forever be "not yet."

10

PILOTING THE COMPASS E-WRITE SOFTWARE AT JACKSON STATE COMMUNITY COLLEGE

Teri T. Maddox

Placement issues are a major concern in higher education. Many states require students who do not have college-level scores on entrance exams such as the ACT or SAT to take precollege developmental classes. Without reliable placement testing, students may be put into classes that are too easy for them and become bored, or worse, they may be put into classes too hard for them and drop out because they don't think they are "college material." Correct placement should mean that students are put into appropriate classes for their ability level so that they will be properly challenged and supported. In short, higher education needs a system of writing placement that is able to measure student ability both efficiently and reliably so that students take appropriate classes. Finding a system that meets all our requirements, however, is not easy. A sign in a downtown business says, "Cheap, Quick, Excellent—Pick Any Two." Jackson State Community College was looking for a writing-placement test that would be quick, cheap, and reliable, but like the business sign, it does not seem that it is possible to have all three.

Jackson State Community College has an enrollment of approximately four thousand, serving fourteen mostly rural counties outside the Memphis metropolitan area. It is a member of the Tennessee Board of Regents, which includes fourteen community colleges and five universities. The system uses ACT English subscores to place students in writing classes. Students who make a 14 and below are enrolled in Basic Writing, which is a sentence to paragraph course; students who score 15–18 are enrolled in Developmental Writing, which is a paragraph to essay course; and students who score a 19 are enrolled in college-level English composition, Comp I.

The board of regents encourages institutions to allow students additional placement opportunities. Jackson State Community College has tried several different placement methods. The first method we used was to require all basic and developmental writing students to write a diagnostic essay the first week of class. If their writing sample was judged to be strong enough by at least two full-time English faculty, students were able to move up a class level. A few students each semester did move up a level, whether from Basic to Developmental Writing or from Developmental Writing to Comp I. However, trying to rearrange those students' class schedules was difficult because classes were often full, so the students' entire schedule had to be changed. A more serious problem with this system was that by the time students had written the essay, the essays had been reviewed, and the students had been given new schedules, they had missed over a week of class. Since they were borderline students to begin with, this system did not seem to give them the best chance to succeed. The process seemed awkward and unfair, so the English department looked for alternatives.

The second placement method we tried was using the COMPASS writing test, an ACT product and much like the ACT English test except the COMPASS is untimed and computerized. We liked the idea that the test is untimed because many students do much better when allowed to complete a test at their own pace, especially nontraditional students. We also liked the idea of the computerized test because it is adaptive; that is, it adjusts the order of questions according to student answers. If a student answers a question correctly, he or she is taken down a different path than a student who answers the question incorrectly. Unfortunately, like the ACT English test, the COMPASS writing test seemed to be more of a revising test than a composition test because there is no actual writing involved; both are indirect tests of writing, and students still choose from multiple-choice options. Our English faculty wanted a test that would directly measure actual essay writing, so we were not completely satisfied with the COMPASS writing test either.

Jackson State Community College had been using COMPASS for five years when ACT publicized its new computer grading software, e-Write. According to ACT product information (2003), electronic scoring is

- fast—The samples are scored and the reports produced within seconds to allow immediate feedback and advising.
- reliable—Research demonstrates close agreement between electronically generated scores and those assigned by expert human raters.
- affordable—For information, contact your nearest ACT office (www.act.org/e-write/).

Students are given a prompt (one of six) and asked to type a multiple-paragraph essay. Institutions can set a time limit for the writing if they choose. Students submit the essay, and it is graded in seconds with an overall score between 2 and 8. In addition, the computer will also score the essay in five different areas: focus, content, organization, style, and mechanical conventions, on a 1–4 scale.

It looked like using e-Write would be a good solution for us. First, we could test students before the semester began so they would be more likely to be placed in the appropriate class at the beginning of the semester. Second, students would be writing an actual essay and not choosing multiple-choice answers. Third, results would be virtually instantaneous, so students could test, receive their scores, and immediately complete a class schedule. Finally, the cost was realistic. In fact, it would cost us about the same to use e-Write as it would to rely on trained holistic graders. Therefore, the software looked like we could say, "Cheap, Quick, Excellent—Have All Three."

The English department voted to pilot the e-Write software for three testing periods, before spring, summer, and fall semesters in 2003. Following ACT suggestions, we required students to take both the COMPASS writing test and e-Write, which gave them a combined writing score. Students took the COMPASS writing test first, which was untimed, and then we decided to give them a time limit of two hours to complete the e-Write topic. The cutoff scores for the combined writing test results had to be the same as the already standardized COMPASS scores set by the Tennessee Board of Regents to allow for transferability and continuity: Basic Writing, 1–28; Developmental Writing, 29–67; and Comp I, 68–99.

Challenge Day is an opportunity Jackson State gives students before each semester to try to raise their placement level. Students pay $20 and may take math, reading, and/or writing-placement tests, depending on their placement. We used the e-Write for writing, the Nelson-Denny for reading, and the COMPASS for math. (Students who have a grade in a class are not allowed to challenge that class; they must retake the class to replace the grade.) The testing went smoothly in spring and summer, but the number of students tested was low; only fourteen in spring and twenty-four in summer tested for writing so we did not have a good feel for the success of the computer program. We did have some concern since a higher percentage of students tested up a level in writing than did so in reading and math, but we wanted to wait and see what would happen with

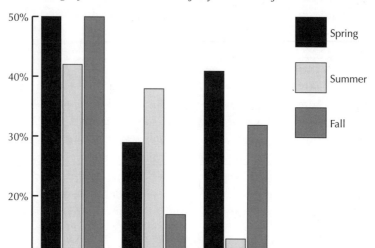

FIGURE 1

Percentage of students who successfully tested out of their DSP classes

a larger student population. The figure above depicts the differences in the percentages testing up a level in writing, reading, and math.

The main event came in the fall semester of 2003, when 107 students showed up at Challenge Day to try to improve their writing placement. We experienced several problems on that day with e-Write. It did not seem to live up to our expectations, especially in the areas where the advertisement promised "fast" and "reliable" results.

Our first concern was that thirty-five students did not get immediate results. One of the reasons we were interested in e-Write was because it would give us quicker results than would human readers. However, twenty-nine scores arrived several hours after the testing was completed, and human readers on our campus could have scored those essays much more quickly. We never got any results at all that day from seven essays. Because those scores were so late, we had to use just the COMPASS writing score to place those students, the method we had used in the past and were trying to replace. The students whose essays were not returned on time were told that when their essay scores were returned, we would contact them if their placement had changed.

In the software instructions, ACT states that essays would not be returned immediately if they were off topic or too short. In those cases the essays would have to be read by human readers, and scores would be returned within forty-eight hours. We assumed that the late essays must have been "problem" essays, but apparently that was not the case; when the essay scores were returned, five students actually tested higher, so their essays could not have been too short or off topic. We had to notify those students to come back to campus and change their schedule—something we were tying to avoid by using a computerized scoring system. Our students often have to drive over an hour to get to campus, and these five had to make one trip to campus to take the test and then come back on another day to complete their schedules. One real advantage the computer has over human readers is speed, but the machine did not come through for us in that respect.

Our second concern was the lack of variability in the essay scores. The e-Write software scores essays between 2–8, with a score of 6 considered to be a college-level essay (www.act.org/e-write/). Seventy-nine percent of the hundred students who received a score made a 5 or a 6, which seems too narrow a range. The table below illustrates the frequency of each of the scores.

It might be argued that the students who came to test on that day were all about the same level of proficiency, so we decided to compare the above e-Write scores with the other measures of student writing that we had, which included their ACT English subscore and their COMPASS writing score. A database was created that included those two scores and the e-Write score as well as students' combined COMPASS/e-Write score, the time they spent on the COMPASS writing test and on e-Write, and whether students placed into a higher level.

The comparative data located nineteen suspicious e-Write scores, 20 percent of the tests that day: that is, instances where the e-Write score seemed high compared with the other measures of writing. For example, five students made below a 15 on the ACT and scored a 6 on the e-Write, which is college level. Since the ACT, COMPASS, and e-Write are all ACT products, we would have hoped there would be more consistency among the tests. Most troubling was a student who spent one minute on the e-Write and wrote an essay that was scored a 6.

Another concern was that as in the spring and summer testing periods, the percentage of students testing up a level on the writing test was higher than the percentage testing up on the reading and math

TABLE 1

E-Write scores (N=100)

E-Write score	Frequency
2	1
3	2
4	8
5	39
6	46
7	4
8	0

challenge tests we gave that day. We used the COMPASS math test and 32 percent of the students placed into a higher class, and we used the Nelson-Denny reading test and 17 percent tested into a higher class. With the COMPASS/E-write, 50 percent tested into a higher class. The majority of those students moved up one writing level, although five students moved up two levels, from Basic Writing to Comp I.

Our final concern about e-Write was its reliability, the most important of the key issues for us. The speediness of the results and the cost are not important at all if we can't trust the results. ACT informational material (2005) states, "Research shows strong agreement between COMPASS e-Write scores and those assigned when essays are rated by two expert readers. *100% of COMPASS e-Write scores are within one point of the reader-assigned scores. About 76% of COMPASS e-Write scores match the raters' scores exactly*" (emphasis in original). Unfortunately, ACT does not make student essays available, so we could not have the nineteen questionable essays read by our trained readers.

Consequently, the only way to adequately measure the placement accuracy was to track students through their next writing classes, so we tracked the students who had been placed in a higher class through the next four semesters. Nine students tested into Developmental Writing from Basic Writing, and of those nine, three passed Developmental Writing, a success rate of 33 percent. Four students attempted Developmental Writing and did not pass, and two students did not enroll in school at all. The four students who did not pass the class have now dropped out. So we do have to worry about their placement. Is one of the reasons they dropped out that they were placed too high?

Five students tested into college-level writing, Comp I, from Basic Writing (a move up of two levels), and of those five, two withdrew from college, two passed with a C, and one made an F in the class and then withdrew from college, so the success rate is two out of five, or 40 percent.

Thirty-nine students tested into college-level English from Developmental Writing. Of those, twenty-four made a C or above in Comp I, a 61 percent success rate. Of those students, fourteen made Cs, and one of our worries is what those Cs mean. Were the students really prepared for Comp I and properly placed, or were they struggling just to barely make a C? Most teachers must adapt their curriculum based on the needs of their students, so did the teacher have to change the curriculum so that even misplaced students could be successful? We have no way of answering these questions, but they do remain part of the placement issues for us.

According to a study by Boylan et al. (1992), which included postremediation performance in college courses of a sample of six thousand students at 150 institutions, 91.2 percent of students who passed remedial writing classes passed their subsequent college-level English course. According to the above numbers from e-Write, the students who placed into Comp I from e-Write had a 61 percent success rate, a rate far below the national study.

I had encouraged the English department to pilot e-Write last year for our Challenge Day because I believed it would be a better alternative for us than the other methods we had tried in the past, better in terms of cost, speed, and accuracy, "Cheap, Quick, Excellent." When the English department looked at the overall results, it voted to stop using e-Write as a placement tool. The department members will be reading student essays themselves at Challenge Day, using a holistic scoring system.

11

THE ROLE OF THE WRITING COORDINATOR IN A CULTURE OF PLACEMENT BY ACCUPLACER

Gail S. Corso

Sarah Freedman, in research carried out during the 1980s, found that holistic ratings by human raters did not award particularly high marks to professionally written essays mixed in with student productions. This indicates that there is room here for AES to improve on what raters can do.
—Bereiter

Placement processes into college writing and developmental writing courses include diverse options. Processes include use of external exams and externally set indicators, such as SAT or ACCUPLACER scores; use of locally designed essay topics for placement that are assessed by human readers using either holistic or analytic trait measures; use of directed self-placement (Royer and Gilles 2002) or informed self-placement (Bedore and Rossen-Knill 2004); and use of electronic portfolios (Raymond Walters College 2002). Whatever process for placement an institution uses needs to align with course and program outcomes, institutional assessment outcomes, the mission of the school, and, most significantly, the needs of the students.

Historically at my small, private college, the Academic Resource Center has managed placement processes into developmental math, developmental writing, and reading courses. My role as writing coordinator (1999–present) and writing specialist (1992–1998) has required my attention to placement as well as assessment processes for the program. For placement into writing courses, I have functioned as a consultant, information manager, and judge, assisting in adjustments for possible misplacements at the end of the first week of each semester. This year, for the first time, I implemented a portfolio appeals process for placement; as part of this process, a brochure about appealing placement decisions for writing now is included in each parent's advising folder on registration/advising days.

In most recent years, processes for checking placement have required my close attention to writing performance, including dialogue with the dean of Arts and Sciences, the director of the Academic Resources Center the vice president for Academic Affairs. My role requires dialogue with those with administrative access to information in the system's electronic database; through ongoing dialogue with the director of the center, we have attempted to adjust placement decisions by ACCUPLACER.

My role has required attention to details and management of information and engaging in dialogue with faculty members and students—thus strengthening my idealistic vision for a placement system that best represents both my college's mission and the uniqueness of each individual student. With the mission in mind, an electronic-portfolio placement system aligning with an institutional system for assessment of learning in the core program and all of the major programs seems warranted. Since this vision is not yet collectively shared by the college community, I am advocating for adjustments to placement in all cases where students, faculty members, the director of the center, or I suspect such changes may be needed.

For now, the placement system by ACCUPLACER, which allows the advisor to register the incoming student in a timely way on four or five scheduled dates, is valued by my college. For writing placement in earlier years, however, select faculty members in the English program or select staff members of the center read essays when students registered at their convenience. If two raters disagreed, a third reader read the essay. With growth at the college and expansion of programs, in 2000 a consultant group for the college recommended that placement into writing courses be determined by examining the SAT combined math and verbal scores. At that time, I argued that this indicator seemed less valid and reliable as an indicator for performance in core writing classes, but the recommendation by the external consultant for enrollment management was implemented.

In spring 2003 at my college, a new system for a more integrative approach for placement, advising, and registration on several pre-planned dates was introduced. This shift to a program for placement, advising, and registration on the same day coincided with faculty members being introduced to online registration of students through the college management of information system, Datatel. The program for placement that was introduced in 2003 was ACCUPLACER. Students whose verbal SAT scores were higher than 450 automatically placed into the first-year composition course, English 101, Effective Writing with Computers. Since that initial exam in spring 2003, students whose SAT verbal scores are lower than 450 have been required to take the ACCUPLACER essay exam. Those students with scores lower than a 7 on the ACCUPLACER exam place into developmental writing. In retrospect, I can only surmise that the college approved ACCUPLACER with its promise of a timely management of and communication about data to facilitate placement processes, advising, and registration, and also to respond to an implied need for enrollment-management processes by the college.

The pilot use of the system for fall 2003 first-year students has warranted ongoing examination of writing from semester to semester as well as ongoing dialogue with the dean of Arts and Sciences, the vice president for Academic Affairs, and the director of the center, unlike the previous system, with only two human raters in the center and a possible third to settle differences in readings of essays. As we are engaged in the third year of ACCUPLACER for placement, I feel compelled to share this story about the need for human intervention in more timely ways for whatever placement system—but especially for placement by ACCUPLACER. My reservations about this automated essay-assessment system have centered on the need for a system of checks and balances by a human reader to be set in place *before* students receive their placement results. With the current system as well, all students ought to write a placement essay, and special arrangements need to be made for students with learning disabilities or for those with English as a second language. At present, the students who take the ACCUPLACER exam submit their essays electronically to the assessment system, virtually instantaneously receive their scores with a summary of their evaluation, print out the ACCUPLACER summary of feedback, meet with their advisor, and register online for fall classes—all on the same day. The culture of immediate results for placement, advising, and registration, while convenient for management of information by staff in the center, and even more convenient for faculty advisors, complicates the process of checking for accuracy of placement, not allowing any time for a human rater to read the essays and to verify how well the system is placing students into writing courses *before* the advising system occurs.

In the past several years, the college, with 1,710 full-time undergraduate students for fall 2004 and a 2,682 total head count for all students at all levels of instruction, has been in a dynamic state of transformation. Students from an ever-wider recruitment area find its location, programs, and emphasis on educating the whole person attractive. As a result of rapid growth in enrollment accompanied by expansion in program offerings, ACCUPLACER seems to have satisfied a need to place a reasonable proportion of students into courses requiring remediation (CA 094 and EG 094).

The rise in enrollment shown in Table 1 forced an increase in the number of faculty members teaching developmental and core writing courses from 1992 to 2004. With such growth, the college administration has sought out more automated methods for placement and registration for incoming students, so that those faculty members also in support-service roles could attend to other time-intensive tasks such as advising more diverse students, many of whom are the first generation in their family to attend college.

While the ACCUPLACER system seems to attend to the needs of the student and advisor to complete registration in person on one of five designated registration days, the college has neglected to consider how the system sends an indirect message about writing, how the time invested in a process approach to writing is de-emphasized, and how possible misjudgments by the ACCUPLACER system could be left uncritically examined if human intervention is not in place. Moreover, the 450 SAT verbal score as a primary indicator for placement into first-year composition presents even more problems with issues of content and system validity than placement by ACCUPLACER. Royer and Gilles (2002) argue strongly for locally designed measures for placement, as "[m]ost assessment theorists agree that a placement method should be derived from the curriculum itself in order to increase its validity" (267). To ensure systemic validity, they explain, the scope of any placement process needs to be envisioned as part of "the context of the entire institution and the consequences that it creates for students" (267).

An examination of records for a number of students not succeeding in first-year composition and showing a low GPA for the first semester overall in fall 2003 and 2004 suggests that the cutoff of 450 for SAT verbal is either too low or that ACCUPLACER is not functioning properly as an indicator of placement. Some of these students, of course, may have benefited from placement into developmental writing. Research repeatedly shows that students who are placed in basic writing classes "graduate in greater numbers than students who are not required to be in basic writing programs or chose to ignore a recommendation to participate in such programs" (Matzen and Hoyt 2004, 8). Instead of the SAT and ACCUPLACER external systems for placement, I recommend

TABLE 1

Fall enrollment numbers for first-year composition (101)
and developmental writing (094)

Semester	Placement adminis-tered by the Academic Resource Center	Enrollment CA 094 or ENG 094	Enrollment CA 101 or ENG 101
Fall 1992	Two human readers with a possible third	3 (4%)	64 (96%)
Fall 1996	Two human readers with a possible third	7 (1%)	97 (99%)
Fall 1999	Two human readers with a possible third	26 (1%)	235 (99%)
Fall 2000	SAT	70 (24%)	225 (76%)
Fall 2003	ACCUPLACER	56 (11%)	436 (89%)
Fall 2004	ACCUPLACER	84 (18%)	387 (82%)

a more person-centered placement by portfolios that aligns with the learning outcomes for the core writing program. While I value such a locally designed and implemented electronic-portfolio process for placement, I recognize that it will take a collective effort, involving more persons than the writing coordinator to make that kind of system for the entire college community more appealing than ACCUPLACER.

WHAT IS ACCUPLACER?

In the College Entrance Examination Board's brochure about ACCUPLACER (based on the IntelliMetric platform), its marketers explain how a "variety of computer-adaptive tests covering the areas of reading, writing, and mathematics . . . have been developed to create the most reliable score in the least amount of time" (College Entrance Examination Board 2001). This writing-placement test, WritePlacer *Plus*, the College Board's promotional material asserts, "is the only direct writing assessment that provides immediate feedback and scoring within a complete testing and placement system." WritePlacer *Plus* claims to evaluate the writing sample online for five features of writing: focus, development, organization, sentence structure, and mechanical conventions. The student's placement into one of various writing courses is determined by the individual college using ACCUPLACER's scores and descriptors for writing, each on the scale of 2–12. The student, shortly after completing the exam, receives a printout with scores for each of the five dimensions or features of writing as well as an overall score on a scale from 2–12 and a statement about placement into either developmental writing or regular first-year composition. With this information, the student then meets with an advisor for placement into fall courses; the placement, advising, and registration processes occur all in one day.

WHO DETERMINES THE ESSAY TOPIC FOR ACCUPLACER PLACEMENT?

ACCUPLACER allows for colleges to select one or several essay topics already tested in its system, to determine amount of time for the essay part of the exam, and to set a passing quality score on the scale of 2–12. For the first year of ACCUPLACER placement at my college, the coordinator of first-year advising selected three topics from ACCUPLACER's repertoire and allowed students an unlimited amount of time to respond. For the second year of placement by ACCUPLACER, the director of the Academic Resource Center asked me to select a topic. I suggested one topic and set the time limit at one hour. Students with documented learning disabilities could request additional time.

SPRING 2003, FOR ACADEMIC YEAR 2003–2004

In spring 2003, I attended part of a workshop at my college delivered by representatives of the College Board who explained aspects of the ACCUPLACER system. To better understand how ACCUPLACER would work, I asked to read several sample placement essays, which the director of the center shared with me. After I rated each, she then showed me the ACCUPLACER score and assessment narrative for each trait and the overall score. Using the rating scale of 2–12, I rated each essay and from this sample set, determined that a minimum of a 7 appeared to be the reasonable standard for students at my college to place into English 101, the regular first-year composition course. One essay that I rated high, as a 10 or 11, the ACCUPLACER system had rated as an 8. This essay, I later found out, was written by one of my colleagues, a published author.

For the first round of ratings for fall 2003 placement, staff from the center set the standard for placement into our first-year composition class at a score of 6. At the time, a standard of 6 was described by WritePlacer *Plus* as follows:

> This is a writing sample in which the characteristics of effective written communication are only partially formed. Statement of purpose is not totally clear, and although a main idea or point of view may be stated, continued focus on the main idea is not evident. Development of ideas by the use of specific supporting detail and sequencing of ideas may be present, but the development is incomplete or unclear. The response may

exhibit distracting errors or a lack of precision in the use of grammatical conventions, including sentence structure, word choice, usage, spelling, and punctuation. (College Entrance Examination Board 2001)

After the placement, advising, and registration process for the first group of students in spring 2003, I examined forty essays by students who placed into two of the five or so projected sections of developmental reading. From this examination of the writing of about 40 percent of students who placed into developmental reading for 2003–2004, I suggested that a score of 7 be set as the standard for placement into first-year composition. For all subsequent placement processes that spring and summer of 2003 for fall 2003 incoming students, the standard was altered to 7. The score of 7 as defined by ACCUPLACER is:

> The writing sample partially communicates a message to the specified audience. The purpose may be evident but only partially formed. Focus on the main idea is only partially evident. The main idea is only partially developed, with limited supporting details. Although there is some evidence of control in the use of mechanical conventions such as sentence structure, usage, spelling, and punctuation, some distracting errors may be present. (College Entrance Examination Board 2001)

Reading a representative sample of placement essays by students who had placed into developmental reading, I identified concerns about the quality of writing in these and other select samples; based on my recommendation, the director of the center adjusted the score for placement into first-year composition from 6 to 7. Final grades in first-year composition were evidence in support of this decision: students with a score of 6 or with an SAT verbal score slightly higher than 450 received lower grades than those with a score of 7.

SPRING 2004, FOR ACADEMIC YEAR 2004–2005

A major problem with ACCUPLACER appears to be cases of misplacement, requiring administrators to spend time and effort on adjustment. For academic year 2004–2005, the process for administering the ACCUPLACER exam changed slightly to facilitate more timely adjustments for misplacement. The vice president for Academic Affairs, the dean of Arts and Sciences, the director of the center, and I agreed to add a clause about placement adjustments to the exam; this clause would justify moving a student if, for one reason or another, the placement result by ACCUPLACER was perceived by the instructor or the student as a possible misplacement, into either first-year composition or developmental writing. A faculty member or student could initiate this dialogue about possible misplacement during the first week of instruction, requiring the writing program coordinator to examine the evidence and to respond before the end of the college's drop/add period—the Friday of the first week of instruction.

While this human intervention seemed proactive, the ACCUPLACER system, with its instantaneous delivery of feedback, appeared difficult to counteract, as its on-demand results set in motion a convenient registration process for advisors and students. It becomes difficult, though not impossible, to change schedules after the semester has started. This adjustment process, predicated on assumptions that faculty members can determine whether or not a student can accomplish the goals of first-year composition at a minimum of a C standard, adds stress to the role of the instructor. Internalizing the range of writing expectations can be quite complicated for new faculty—full-time, part-time, and adjunct—who are new to expectations for writing within the college's writing program.

As a result of this procedure, in the first week of instruction faculty members recommended that thirteen of eighty-four students be moved from a developmental writing course into a first-year composition class. After examining the essays written in class during the first week of instruction and listening to the recommendations by the faculty members, who initially discussed possible changes with students, I intervened by placing these students into several sections of first-year composition by the end of the drop/add time—the end of the first week of instruction. I discussed these possible changes with the director of the center and the dean. Yet another student, with English as a second language, who was a possible fourteenth misplacement, decided to remain in the developmental writing course. At the end of the semester, performance by these fourteen students indicated that the choices were beneficial. Many received As or Bs in first-year composition, and their overall GPAs indicated success.

While the system for placement adjustment during the first week of instruction has worked for individual students, this system in fall 2004 created slightly overcrowded teaching and learning environments for two sections of first-year composition, doing an injustice to students and faculty, moving beyond recommended class sizes in a program that values conferences, multiple revisions of drafts, and other person-centered pedagogy. While those students who moved into the first-year writing course succeeded during that semester, they were stressed by this late system for adjustment during an already anxious first week of college.

In June 2004, after another ACCUPLACER placement session for incoming fall 2004 students, I read sixty-two essays to check placement results. I identified sixteen that warranted reevaluation case by case. While the policy to adjust for possible misplacement was wise to initiate, I then recognized how waiting until the first week of instruction to adjust some obvious errors or oversights would complicate the advising and scheduling process and exhaust resources. Sixteen of sixty-two students possibly misplaced from this third or fourth group of students for placement into the first-year class seemed to me sizeable enough to warrant earlier attention by the college.

SPRING 2005, FOR ACADEMIC YEAR 2005–2006

During each phase of this process, I communicated my observations and recommendations to the administration. The current adjustment for 2005–2006 students allows me to intervene as soon as possible before, during, and after placement to adjust possible misplacement by ACCUPLACER. For the fall 2005 class, after I read seventy-eight essays from that group, the director of center and I identified seventeen students to contact about their placement results by ACCUPLACER. I contacted the students, asked about their experiences with writing in high school, described the expectations for each course, and adjusted most of their schedules to either first-year composition or developmental writing. Each possible case of misplacement needs to be discussed with the student, so that changes in the schedule can be made before the next group of summer-placement students register for sections of courses that might soon meet enrollment limits.

At this time, the placement system seems to need more human oversight before advising and registration. Adjustments to schedules after the semester starts, even if these adjustments are for only ten students, require reconsideration of several already carefully designed plans—students with special needs have predetermined special advisors; students in certain intended majors, too, have advisors in those majors. If too much time lapses, or if students are placed into several special advising programs with a designated first-year advisor or placed into some writing or advising courses by intended major, adjustments to placement into writing could disrupt already carefully planned programs; disrupting relationships already established for first-year students seems to create another kind of dilemma for persons and programs. In short, any adjustments to schedules for students who possibly have been misplaced may take a great deal of time and readjustment on the part of all involved.

To address some of these issues, for 2005–2006 the director of the center, the vice president for Academic Affairs, the dean of Arts and Sciences, and I approved a new procedure for an appeals process that can be initiated by a student or the writing coordinator before a student's arrival on campus for the fall semester. Also, if a student submits samples of writing showing why placement may be inaccurate, the writing coordinator can examine the case and make appropriate changes. The writing coordinator, also, can initiate a change based upon examination of the ACCUPLACER writing sample, and/or any submitted evidence of a student's writing competence after a dialogue with the student. While these processes after placement and registration seem complicated and time intensive, for now they integrate the essential aspect of human oversight for part of the placement program (excluding possible misplacements by SAT criteria).

Human intervention is essential in placement processes, as it reflects the intended mission of my college. Instead of the ACCUPLACER system, I recommend a locally designed and implemented electronic-portfolio placement system, one that would value the following human interactions, which are more valid: for placement submissions, human raters who teach in the specific writing program; faculty and coordinator of writing designing local survey questions to assess the student's orientation to a process approach to writing; human raters in the writing program assessing a student's response to a locally designed topic on an issue related to the college's annual values-based theme. This kind of system, aligned with an institutionwide portfolio system for learning, would seem more purposeful and valid, more intentional and instrumental for measuring growth of each learner from placement through select performances in the core program and into the major program.

As the institution grapples with assessment outcomes, faculty members and administrators need to consider greater issues about assessments in relation to the mission of the college. Such an institutionwide system, which could align with the college's mission and values to respect the uniqueness of each student and to promote healthy relationships, would also need to relate to placement processes.

Such systems do exist, empowering human raters and fostering negotiation with the student about placement decisions. Such online portfolio-placement systems provide useful baseline information for measurement of individual growth in writing, orientation to the values of a college and, overall, stimulus for the growth of a student writer as a reflective learner. Small-college programs, such as the one that I coordinate, probably would improve their courses, their core program, and their major programs by examining placement processes and asking, how do all processes align? How do placement processes, course outcomes assessment, core program outcomes assessment, and major program outcomes assessments relate?

CONCLUSIONS

With each administration of the ACCUPLACER system, I wonder about students' first impressions of literate practices at the college and about methods for the advisor to examine complex information about the student for course selection and placement. In a college culture that already has in place an evolving portfolio system for measuring end-of-semester writing competence, I wonder whether students receive some mixed messages about ACCUPLACER placement, with its instantaneous response and assessment, in contrast to the program that they will experience, a program that values conferences, revisions, peer reviews, and other time-intensive interpersonal communication processes. The ACCUPLACER placement process presents a contradiction of sorts. The analysis of an essay by computer-assisted assessment shows that expediency is valued. Compare this to the pedagogy valued in our writing courses: the end-of-semester writing assessments with teams of professional readers, analyzing the quality of essays and sample portfolios for a range of performance from nonpassing quality to excellence. While these end-of-semester processes occur regularly each semester, the initial impression of writing at the college since the inception of placement by ACCUPLACER would suggest something quite different for incoming students and their parents or guardians, who also are present on the days of placement and registration.

If my understanding of the mission of my college is correct—respect for the individual, care and concern for others, to name just two of its core values—then a placement system that values the person's writing for a purpose would seem to require a human reader. Fostering this relationship through dialogue *from the outset* would seem preferable for placement processes. By having ACCUPLACER read and rate the placement essays, the college, perhaps unwittingly, sends a message about the value of what the student may be telling us in writing—not just how he or she writes but also what he or she values and believes.

Rather than the ACCUPLACER system, I would recommend for my college, or any other such small college, an electronic-portfolio placement and assessment system, similar to that at Raymond Walters College at the University of Cincinnati (2002). This kind of locally developed system aligns well with a program that values faculty members' insights about reading students' placement essays and interpreting other indicators for the most appropriate placement into a college's core and developmental writing programs. Much more could be measured about students' understandings of values if one or two carefully developed locally designed placement essays could be instituted. At my college this dream for values-driven placement seems possible, as the college has been piloting electronic portfolios in select major programs, and a system for portfolio assessment of learning is one of the recommendations of the 2004–2005 core program self-study.

While this narrative does not detail for the reader a core writing program with its own carefully developed assessment systems, its own faculty-developed internal documents for feedback and assessment, its own mini–resources for shared units of inquiry in first-year composition that integrate well with the college's overall theme each year, its ongoing faculty development workshops for those who teach writing, its numerous collaborative activities with faculty and staff in the Academic Resource Center, its truly caring staff in the center and the dedicated faculty scholars in the writing program, I hope to have shown the importance of situating the human factor in any placement procedure, but especially in an automated system for placement such as ACCUPLACER. For any placement process to work the writing coordinator needs to communicate, collaborate, mediate, manage information, research, and judge. Most importantly, the writing program coordinator needs to advocate for systems, in this case, a placement system for writing that values time and respects the dignity of all persons involved in the placement process and that aligns with other mission-driven assessments for the writing program in the context of a core program and all other major programs.

ACKNOWLEDGMENTS

I appreciate the feedback of my colleague Dr. Sandra Weiss, Coordinator of Biological Sciences and Clinical Lab Sciences.

12

ALWAYS ALREADY
Automated Essay Scoring and Grammar-Checkers in College Writing Courses

Carl Whithaus

INTRODUCTION

Although Ken S. McAllister and Edward M. White call the development of automated essay scoring "a complex evolution driven by the dialectic among researchers, entrepreneurs, and teachers" (chapter 1 of this volume), within composition studies the established tradition points toward the rejection of machine-scoring software and other forms of computers as readers. This tradition culminates in the Conference on College Composition and Communication's (2005) "Position Statement on Teaching, Learning, and Assessing Writing in Digital Environments," where the penultimate sentence succinctly captures our discipline's response: the committee writes, "We oppose the use of machine-scored writing in the assessment of writing" (789). If, however, we step back from this discourse of rejection and consider the ways in which a variety of software packages are already reading and responding to student writing, we begin to see that outright rejection of software as an assessment and response tool is not a viable, practical stand, because software is already reading, responding, and assessing student writing.

These "on the ground facts" of software's presence in students' writing processes range from the ubiquitous grammar- and spell-checkers in Microsoft Word to the use of Intelligent Essay Assessor to assess student knowledge in general-education courses. Once we acknowledge that software agents are intervening in students' composing processes, and that new more helpful, or more invasive, forms of software will continue to be developed, the questions facing writing program administrators and composition instructors transform from whether or not to use automated essay scoring and other forms of software to what types of software to use and how to incorporate these software features in effective and meaningful pedagogies for composition and writing-in-the-disciplines courses.

As a corrective to categorical rejections of software assessment and response systems, this essay examines the teaching and learning environments at Florida Gulf Coast University (FGCU) and at Old Dominion University (ODU). In the case of FGCU, Intelligence Essay Assessor, the latent semantic analysis based software is used to assess students' short essay question responses (350–500 words). At ODU, Microsoft Word is the default word processor used in open campus labs, the English department computer lab, and on many students' home computers. In both environments, software agents are part of the reading, responding, and evaluation processes for large numbers of undergraduates.

By analyzing writing activities at FGCU and ODU, we come to see that practices of using software as a tool for assessing and responding to student writing are already in place. The use of software agents as tools within students' writing processes, however, does not mean that students are not using these same digital writing environments as media for communicating ideas to their teachers. The Conference on College Composition and Communication's position statement justifies its rejection of machine-scored writing in terms of a dichotomy between human and machine readers, between what I have called software used as a medium for communication and software used as a tool for assessment or correction (Whithaus 2004). Stuart Selber's (2004) work on functional literacy, particularly his examination of computers as literacy tools, argues for a more subtle and nuanced reading of software and the multiliteracies within which students work. Further, the cases of software usage at FGCU and ODU suggest that in practice this either/or formulation does not correspond with the daily realities of students' composing processes.

In practice, software is used as both a medium for communication and as a tool for assessment and response. I am arguing for a conceptual shift within composition studies—if our practices combine software's functions as media and tools, then we need to reformulate our conceptions about machines reading and assessing students' writing. The tradition of rejection, reaching back to Ken Macrorie's (1969) critique of Ellis Page's work (Page and Paulus 1968), needs to be revised in favor of theories and practices of writing assessment that acknowledge the range of software's influence as responsive evaluative agents. Acknowledging this range will make it possible to evaluate the validity as well as the reliability of automated essay-scoring systems, not because the systems are valid in and of themselves, but because—drawing on Lee Cronbach's (1988) notion of validity as argument—the use to which the software agents or other forms of writing assessment are put are appropriate. For instance, the writing component on the new SAT exam is not a valid measure of a high school junior's or senior's overall writing ability, but it is a valid measure of how that student writes on a twenty-five minute timed, impromptu writing exam. Will this exam tell us all we want to know about incoming students' writing abilities? Hardly. But it does give a snapshot of a student's ability for one particular moment and for one particular form of writing. Predications based upon the writing component of the SAT, then, will be most accurate for this form of writing; the scores will have less validity as students move on to other, more complex writing tasks. Similarly, in carefully defined writing activities, software can be effectively used to assess short, close-ended responses from students, to quickly respond to surface features of student writing, and to offer the potential for students to develop metacommentary or reflection on the paragraph level.

SOFTWARE AS ASSESSMENT TOOL: INTELLIGENT ESSAY ASSESSOR AT FLORIDA GULF COAST UNIVERSITY

Looking at the use of Intelligent Essay Assessor at FGCU allows us to understand one context within which software could be used to assess short, close-ended written responses from students. Intelligent Essay Assessor is used to assess students' content knowledge and higher-order critical thinking skills through evaluating student writing in a general-education course, Understanding Visual and Performing Arts. This course is WebCT-based with large enrollments (380 in fall 2002, 560 in spring 2003, 541 in fall 2003, and 810 in spring 2004) (Wohlpart 2004b). In addition to assessing short written responses through Intelligent Essay Assessor, students' content knowledge is tested through multiple-choice questions and longer critical analysis essays read by preceptors, paid graders with bachelor's degrees in English.

To understand the impact of Intelligence Essay Assessor on student writing and learning, we need to consider the software within this context of multiple content assessments. Students are not only conscious of having a machine score their writing, they are also aware that a machine is scoring their multiple-choice answers and that human readers are grading their longer critical analysis essays. Students work within a continuum of multiple-choice tests, short essay question responses and longer critical analysis essays. The first two forms of assessment are evaluated by software and the third by a human reader. Students learn not only through video-streamed lectures and reviewing PowerPoint lecture notes but also by preparing for these three forms of assessment. They are given practice multiple-choice tests and analyze short essay question responses; they also develop Web board discussions about the sample essay questions and student responses to these questions. When it comes time for students to take exams with multiple-choice questions and short essay questions, they have already engaged in test preparation, learning activities for those forms of assessment. They are familiar with the concept of the computer as grader for the multiple-choice parts of their exams, and this concept is now extended to their short essay question responses—that extension is not likely to produce the alienation discussed by Anne Herrington and Charles Moran (2001) or the naïveté described by them in chapter 7 of this volume. In addition, the short essay questions on the course exams are contextualized within the course. The structure of the questions reflects the interweaving of course content and the rhetorical forms of students' written responses.

For instance, when a question on the Visual Arts exam asks students to "identify the element of form in Albert Paley's public sculpture *Cross Currents*," the question is prompting students to focus on the concept of *form* in the visual arts. The second sentence in the question continues the focus on form as a key semantic quality by asking, "How does the form of the work create meaning or experience?" Finally, the third sentence in the question asks for a student interpretation or application of the concept of form in relation to both Paley's sculpture and the student's views: "What do you think this meaning or experience could be?" The short essay question is dictating the form of the student's response: (1) identify; (2) explain form in relationship to meaning or experience; (3) think about the meaning or experience in relationship to your own views. Concepts from the visual arts are invoked in the question, and the student must link these together in writing to demonstrate mastery of the concepts. The format of the writing is formulated in the question. The students must take part in a particular "genre" of writing—the short essay question response—that is not uncommon in high school and college courses. Based on the form of this genre, and its narrowed definition within FGCU's Understanding Visual and Performing Arts, Intelligent Essay Assessor scores the ways in which students link the relevant ideas from the course together.

Jim Wohlpart describes the students' written responses to the short essay questions as ways in which they demonstrate a greater mastery of their knowledge of the course content and apply higher-order critical thinking skills than they do in the multiple-choice questions (2004a). The short essay question responses are also not the end of the student's writing activities in Understanding Visual and Performing Arts; rather, they are part of a learning and assessment continuum that moves from multiple-choice questions to open-ended, individualized critical analysis essays. As Wohlpart readily acknowledges, these longer critical analysis essays could not be effectively scored by Intelligent Essay Assessor. Rather than directing students to apply course knowledge in a short, relatively controlled form, students are allowed to analyze an artwork or performance of their choice. Because of their complexity and their variability, these open-ended critical analysis essays cannot be scored effectively by essay-scoring software. Wohlpart compares these critical analysis essays to the types of assignments he gives in first-year composition courses. The students need to write multiple drafts and explore concepts discussed in the class in intimate detail. The current version of Intelligent Essay Assessor would be no more appropriate for assessing these critical analysis essays than WebCT's multiple-choice scoring mechanism would be for scoring the short essay question responses. According to Lee Cronbach's (1988) concept of validity as argument and Huot's (2002, 53–56) development of that concept in composition, for a writing assessment to be valid, not only does the scoring mechanism need to be valid but the use to which the results of the scoring are put needs to be valid and appropriate as well. Using automated essay scoring to score the critical analysis essays, or the types of individualized, open-ended essays written in Wohlpart's first-year composition courses, would make the assessment system invalid. When I argued at the beginning of this essay that composition researchers and teachers need to step back from a discourse of rejection, it is in order to make these finer and more accurate distinctions among types of software and their uses.

When software is used as a tool for assessment or response purposes, we need to decide whether the use of that tool is valid. We need to ask: how does the software tool function? Is it accurate for its claimed purpose? And, are the results of the assessment put to valid use within the larger course or institutional context? When software is used as a tool for assessment, response, or revision, it is not necessarily opposed to effective composition pedagogies. While students do need to use software as media to communicate with each other and with their instructors to improve their composing skills, the use of software as a medium for communicating does not exclude the use of software tools as prompts for sentence-level or paragraph-level revision or as an assessment device for content knowledge. Understanding the context within which Intelligent Essay Assessor is used at FGCU provides us with a wider scope within which to evaluate software's influence on student writing and our pedagogies.

At FGCU, Intelligent Essay Assessor is used as a tool, not as a medium for communication. That is, the multiple-choice questions graded by WebCT and the short essay question responses graded by Intelligent Essay Assessor are software agents as tools. When the students submit critical analysis essays for the preceptors to grade, then WebCT and the word-processing software are being used as media for communication. These distinctions are important, because in both the multiple-choice and the short essay question responses the knowledge that is being tested is close-ended and containable, but in the communication-based critical analysis essays the subject matter, what piece of visual or performing art is analyzed, as well as the rhetorical techniques used to create an effective analysis vary from student to student, situation to situation. Still the question remains: is Intelligent Essay Assessor's evaluation of the short essay question responses about writing? To say that having students write within a very specific format is a high-end way of assessing content knowledge and critical thinking strategies is not the same thing as saying that these short essay questions teach the students how to become better writers.

SOFTWARE AS RESPONSIVE TOOL: MICROSOFT WORD AT OLD DOMINION UNIVERSITY

By analyzing how Microsoft Word's grammar-checker and readability features are used in writing courses at Old Dominion University, we will see a narrower example of software used as a responsive tool for improving student writing. Unlike the use of Intelligent Essay Assessor as an assessment tool and WebCT and word processing as media for communication at FGCU, the use of Microsoft Word at ODU combines the functions of software as tool for correction and evaluation and software as a medium for communication in a single software package. If it was important for us to see the use of Intelligent Essay Assessor at FGCU as occurring within a continuum of assessment tools, it is also important for us to recognize that there is a range of software tools for assessment, scoring, and response to student writing. Automated essay-scoring software does not stand alone, especially from students' perspectives. These software packages, particularly when used as described by Jill Burstein and Daniel Marcu (2004), in classroom settings do not exist in isolation for student writers from more mundane, common software tools such as Microsoft Word. Understanding the use of Microsoft Word's grammar-checkers and readability features in ODU writing courses helps us get a better picture of what it means to use Intelligent Essay Assessor as an assessment agent at FGCU; the impact of grammar-checkers and readability features on composition pedagogies makes acknowledging the fuller range of software's influence on writing instruction possible.

Writing instruction at ODU involves three writing courses for all undergraduates: first-year composition, a second-semester composition course or a science and technical writing course, and a discipline-specific writing-intensive course at the junior or senior level. In addition, the English department offers courses in advanced composition, technical writing, management writing, and a variety of journalism and creative writing courses. Over two thousand students are enrolled each semester in the first- and second-semester composition requirements. In this panoply of writing courses the default word-processing program is Microsoft Word. Eleven percent of the sections meet at least twice a semester in the English department computer lab for writing workshops, hands-on activities in Blackboard, or Web-based research assignments. While the students use Microsoft Word during the writing workshops, most of the instructors do not explicitly address how to use or respond to Microsoft Word's grammar-checker. It is common for instructors to advise students not to blindly trust the grammar-checker; however, more detailed discussion of Microsoft Word's green squiggly lines are not a required part of the curriculum and often do not occur. To be able to explain when to follow Microsoft Word's advice and when to ignore it requires an understanding of both grammatical concepts and software's (mis)application of these concepts. To further complicate matters, it is not only instructors but also the students who need to understand these issues. Within a labor system where 98 percent of the courses are taught by graduate students, adjunct faculty members, or lecturers, the time to focus on grammar and software's application of grammar does not exist. The general sentiment is that composition instructors are teaching writing, not word-processing skills or software usage.

What is funny is that the interface of the word processor, particularly Microsoft Word, is so prevalent in writing instruction at ODU, yet it is infrequently addressed or discussed as an explicit class lesson. The tool exists, but writing instructors are more interested in the computer as a medium through which their students communicate rather than as a tool for correction. Yet, for students, and even for teachers, Microsoft

Word's green squiggly lines often interrupt or at least influence the writing process. Very few go into Word's Tools > Spelling and Grammar menus and deselect the "Check grammar" box. The software is a low-level reader of form and a response agent, but it is untheorized in composition studies and unaddressed, and perhaps underutilized, in our pedagogies.

While it is possible, and useful, to critique Microsoft Word as "the invisible grammarian" as McGee and Ericsson (2002) have done, another response would be to run into the teeth of the machine. In other words, by working with the features in Microsoft Word such as readability and by explaining to students exactly how the grammar-checker works in terms of their language, we make the students' interaction with the software into teachable moments rather than rote acceptance of the software's authority.

For instance, in a junior-level technical writing course, I had students use Microsoft Word's readability feature as a tool for paragraph-level revision. On Blackboard's discussion board, I asked students to:

1. Select a paragraph from your proposal or from your current draft that you would like to rewrite. Paste that paragraph into the discussion board space. 2. Score that paragraph according to reading ease and grade level using MSWord. Paste that paragraph into the discussion board. 3. Revise that paragraph. Score the revised paragraph according to reading ease and grade level in MSWord. Paste that paragraph into the discussion board. 4. Explain why you think the revised paragraph had "better" scores. (Or if the revised paragraph did not have better scores, explaining why you believe it is more effective despite the readability and grade-level scores.)

In this assignment, the software is a response agent to encourage revision. The assignment also contains a prompt to respond to the software by developing metacommentary about the revised paragraph and the software's reading of that paragraph. A student who was working on a technical report about the future of U.S. space exploration posted the following material:

UNEDITED: The security of our nation domestically, internationally, and economically will be ensured through research and developed skills that may help detect and deflect asteroids that may threaten Earth. Since U.S. military strength and economic security rests on our technology leadership, implementation of the space exploration vision will drive technology related disciplines such as medical research, biotechnology, computing, nanotechnology, composite manufacturing, and many others. The report presents the argument that as international leaders, the U.S. that should forge ahead into space exploration, rather than sitting idly by. This competitiveness will require a skilled workforce, and the space exploration vision will work to create a needed re-focus on math and science education in the United States.

EDITED: Our nation's domestic, international, and economic security will benefit from the research and skills developed through space exploration. For example, we may discover a way to detect and deflect asteroids that threaten Earth. Since U.S. military strength and economic security rests on our technology leadership, implementing the space exploration vision will drive technology related disciplines such as medical research, biotechnology, computing, nanotechnology, and composite manufacturing. The Commission's report poses the argument that as international leaders, the U.S. should forge ahead into space exploration rather than sitting idly by. This competitive approach will necessitate developing a skilled workforce. Thus, the space exploration vision will work to create a needed re-focus on math and science education in the United States.

CONCLUSION: The first paragraph scored a 5.0 for ease of reading and earned a rating of grade level 12. I revised the paragraph by removing some passive sentences and nominalizations. It then scored an 11.5 for ease of reading and remained at the grade level 12 (although I got a 0 percent for passive sentences, down from 25 percent). Since the reading ease scale calculation utilizes average sentence length and average number of syllables per word, a piece with longer sentences and bigger words, such as a technical piece with scientific wording and terminology, will score lower and earn a higher grade level rating. I found that the best way to increase readability was to break long sentences into shorter ones and to make sure there were transitional phrases, such as "however," or "thus," to improve the logical flow of the information.

Her commentary is fascinating because it shows an attention to the stylistic details of sentence length and number of syllables. She articulates an awareness of the software's limitations for scoring "a piece with longer sentences and bigger words, such as a technical piece with scientific wording and terminology" and is still able to use the software to increase the readability of her report.

Although this student was able to implement the changes suggested by Microsoft Word's readability scoring, others were resistant to the software. One student submitted three different paragraphs. Her meta-commentary is worth quoting: "Well, finally! The revisions used shorter words and shorter sentences in order to increase the reading ease score and lower the grade level. I am not sure, however, if I will keep this paragraph in my presentation. The second one does flow better than the first, but the third one seems a little too "dumbed down" to me. Maybe I have been in college too long . . ."

She is ranking samples of her own work, using Microsoft Word's scores as one filter and her own sense of audience as another filter. Another student, whose views I believe would be echoed by many composition instructors and researchers, wrote, "Although I do agree that concise writing is more effective, I think this method of scoring readability is too simplistic." On one level this student is surely correct—if writing teachers were only to take Flesch Reading Ease and Flesch-Kincaid grade-level scores into account when judging student writing, then those writing assessments would be far too simplistic. However, when students are communicating multiple complex ideas and using software as both media and tools, then the use of simplistic readability scores as useful abstractions in order to help students see their writing through a different screen becomes more appropriate. In first-year composition courses, in the writing of the analytic essays at FGCU, and in this technical writing course at ODU, I would suggest that the limited use of software as an assessment and response tool is valid and appropriate.

CONCLUSION

Microsoft Word can work as a tool, as a prompt for revision on the sentence level or the paragraph level. Within a sequence of assessment tools, Intelligent Essay Assessor can function as a device for building higher-level critical thinking skills and testing content knowledge. In both cases, the software is a tool, not a medium. However, the ultimate goal of the writing activities is a communicative agenda that involves using software as media for communication as well. I would respectfully want to argue that the Conference on College Composition and Communication's committee on Teaching, Learning, and Assessing Writing in Digital Environments has made a mistake by continuing composition studies' tradition of rejecting software as a reader, responder, and assessor of student writing. The uses of software as tools within courses at FGCU and ODU suggests that, as contextualized tools, there are uses for Intelligent Essay Assessor and Microsoft Word as readers, responders, and assessors. What composition studies needs is not a blanket rejection of these systems but rather data-driven studies of how these different software agents are already being used in postsecondary writing courses. When software works well for a particular task, writing researchers should build pedagogies that incorporate these features. When the use of software produces decontextualized, invalid writing assessments, writing researchers need to point out the faults of these systems. In the end, a blanket rejection of automated essay scoring and other forms of software as readers does not serve composition teachers or students; a more nuanced, situation by situation consideration of how software is used and its impact on writing pedagogy provides a clearer picture of the challenges facing teachers and students.

13

AUTOMATED ESSAY GRADING IN THE SOCIOLOGY CLASSROOM
Finding Common Ground

Edward Brent and Martha Townsend

OVERVIEW

This chapter describes an effort by one author, a sociologist, to introduce automated essay grading in the classroom, and the concerns raised by the other author, the director of a campuswide writing program, in evaluating the grading scheme for fulfillment of a writing-intensive (WI) requirement. Brent provides an overview of existing automated essay-grading programs, pointing out the ways these programs do not meet his needs for evaluating students' understanding of sociology content. Then he describes the program he developed to meet those needs along with an assessment of the program's use with six hundred students over three semesters. Townsend provides a brief overview of the campus's twenty-year-old WI graduation requirement and illustrates concerns raised by the Campus Writing Board when Brent's course, employing the machine-graded system, was proposed for designation as WI. In this point-counterpoint chapter, the coauthors highlight areas of concordance and disagreement between the individual professor's use of machine-graded writing and the established writing program's expectations.

INTEGRATING AUTOMATED ESSAY GRADING INTO AN INTRODUCTORY SOCIOLOGY COURSE: BRENT'S PERSPECTIVE

I have taught introductory sociology for many years to classes of 150 to 250 students each semester. By necessity, my course has relied almost exclusively on in-class multiple-choice tests for evaluation. Students often express frustration at taking such tests, and I find it very hard to measure higher-level reasoning on these tests. My objective is to incorporate more writing into this large-enrollment course despite limited TA resources.

Using writing for learning and assessment offers a number of advantages over multiple-choice tests (Bennett and Ward 1993). Essays are more "authentic" than multiple-choice tests because they "present test-takers with tasks more similar to those in the actual educational or job settings" (Yang, Buckendahl, and Juszkiewicz 2001). Essays permit students to demonstrate higher-order thinking skills such as analysis and synthesis (Rudner and Gagne 2001), requiring students to construct arguments, recall information, make connections, and support their positions (Shermis and Burstein 2003).

However, grading essays is expensive and time-consuming (Rudner and Gagne 2001). Feedback is often delayed, limited in scope, and of poor quality (Yang, Buckendahl, and Juszkiewicz 2001). Adding significant writing assignments to this large-enrollment introductory course required a new, more cost-effective strategy, so investigating automated essay grading programs seemed worthwhile.

Automated Essay-Grading Programs

A number of commercially available essay-grading programs are used in some very high-profile applications. Several large-scale assessment programs now include one or more measures based on writing, including "the Graduate Management Admissions Test (GMAT), the Test of English as a Foreign Language (TOEFL), the Graduate Record Examination (GRE), Professional Assessments for Beginning Teachers (Praxis), the College Board's Scholastic Assessment Test II Writing Test and Advanced Placement (AP) exam, and the College-Level Examination Program (CLEP) English and writing tests" (Burstein 2003, 113). Many of these tests also have students submit essays by computer, including the GMAT, TOEFL, GRE, and Praxis, making the use of automatic-scoring programs feasible for those tests. Commercially available essay-grading programs used in these tests include the Intelligent Essay Assessor, the erater, developed by Burstein and her colleagues at the Educational Testing Service, and the IntelliMetric program .

Some of these programs employ a statistical approach for developing and assessing the automated-grading model. In each case human graders must first grade many (usually several hundred) essays. Those overall grades are then used as the "gold standard" to fit or "train" statistical models predicting scores assigned by human graders from features of essays measured by the programs (Yang, Buckendahl, and Juszkiewicz 2001). Once trained, the resulting model can then be used to assign grades to papers in the test set without using human graders.

Other programs for automated essay grading take a rule-based or knowledge-based approach; in these, expert knowledge provides the standard for assessing student performance. One or more experts creates a knowledge base for the content area along with a grading rubric indicating the kinds of knowledge and reasoning students should display. Student essays are examined for evidence of such knowledge, with better scores being given to students whose writing most closely expresses the expert knowledge. A rule-based or knowledge-based program can be tested on a much smaller number of cases, thereby reducing development costs. This approach obviously requires an expert to explicitly determine the knowledge-based criteria

Concerns and Standards for Essay-Grading Programs

Automated essay-grading programs appear to offer a number of advantages over manual grading of essays. They are much faster than human readers, often being able to score essays in only a second or two. Hundreds or even thousands of essays can be graded very quickly and efficiently, with less cost than manual grading, and the scores are immediately provided to students (Rudner and Gagne 2001; Yang, Buckendahl, and Juszkiewicz 2001). However, a number of criteria must be considered in deciding whether and which automated-grading program to use, including the nature of the writing task, cost-effectiveness, an appropriate standard for assessing writing, and the quality of feedback provided to students.

The Writing Task

Statistical programs work for standardized writing assessment, in which the "mechanics" of writing—spelling, punctuation, subject-verb agreement, noun-pronoun agreement, and the like—are being scored, as opposed to substantive, discipline-based knowledge. Essays with very general topics often have few or no "content" constraints, in order to permit students from a wide range of backgrounds to answer the given prompt. They typically address broad questions having no right or wrong answer while giving writers an opportunity to construct an argument, organize their thoughts, and show that they can reason about the problem. In this kind of assessment, mechanics along with some organizational and reasoning abilities are more important than discipline-based content. For such tasks, statistical programs that assign grades based on the grades assigned to similar papers by human graders may be appropriate.

In contrast, in most writing tasks for discipline-based courses dealing with substantive knowledge in the field—whether they be term papers, shorter formal or informal assignments, or answers to tests—there is greater emphasis on content. Mechanical skills such as spelling and punctuation are secondary to being able to construct an argument, reason in accepted ways, and understand specific content. Writing tasks for discipline-based courses are usually designed to assess students' understanding and knowledge of the substantive domain of the course, along with their ability to perform the kinds of higher-order reasoning that are important for that discipline. For example, in sociology we want students to be able to develop and understand a causal argument, to recognize specific theories and the concepts and proponents associated with them, to identify examples of a concept, to interpret specific events from different theoretical perspectives, and to understand and critique the methods used in studies. The ability of students to construct arguments using these forms of reasoning and specific substantive knowledge is best measured with rule-based programs.

Cost-Effectiveness

We would expect automated essay-grading programs that can grade literally hundreds or thousands of papers an hour without human intervention to cost much less than grading those same essays with human graders. However, the cost and time required to develop machine-scoring systems can be prohibitive (Yang, Buckendahl, and Juszkiewicz 2001). In an actual trial of machine grading, Palmer, Williams, and Dreher (2002) found the cost of machine grading to greatly exceed the cost of grading by human graders for a few hundred essays due to high up-front development costs. Automated grading is most cost-effective for large numbers of essays where minimal costs are required for training the program and the users pay a one-time fee for use of the program. Commercially available automated-grading programs are usually not cost-effective for small classes and nonstandardized teaching and assessment.

The economics of statistical approaches and rule-based approaches are somewhat different. The statistically based programs generally require that a few hundred student essays be graded by competent human graders, then those data are used to estimate parameters of the regression equations for the model. In contrast, knowledge-based approaches require that an expert in the discipline specify the correct knowledge. In this case only a few essays need to be graded to test the program's ability to detect information in student essays correctly. Hence, rule-based programs are more likely to be cost-effective even for moderately large classes.

An Appropriate Standard for Assessing Performance

Statistical programs for automated essay grading use the grades assigned to similar papers by human graders as their standard for judging essays. However, "the correlation of human ratings on (essays) is typically only .70 .75" (Rudner and Gagné 2001), and exact agreement among human judges is often in the 50 percent to 60 percent range. "Thus, correlating with human raters as well as human raters correlate with each other is not a very high, nor very meaningful, standard" (2). A more appropriate standard for judging writing is whether it displays important features we expect in good writing rather than whether it displays indirect measures that correlate with human readers' scores (Page 1966; Page and Petersen 1995) or whether it matches documents having similar scores (Landauer et al.1997). The important issue is not consistency with human graders but the validity of the scores. Hence, rule-based essay-grading programs provide a better standard for judging student work (Klein et al. 2001).

Quality of Feedback

Essay-grading programs based on statistical modeling have often been criticized for being unable to provide good feedback (Kukich 2000), giving students little or no advice on how to improve their scores. Those programs sometimes produce only a single summary grade, or at most only a few summary measures. Poor feedback may be a fundamental weakness of statistical approaches because they are based on complex patterns of statistical relationships that may be hard to interpret and indeed may have little meaning to either readers or writers. Also, most currently available programs for automated essay scoring are proprietary commercial systems, and their algorithms are treated as trade secrets, described only in generalities. We do not know, for example, the specific variables used in any model nor their weights in predicting the overall score (Rudner and Gagné 2001; Shermis and Burstein 2003).

In contrast, in rule-based programs the criteria are determined based on experts' knowledge; criteria are chosen because they reflect meaningful knowledge the writer should be able to display. In many cases, rule-based programs have an explicit rubric indicating what features should be present and how many points are assigned for each. For this reason, rule-based programs like the Qualrus-based SAGrader program are able to provide very explicit and detailed feedback to students and instructors that clearly states what they did right (or wrong) and how students can improve their grades.

For all these reasons, I chose to use a rule-based program for auto-mated essay grading rather than a statistical one. For this purpose, my colleagues and I developed our own essay-grading program, SAGrader. This program builds upon a general-purpose qualitative analysis pro-gram, Qualrus, which we also developed and which is widely used in both industry and academia for analyzing unstructured data. Both of these programs are available commercially from Idea Works, Inc.

A Substantive-Based Approach to Automated Essay Grading

My objective is to assess students' discipline-based substantive knowl-edge and reasoning by having them write several brief focused papers addressing specific substantive objectives. This approach emphasizes substantive content over writing skills and focuses on students' knowl-edge of sociological concepts, theories, and methods; the approach also emphasizes students' ability to use this knowledge to reason socio-logically about the world around them. The Qualrus-based SAGrader program developed for this course expresses substantive knowledge as a semantic network linking key concepts, theories, authors, studies, and findings from sociology. The structure of that knowledge base gives the program relevant information that can be used to help identify student misunderstandings and generate individualized student feedback. It then uses rudimentary natural-language processing to recognize key terms and phrases in text that reflect relevant elements such as concepts or theories based on those available in the semantic network for each chapter. It uses the grading rubric (and the relatively structured assign-ment) to create a template describing the rhetorical objectives for the writing assignment. By comparing each student's written input with the set of requirements for the assignment, the program is able to grade essays. For example, in the program's substantive knowledge base, the labeling theory of deviance has concepts and theorists related to it as shown in figure 1 (next page).

One writing assignment asks students to briefly describe one theory of deviance. If they chose this theory, the program would look for these concepts and theorists, giving students points when they correctly iden-tify concepts and theorists associated with this theory, subtracting points when they leave out important items or include incorrect concepts or theorists from other theories. The grading rubric specifies how many points are assigned for each element.

For the writing-intensive course (WI) there is one written paper (fif-teen pages long) plus four two-page writing exercises requiring students

FIGURE 1

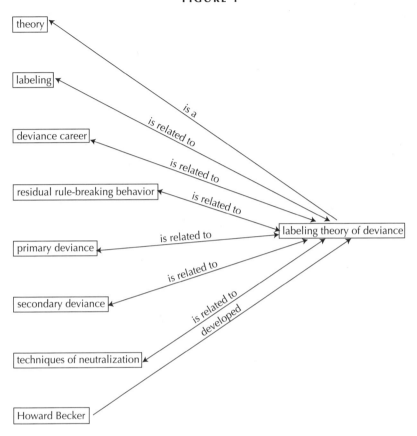

to address specific issues. The two-page exercises employ common forms of sociological reasoning to address a range of specific substantive concepts and perspectives. For example, the second assignment asks students to write about crime and theories of deviance (see figure 2).

The four writing exercises and term paper demand increasingly higher levels of reasoning as the student progresses, with later exercises requiring students to interpret a description of a community sociologically and to use sociological concepts and perspectives to describe and understand their own families. In the future I hope to provide additional writing exercises and permit students to select which ones they will do.

To submit their work, students enter WebCT and use a hyperlink on the syllabus to open the submission form in their Internet browser. There they enter their names and student numbers, then paste their

FIGURE 2.

Writing Exercise 2: Crime and Theories of Deviance

20 points, 2 drafts, 2 pages each time, first draft reviewed by computer (optionally by TAs as well), second draft reviewed by TAs. The final score is the weighted average of first (1/3) and second drafts (2/3).

Assignment: Select a type of crime discussed in the chapter on deviance and social control. Briefly describe this type of crime, give examples of it, and indicate any other types of crime it might be closely related to. Then take one of the theories of deviance discussed in this same chapter, briefly summarize the theory, and discuss how well that theory can account for the type of crime you have chosen. Your answer should identify the theory, one or more proponents of the theory, and four or more key concepts from that theory.

Learning Objectives: To become familiar with the components of theories, concepts, proponents, and how those theories can be used to explain specific phenomena.

Substantive Topics: Theories of deviance, types of crime.

papers into a text box. Once this is done, they press a "submit" button at the bottom of the page and the paper is sent to the Qualrus server, where it is graded and detailed feedback is displayed on a second Web page. The time between submitting the paper and receiving detailed feedback is usually two seconds or less, depending on network transfer speeds. A sample of student writing and the feedback the program provides on the deviance assignment is shown in figure 3 (next page).

The program feedback is detailed and specific, showing students not only their scores for specific components but also specific ways they can improve their score.

Strengths and Weaknesses of This Approach

This essay-grading program offers the promise of speeding up the grading process, reducing costs, and giving students the opportunity to write in a large lecture class. However, the program has limits and, to be successful, must be carefully integrated into the course to overcome those limits.

The approach has the advantage of providing very explicit criteria for judging the essay that are consistent with the learning objectives of the course. Consequently, the program can provide students with a detailed breakdown of credit received and missed based on their answers along with detailed feedback of how their answers do and do not meet the assignment objectives. Since the feedback is nearly instantaneous, it can provide a much better learning environment for students than they experience when human graders take days or weeks to grade their papers.

Each assignment combines specific substantive content represented in a semantic network (such as descriptions of a theory or a study)

FIGURE 3

SAMPLE ANSWER (Abbreviated)
Qualrus Grading Server
The Nature of Crime
by: Samuel Adams
    Crime affects everyone in the United States. There are many types of crime. I will focus on white-collar crimes such as crimes committed by someone who knowingly pollutes a stream from runoff from their hog farm. White collar crime can be understand in terms of labeling theory. Labeling Theory labels deviants. The labeling has two different types. One is primary deviance and the second is secondary deviance. Primary deviance is goes undetected by authorities and secondary deviance is known by the authorities and they accept that title. Once people get labeled as a deviance they have a hard time getting rid of the title.

SAMPLE FEEDBACK (Abbreviated)
Qualrus Grading Server
Essay Grader
Copyright © 2002, Idea Works, Inc.
Student Feedback for Samuel Adams

Number of Concepts from the Chapter: +2 out of 7 points
You appear to have included only 5 concepts from this chapter, instead of the 10 required. The concepts you included that are from this chapter are crime, labeling, primary deviance, secondary deviance, and time . . .

Overall Treatment of Theory: +3 out of 4 points
You were asked to discuss one theory, including at least one proponent of the theory and four or more concepts associated with the theory. This paper considers labeling theory of deviance. The paper's treatment of labeling theory of deviance is inadequate. This paper does not discuss Howard Becker, Thomas Scheff, Thomas Szasz, and William Chambliss, who are related to this theory. This paper discusses labeling, primary deviance, and secondary deviance, which are related to this theory. This paper does not discuss . . .

Type of Crime: +1 out of 1 point
You were asked to identify one type of crime and interpret it with a single theory. This paper appears to focus on toxic pollution which is mentioned 1 times . . .

Overall Score Summary:
20 points possible
+ 2 for concepts related to the theory
+ 2 for identifying the theory
+ 2 for summarizing the theory in a paragraph
+ 3 for overall treatment of the theory
+ 1 for identifying the type of crime
+ 3 for relating the type of crime to this theory
Your score is 13.

with a program module that identifies specific kinds of reasoning and relationships among those concepts and applies the grading rubric. Each program module can be applied to a wide range of substantive topics represented by different semantic networks. For example, the modules designed to assess the deviance exercise could be used for a similar exercise regarding the family or political life. Thus, this basic essay-grading program can be extended to generate literally hundreds or thousands of exercises combining different substantive content with different learning objectives. This should dramatically reduce further development costs for additional essay-grading modules both within sociology and in other disciplines.

Several logistical problems must be addressed for automated essay grading to be practical for a course. Students must have access to computers in order to produce papers in machine-readable form (Yang, Buckendahl, and Juszkiewicz 2001; Palmer, Williams, and Dreher 2002). Those papers must be formatted to meet certain standards. For example, hard returns at the end of each line rather than at the end of each paragraph may make it difficult for programs to recognize when paragraphs begin and end. Some system for file management is required to handle the many different student papers. A grade-recording system is needed to track student performance and report scores both to the students and to others. The University of Missouri, where this program is in use, has many computer labs for students and most students also have their own computers, so access is not a problem. The SA-Grader stores every student draft in a database along with the comments generated by the program and a summary file of scores. Instructors can review each draft and see how students have changed their papers in response to feedback. A reminder to students not to put hard returns in their texts has been sufficient to avoid formatting problems.

Potential for Deception and Cheating

A continuing concern about machine-scored essays is whether sophisticated writers can take advantage of the program's features to deceive the program into giving them a better grade than they deserve (Baron 1998; Kukich 2000; Powers et al. 2001; Rudner and Gagné 2001; Yang, Buckendahl, and Juszkiewicz 2001; Palmer, Williams, and Dreher 2002). Because the Project Essay Grade (PEG) program (Page 1966) emphasizes surface features and syntax while largely ignoring content, "a well-written essay about baking a cake could receive a high score if PEG were used to grade essays about causes of the American Civil War" (Rudner and Gagné 2001, 2). On the other hand, the Intelligent Essay Assessor (IEA) emphasizes content and largely ignores syntax. So, "conceivably, IEA could be tricked into giving a high score to an essay that was a string of relevant words with no sentence structure whatsoever" (2). (See McGee, chapter 5 in this volume, for an example of tricking the IEA scoring machine.) For this reason and others, many current applications of essay-grading programs for high-stakes assessments such as the GMAT have every essay read by at least one human reader in addition to an assessment by a grading program (Kukich 2000).

In its current form, the Qualrus-based SAGrader program cannot discriminate between papers that are well written and those that string together key concepts. However, it does look for structures like paragraphs containing summaries, sentences linking concepts to theories, and so on. Future versions will certainly attempt to expand these capabilities to assess other aspects of writing style and rhetorical strategy. Until the program can do all these things, though, every grade assigned in the WI course by the automated essay grader will be reviewed by a human grader. In the current course, students were informed that the instructor would read every paper in addition to the machine scoring and their score from the computer was only an initial estimate of their grade. This seemed to be sufficient to encourage them to write sensible papers rather than simply string together words.

Automated Screening for Plagiarism

The program includes a built-in test for plagiarism. Each paper submitted to the automated essay grader in the WI course is compared with the database of all papers submitted for the same assignment. Papers displaying suspiciously high similarities are flagged for review by the instructor or TAs to assure that students are not plagiarizing the work of others. Of course, the system does not address all forms of plagiarism, such as copying materials from the Internet. This feature is new and has not been tested in application yet. However, we've told students the program can do this; we'd much rather prevent plagiarism than discover it.

Limitations of Scope and Depth

Perhaps the greatest concern we have about essay-grading programs is what they do *not* address. This program is able to assess important elements of student essays such as their understanding of the relationships among key concepts, their ability to use sociological concepts and perspectives to interpret their own experiences and those of others, and their ability to understand and critique empirical studies. But there are many aspects of a written paper that are not yet addressed by SAGrader or other programs. It seems likely these programs will continue to become more sophisticated and to broaden the scope of issues they examine. So far, though, SAGrader has proved to be very flexible, and we have been able to create writing exercises of considerable diversity. But there are likely to remain, at least for the foreseeable future, important aspects of student writing that only human graders can judge.

Pilot Testing: Performance and Student Assessments

We piloted the program and the essay-grading procedures for two semesters using the deviance exercise as an extra-credit project in my section of Introductory Sociology. In a third semester we incorporated the deviance exercise, the "what is sociology" exercise, and the "evolution of community" exercise into the course as part of the required assignments. These three semesters have provided an excellent opportunity to test most of these exercises and assignments (or variations of them) and further improve them. They also permitted us to test the logistics of the process to make sure it worked smoothly.

Students were able to conveniently and easily submit their papers over the Web and receive immediate and detailed feedback. Students were asked to e-mail me if they felt they were graded unfairly; fewer than 5 percent did so. Roughly half of those were minor problems such as a phrase that was not properly recognized. Those problems were easily corrected and such problems had essentially disappeared by the third semester of pilot testing. The other half of students' complaints did not concern problems with the program. For example, one student complained that she had used other terms to indicate some of the concepts instead of the precise terms and hence she felt the program was at fault. I explained to her that part of the learning objectives of the course was to learn the appropriate technical terms.

Appended to the feedback on students' papers is a brief questionnaire in which students are asked how fairly they thought the program graded various components of the assignment and what they did and did not like about this project. In pilot tests of the deviance writing exercise, for example, students liked the essay grading, even though this was our first trial of the program and there were some imperfections in its grading. Students appreciated the immediate feedback (92 percent liked it, with 60 percent liking it a lot), the opportunity to revise their paper (92 percent liked it, with 66 percent liking it a lot), and the detailed comments (88 percent liked this aspect, with 43 percent liking it a lot). Most (65 percent) thought the initial grading was fair; 35 percent disliked the initial grading. They preferred this form of evaluation over multiple-choice tests by almost 2:1, with 47 percent preferring automatically graded essays, 26 percent preferring multiple-choice tests, and 26 percent undecided.

INTEGRATING AUTOMATED ESSAY GRADING INTO A WRITING-INTENSIVE SOCIOLOGY COURSE: TOWNSEND'S PERSPECTIVE

As director of the University of Missouri's Campus Writing Program, one of my responsibilities is to facilitate communication between the Campus Writing Board, which certifies writing-intensive (WI) designations, and discipline-based faculty, whose courses are needed from across the curriculum to satisfy the university's two-course WI graduation requirement. My writing program colleagues and I are charged with helping faculty develop academically rigorous WI courses that meet the board's criteria. In this particular case, Brent volunteered the course, but the board, faced with certifying its first machine-graded WI course, balked. Among the concerns raised were whether the machine scoring would be accurate, fair, able to provide high-quality feedback that leads to substantive revision and, not least, what "messages" would be sent to students about academic writing. In this section, I describe the process of finding common ground between the instructor and the board, a process that involved articulating skepticism diplomatically, broadening understanding on both "sides," learning new technologies, and fostering experimentation.

Writing program staff members don't recall exactly when we became aware of Professor Ed Brent's work with machine-assisted grading of writing. But the grapevine on our campus—where writing is reasonably well attended to for a large research university, in both WI and non-WI courses—had brought us news that he was up to something out of the ordinary. None of us had met him, though, on any of the committees that typically draw faculty who are interested in pedagogy and/or writing. He hadn't taught any WI courses. And although he had attended one of the faculty writing workshops we offer twice a year, it was way back in January 1987. So when he called us to inquire about the process for having his large introductory class designated as WI, we were mildly surprised and, I must admit, skeptical and even a little put off. How was it, we wondered, that a faculty member who, to our knowledge, hadn't shown recent interest in student writing could want WI status for his course—and not just any course, but one that typically enrolls 250 students? Jo Ann Vogt, our liaison to MU's classes in the social sciences and to whom I passed along this information, reacted with incredulity. "Let me get this straight. A professor wants to offer a WI class, but doesn't want to engage with the students' writing himself? Wants a machine to do the work for him? Isn't there something odd about this?"

Ed was prepared for our skepticism, though. He described his several-years'-old experiment with machine-scored writing and said he believed his project was far enough along to try out in the WI setting. No doubt discerning hesitation in my voice when I explained the WI proposal process, he offered to come to my office to demonstrate his program. I accepted, even as I wondered what the writing program was getting into. The program has a proud history of opposing standardized writing assessment. In the early 1990s, I had chaired our campus's Assessment Task Force whose main focus, it seemed, was educating faculty and administration about the drawbacks of standardized assessment of many kinds. We actively resisted a statewide impetus to assess general education (including writing) with an "off the shelf" instrument. I still see the task force's most significant achievement as having persuaded our chancellor to seek the Board of Curators' rescission of their mandate that MU students take an expensive and ineffective standardized test of general education. The curators did indeed rescind the mandate, and MU has engaged in a more responsible form of general-education assessment ever since. Additionally, for the twenty years that our WI requirement has been in place, we've successfully avoided one-size-fits-all tests of writing. So, to find myself discussing a possible WI course that would feature machine-scored writing was unexpected, to say the least.

February 18, 2004

Laptop in hand, Ed arrives at my office at the appointed hour. Our opening hellos are friendly and comfortable since, despite our not having worked together at MU, we know one another through our significant others, who both work at the local high school. We sit down, he more confident than I (in my perception) because he knows what he's going to demonstrate and I'm still skeptical, though by this time I'm also more curious than before. In lay language, Ed gives me a quick background on how the system works; still curious, I begin to wonder whether I'll follow what seems to me a technical explanation beyond my ken. "Statistical versus rule-based approaches," "parameters of regression equations," "substantive knowledge expressed through a semantic network linking key concepts," "rudimentary natural-language processing." I recognize the words, but can't think fast enough to comprehend them in the new and unfamiliar context. I flash back to David Bartholomae's concept of students inventing the university (1985) and wonder if I can invent enough leaderly acumen to maintain credibility with Ed, a senior colleague who's been a full professor for longer than I've had my Ph.D. Realizing that a concrete example is called for, Ed opens the program on his computer and shows me a sample writing assignment, a two-page sample student response to it, and then a sample of the feedback his Qualrus system provides to the student. I follow along, though still unsure about formulating intelligent questions. He continues with an explanation of the array of responses the system can provide, based on the range of text students might enter.

Finally, something clicks and I comment, "But this assignment and the student's short response involve mainly straightforward reading and recall cognition. This isn't the in-depth critical-thinking writing that WI courses call for."

And this is when our breakthrough, of sorts, occurs. "Well, no," Ed replies. "These are exercises students do to help them acquire familiarity with the founders of sociology, the historical contexts within which they worked, their key concepts, the theories that dominate the field, and so on." Tightly structured questions that require focused responses, he points out, allow students to "rehearse" what they're learning. And if their responses don't conform to the narrow prompt, the computer tells them what's missing, and they can add to their responses to improve their scores, scores that comprise only a minor portion of their overall grade. "I'm not looking for deeply analytic thought, nor do I care about grammar and spelling with these exercises. With writing, students can assimilate ideas that simply reading or even reading with multiple-choice quizzes can't accomplish. But with 250 students each semester, machine feedback is the only way I can do it."

"Writing-to-learn," I say. "You're machine scoring revised microthemes to promote learning." Now it's Ed's turn to process my discipline's discourse. I describe the writing-across-the-curriculum pedagogies he has unknowingly adopted: short writing assignments focused on specific problems, attention to concepts over mechanics at the early stages of the process, rewriting to clarify one's ideas (e.g., Bean 1996). I am tempted to cite some of the seminal literature (Britton et al. 1975; Emig 1977) and a few of the movement's founder-practitioners (Fassler [Walvoord] 1978; Bazerman 1981; Maimon 1981; Fulwiler 1984), but I refrain so as not to appear overly eager. As we engage in further exploration of one another's work, I learn that he uses four of these short exercises to help prepare students to write a longer paper requiring synthesis and application of sociological content, and that in addition to the machine scoring, both short and long papers are read, discussed, and graded by Ed and two graduate teaching assistants in twenty-five-student once-a-week discussion sections that accompany the twice-a-week lectures.

Before long, I realize that Ed isn't an educational charlatan using machines to do the work that he doesn't want to, as we imagined might be the case. He's a serious educational researcher whose two-decade research agenda has focused first on social interaction and later on developing computing technologies to practice research and train others to reason sociologically. He's actively working toward a future in which the two will converge, and he's anticipating the implications for both research and teaching. More relevant to the writing program's purposes, he's closer than we imagined to offering the kinds of writing and learning experiences that WI courses encourage. I ask if he'd be willing to repeat the demonstration for the writing board at its next meeting.

March 18, 2004

The Campus Writing Board, having a year earlier tabled a previous WI proposal from Ed based largely on skepticism about the machine-grading component, convenes to see his presentation. In between this meeting and his earlier demonstration for me, Ed and I have had our proposal accepted for this very chapter in Ericsson and Haswell's book; knowing this, board members listen with keen awareness of the stakes involved. He acknowledges the hesitancy they bring and the controversy that machine scoring engenders, but points out that with only two TAs for a class of 250 students, it isn't possible to assign and respond to writing in a timely enough way for students to benefit, nor can he assure that TA responses are consistent. He explains that he has developed this system because he wasn't satisfied with students' learning when he used objective tests and that machine scoring is one attempt to resolve this dilemma.

Board members observe how students enter short papers via WebCT, how the scripts Ed has written for that assignment review the text to identify required concepts, and how quickly students receive detailed feedback—usually in one or two seconds. He explains that students are invited to consult with him or their TA whether or not they have questions about the machine score (which is always tentative and subject to TA review for accuracy). After revision, students can resubmit the paper for additional machine scoring before it goes to the TA for a final score. The student's grade is the weighted average of the machine-scored draft (1/3) and the subsequent TA-scored draft (2/3). Together, the four papers account for 30 percent of the course grade. One longer paper accounts for 45 percent. Writing, in other words, accounts for 75 percent of the total course grade. Participation in the discussion sections is 25 percent. There are no exams and no quizzes.

Questions ensue. How do the "scripts" work? How structured must the assignments be? Can assignments involve problem solving? Can students subvert the system with content-free responses? Given the tight structure of the assignments, does the program check for plagiarism? What about false positives for plagiarism? What do students think of machine scoring? How long does it take to set up a new assignment and the scripts that respond to it? Why did you rule out the existing software and design your own? Can you envision a program that discerns whether students understand hierarchies of relationships among related ideas? Could you use your system in upper-division courses as well as the introductory course?

Ed thoughtfully answers each question in turn, acknowledging the limits of the technology and its use in the classroom. Scripts contain key words, qualities associated with them, and certain patterns of argument; the computer looks for these words and patterns in the same sentence. Eventually, Ed hopes to develop scripts with the ability to identify causal and functional explanations. Assignments must be highly structured to be machine graded. Not all writing assignments should be structured this way, he says, but certainly some can be. These work to tell him whether students are learning something about sociology. Eventually, Ed hopes to develop scripts that provide feedback on transitions, paragraph length, and so on. Yes, problem-based assignments are possible. Ed tries to start with basic sociological principles and move gradually toward more intellectually challenging topics like gay marriage, for example, which have no "right answer." Yes, students could fool the system with content-free prose, but they know that Ed and the TAs skim the papers in any case; so far, no students have tried it. Yes, the program does check for suspicious similarity among papers. Given the tight structure of the assignments, there is some uniformity to them; but students are "amazingly creative" in applying different theories and organizing content differently. The questions have enough room for students to use material from a given chapter in a variety of ways. Students' evaluations show that they don't trust machine scoring as much as they trust Ed and the TAs. There's a tension, he says, between students thinking, "I got a low score, so the program is worthless" versus "I got a low score, so I better make some changes." He doesn't know how that will work out, but says it could be a problem.

Board members also want to know long it takes to set up new scripts. Ed says that now that the system is worked out, he can add new code and comments quickly. The scripts are fairly general so most of the effort goes in to changing the content, not the form, of the script. Ed ruled out existing software because most employ statistical approaches to automate the grading model; they work well for standardized writing assessment in which "mechanics" are scored, but they don't work well for his purpose, which is scoring substantive, discipline-based knowledge. Eventually—if there are certain phrases that would indicate hierarchy of ideas—Ed could code for them, but there will never be a program that looks for everything. However, many concepts in sociology are standard enough that the system works fairly well now. It wouldn't be adequate for the humanities; it might work in the physical sciences. Finally, Ed says, he couldn't claim that the program would work well in upper-division courses. He'd have to consider the course objectives and, while the present version might hold some promise at that level, it's still evolving. Over time, with a given course, it can become more useful, but no machine-scoring system will ever do everything.

Board members also want to know how the scripts are developed; who does the work? In his course, Ed developed them himself. Other content-area instructors using SAGrader could develop their own or use concept maps developed by other expert authors. He is working with publishers to make versions available in other disciplines. Board members wonder how much time is saved if all the essays are also read by human graders. Since WI courses require students to submit multiple drafts, Ed points out that he will use the program to grade first drafts of the writing exercises, and he and the TAs will grade the final drafts. The program should reduce their grading time by about half. More important, because the program gives students immediate feedback and permits them to revise and resubmit papers several times, students can submit as many as five or six versions, something they could not do with human feedback. Finally, a board member from education asks how this kind of machine scoring might translate to K–12 settings. Ed explains that since the program scores essays based on substantive content as expressed in the semantic diagrams, as long as diagrams express knowledge taught in K–12 settings, the program should work. In some cases, slightly more simplified versions of the semantic diagrams could express content appropriate for a wide range of educational levels. In other cases the semantic diagrams need not change at all; a simpler statement of the assignment with expectations appropriate for each grade level could make the program appropriate for K–12 classes.

By the end of the demonstration, Campus Writing Board members and program staff are convinced that the manner in which Ed uses machine scoring, combined with the overall design of Sociology 1000, not only does not violate the WI guidelines established in 1985, but in fact it addresses them in new and innovative ways. They vote unanimously to designate the course WI for 2004–5 and ask that Ed submit an assessment at the end of the year. Shortly after the presentation, Ed e-mails to thank us to arranging it. "I appreciate the questions and comments I got from the board members. They raised legitimate concerns, and I hope they can see that I share them. I believe the only way this program can be effective is as part of a complete course structure that provides the kinds of checks and balances needed to assure quality."

December 10, 2004

At the end of fall semester, with the first machine-graded version of a University of Missouri WI course completed, Ed reports that it "went well—but not perfectly." Some students continue to focus on format—single or double space? font and margin size?—not yet understanding that the program doesn't even look at these; sociological concepts are the primary learning goal. Some students are having difficulty submitting papers to the Qualrus server. Others are irritated by the machine scoring's imperfections, for example, not recognizing an unusual concept and awarding fewer points than deserved or not recognizing concepts that are used incorrectly and awarding more points than deserved. "Oddly enough," Ed comments on the class listserv, "few students complain about the latter."

What turns out to be the most troublesome aspect for Ed and his TAs is machine grading drafts of the longer, more complex paper. It comprises three parts: (1) identifying an important technological problem that influences work in America; (2) proposing a solution for it; and (3) designing a research study to assess the impact of the solution. Because Qualrus looks only at the whole rather than at individual parts, machine feedback is compromised. Ed notes, "We weren't happy with the program's performance on test drafts, so we graded the first draft of the term paper by hand. We will continue revising and improving the program so that it can be used more effectively for the first draft next semester."

May 26, 2005

Things go more smoothly the second time around. Ed and the TAs modify some of the writing assignments to incorporate more content from the textbook they are using, and the Internet connection to the server is more reliable, producing less stress for students who submit on the last day. A few students, however, do not understand that the final essays are graded by course staff and are more intent on trying to fool the program than improve their papers. Ed will reduce this tendency next time by having final drafts submitted through the server just as the first draft was, so he and the TAs can call up the paper, view the program's grade and comments, and make necessary changes in the final grade. In addition to soliciting students' reactions about the grading system's fairness, Ed is adding a check item for students to indicate if they want to appeal the program's score and a text field where they can specify what they believe the program did wrong. This will provide an ongoing mechanism for quality improvement and help isolate remaining weaknesses in the program. Ed reports that, on comparing many of the first and last drafts submitted to the program, "it's encouraging to see that they often improve substantially." Students continue to like the immediate and detailed feedback, he says, as well as the opportunity to revise their papers. At this point in the experiment, Ed and his TAs believe the system offers a sensible way to offer students writing opportunities that replace multiple-choice tests in large-enrollment classes.

As we submit our chapter, the Campus Writing Board still awaits the results of this first year's trial with machine-scored writing at our university. A specially convened summer board meeting will determine whether machine-scored WI versions of Sociology 1000 will be offered in 2005–6. At this same time, however, other questions also loom for the field of composition studies. We see that recent policy statements that attempt to shape good practice in writing assessment and machine scoring may not have fully anticipated the pedagogical applications of technology. Ed's work problematizes these new policies. For example, the section on electronic rating of placement tests that is part of the Conference on College Composition and Communication's "Position Statement on Teaching, Learning, and Assessing Writing in Digital Environments" (2005) states unequivocally that "all writing should have human readers, regardless of the purpose of the writing" (789). This section also claims that (1) "writing to a machine . . . sends a message [that] writing . . . is not valued as human communication"; (2) "we can not know the criteria by which the computer scores the writing"; and (3) "if college writing becomes *to any degree* [emphasis added] machine-scored, high schools will begin to prepare their students to write for machines." The overall statement ends by noting that machine scoring is being considered for use in writing centers and for exit tests, and its unambiguous conclusion is, "We oppose the use of machine-scored writing in the assessment of writing."

The CCCC "Position Statement on Teaching, Learning, and Assessing Writing in Digital Environments" seems not to anticipate classroom use of the kind to which Ed Brent is applying machine scoring. In his class, machine scoring is a complement to human reading, students do know the criteria by which the computer arrives at their feedback, and if high school writing teachers did inculcate the advantages of writing-to-learn and prepared students to respond to content-driven microthemes, students would likely benefit. In its strident "regardless-of-the-purpose" stance, the digital position statement does not acknowledge that—*when used responsibly* (as I would argue Ed is doing in Sociology 1000) *and when not used as the sole or even primary determiner of grades* (as Ed is not doing)—machine-scored writing might assist and enhance learning, as is its purpose in his large-enrollment course. Ironically, the other choice available for Sociology 1000 is scantron-graded multiple-choice tests, a machine-scored form of assessment that does not enhance learning. Given the impediment of responding to writing in a class of 250 students with three instructors, using technology to assist learning rather than test objective knowledge seems the preferred alternative.

The earlier CCCC "Writing Assessment: A Position Statement" (1995) lays out the profession's best thinking on ways to "explain writing assessment to colleagues and administrators and secure the best assessment options for students" (430). Few would disagree with this statement's cautions against high-stakes, standardized assessment of writing. But many would probably be surprised by the number of positive correlations between the statement's recommendations and Ed Brent's use of machine-scored writing in Sociology 1000. Using the language of the statement, a partial list includes: providing assistance to students; its primary purpose governs its design and implementation; students clearly understand its purpose (learning objectives appear on each assignment); it elicits a variety of pieces over a period of time; it is social (students freely discuss their machine-scored writing experiences online and in discussion sections); reading is socially contextualized (reading the course material is necessary for the machine-scored writing); a variety of skills in a diversity of contexts is employed (different genres, audiences, occasions, and readers are involved); the assessment is used primarily as a means of improving learning; it does not focus on grammatical correctness and stylistic choice and does not give students the impression that "good" writing is "correct" writing; large amounts of institutional resources were not used to design or implement the machine scoring; students are encouraged to plan, draft, and rewrite; students write on prompts developed from the curriculum that are grounded in "real-world" practice; students know the purpose of the assessment, how the results will be used, and how to appeal a score; the faculty member played a key role in the design of the assessment; the faculty member participates in reading and evaluating student writing; the faculty member assures that the assessment supports what is taught in the classroom; and the faculty member continues to conduct research on writing assessment, particularly as it is used to help students learn and to understand what they have achieved. This is a long list of positive correlations between composition studies' professional recommendations and the program Ed has designed and is using.

In light of the challenges that Ed's example offers to the thinking in composition studies to date, it is time for composition specialists to revisit our professional policies and practices. Such revisiting is to be expected, given the changes that technology has wrought in the teaching of writing, not just in the past couple of decades but over the centuries.

CONCLUSION

Ed began this chapter by pointing to the promise of automated grading programs for writing. Indeed, impressive claims can be made for them. Pilot tests of SA-Grader suggest that it can reduce costs for large classes, provide immediate and detailed feedback in a manner students appreciate, and apply to a wide range of exercises addressing substantive concepts and theoretical perspectives. However, there are serious issues to be considered if automated grading is to be used both appropriately and successfully. Ed and I both believe there is a place for machine-scored writing, so long as the concerns we raise are carefully considered. The role of machine-scored writing will likely always be limited, but that role will surely evolve as technologies mature. We don't believe that essay-grading programs will ever become a panacea for writing classes, nor that they should or will replace human teachers. But *when used responsibly* they can make writing assignments such as the writing-to-learn exercises we described above feasible in a wider range of courses. And, when incorporated into courses in ways that minimize their weaknesses, they can provide a meaningful enhancement to student performance.

14

AUTOMATED WRITING INSTRUCTION
Computer-Assisted or Computer-Driven Pedagogies?

Beth Ann Rothermel

Elsewhere in this collection William Condon (chapter 15) exposes the losses college writing programs may experience when employing machine scoring in the assessment process. Contrasting machine scoring with a host of other more "robust" forms of assessment, such as portfolio-based assessment, Condon reveals how machine scoring fails "to reach into the classroom;" using machine scoring for student and program assessment provides administrators and teachers with little of the necessary data they need to engage in effective internal evaluation. This essay examines another recent application of commercial machine scoring—its use with Web-based writing-instruction programs currently marketed to K–16 writing teachers.

I look at Vantage Learning's new "writing development tool," MY Access! which, like WritePlacer *Plus*, uses Vantage Learning's general-purpose program IntelliMetric. Students employing MY Access! engage in online writing to specific prompts and then submit their writing for a grade; the program then provides students with immediate feedback on ways to improve as well as opportunities to rewrite and resubmit. All of the students' work is maintained in a Web-based "portfolio" that may be reviewed by the instructor when assessing individual and class progress. In other words, MY Access! appears to take up where assessment programs such as WritePlacer *Plus* or e-rater leave off, reaching more directly into classrooms to shape the learning and teaching process.

Scholars writing for this collection have noted the extent to which companies developing computer-assisted writing assessment programs ignore, and even show disdain for, the perspectives of scholars and teachers in the field of rhetoric and composition. I would add that these companies show similar disdain for classroom teachers working at the primary and secondary levels. Much of the marketing produced by companies like Vantage Learning focuses on upper-level management. A literature search shows that advertisements and industry reviews of MY Access! appear frequently in journals for K–16 administrators. I first learned about MY Access! when my college's academic dean asked me to review the program after he received e-mail promotional information sent out to colleges across the state. Marketing pitches made by the company are tailored to administrators' concerns about efficiency and reliability. In its online product sheet, Vantage Learning (2004d) asserts that MY Access! is "proven to be more consistent and reliable than expert human scorers." It is also "less expensive than traditional offline administration and handscoring."

Yet promotional materials are also finding their way into the inboxes of teachers, and these materials take more into account the interests and needs of classroom educators, particularly those teaching writing at the secondary level. A review of MY Access! materials on the Vantage Learning Web site shows the company playing on teachers' fears and anxieties over workload and student (hence institutional) success. But Vantage Learning also makes claims that appeal to the field's current investment in process-writing instruction and many a contemporary writing teacher's desire to create a student-centered, interactive learning environment. Drawing on terms and concepts associated with the process-writing movement, Vantage Learning (2004d) claims to encourage "improvement through a continuous, iterative process of writing and revising," thus empowering students and teachers.

A closer examination of the product as well as a review of current scholarship leads me to argue that the language with which Vantage Lesarning represents MY Access! masks a different ideology, one that defines not just writing, but also teaching and learning, as formulaic and asocial endeavors. I argue that rather than developing a space rich in dimension, conducive to complex interactions between students, teachers, and curriculum, MY Access! constricts and narrows the learning environment. Using the program in the way that it is intended to be used potentially disempowers teachers and limits student access to the multiple print and technological literacies they in fact need. Given the extent to which MY Access! is being marketed to secondary school teachers, I conclude by considering the implications such programs have not just for K–16 writing teachers, but for those charged with preparing preservice writing teachers for the schools.

The data on who and how many schools are actually employing MY Access! are sparse. In the promotional brochure I was first mailed, Vantage Learning (2003a) claimed to provide service to 17 million students per year.[1] Teacher comments along with various press releases on the Vantage Learning Web site suggest that most of these students are in

Pennsylvania and California, although several districts in Texas have also recently adopted the program. Many of those schools using the program appear to serve at-risk students. Vantage Learning has, in fact, touted its foundation's "dedicat[ion] to providing at-risk schools" "access" to the "same online reading and writing tools now used in more than 49 US states" (United States Distance Learning Association 2002). In one California class of English-language learners, MY Access! came to the students bundled with other software as part of Apple's mobile assessment cart project (a cart containing twenty-five Apple iBook computers that may be rolled into classes on demand) (Vantage Learning 2003a).

While a Vantage Learning representative informed me in 2004 that only one district in my home state of Massachusetts had adopted its program, promotional materials are in the hands of administrators like the academic dean at my institution. Some of these materials directed at administrators note that English teachers are likely to hesitate if asked to use MY Access! Perhaps as part of a campaign to overcome such hesitation, Vantage Learning is producing and distributing other promotional materials that speak more directly to the skeptical writing teacher.

Vantage Learning (2004d) begins what it labels its "challenge" to writing teachers by showing cognizance of their day-to-day classroom realities and concerns, particularly those of teachers working at the secondary level. While calling attention to recent studies asserting that educators *must* provide students with more opportunities to write, Vantage Learning notes that teachers "instruct a minimum of 120 to 200 students weekly. Assigning and hand-scoring one writing practice per week requires at least 25 hours of teacher time." Such assignments are also crucial in preparing students for the various state writing assessments now often "required for graduation or grade-level advancement." References to the teacher's burden—which is defined as coming up with assignments, responding to them, and examination preparation—and that burden's inevitability are common in literature on computer-assisted writing assessment more generally. In his essay for the Shermis and Burstein collection, Miles Myers (2003, 13) writes that the "average secondary teacher . . . has a student load each day of 150 or more students. In a book-bound classroom, without computers, the management and cursory monitoring . . . of the special needs of students for information and practice in Composition Knowledge is a nearly impossible task." Not surprisingly, reviews of MY Access! continually highlight its effectiveness in bringing up the scores of students taking state-mandated tests. In a recent article about ETS Technologies' program Criterion Online, a program that resembles MY Access! linguist Julie Cheville (2004, 47) argues that the context of high-stakes assessment contributes significantly to the "privileging" of automated essay-scoring tools in the classroom.

However, Vantage Learning also pitches its product by playing on teachers' potential investment in process-writing instruction and their commitment to enabling students economically, socially, and personally through literacy learning. Vantage Learning (2004d) follows up its appeals to fear and fatigue by emphasizing how the program "engages and motivates students to want to improve their writing proficiency." Students are motivated to "write more frequently." Adopting the program will help teachers to more effectively respond to the individual needs of students, to engage in "informed intervention." "MY Access!" an "innovative" new tool, "empowers students to participate in their own learning journey" (Vantage Learning 2003a).

Looming behind such claims appears an awareness of recent concerns like those articulated by the National Writing Project and Carl Nagin in *Because Writing Matters: Improving Student Writing in Our Schools* (2003, 18). For example, in Vantage Learning's claims I hear echoes of the credo of process-writing movement leaders like Peter Elbow, who link student empowerment with a desire to write. Known for commitments to the process-writing movement and to the professional development of writing teachers, the National Writing Project and Nagin make a number of recommendations for improving writing instruction in the schools that are also addressed in Vantage Learning's claims. They call for more school-related opportunities for students to write (12), something Vantage Learning, with its frequent reference to improving student "access," says it will provide. In addition, the National Writing Project and Nagin call for "mastery of diverse writing tasks" (13), reflected in Vantage Learning's assertion that MY Access! allows students to work with different types of discourse (it lists informative, literary, narrative, persuasive forms) and for varied audiences (Vantage Learning 2004c). The National Writing Project and Nagin also argue that instructional feedback is essential to student growth and that teachers should offer more by way of constructive analysis and not criticism when responding to student writing (14). Vantage Learning (2004a) suggests that its program will help teachers achieve such a goal by providing "instant," "diagnostic" feedback aimed at individual improvement. One recent user, whom Vantage Learning (2004a) quotes, underscores the motivating power of quick feedback: "The immediacy of the response is a remarkable reward. It's quite amazing: once [the students] get going, the hum of writing and thinking and crafting permeates the space. How wonderful!" Similarly, in his report on the program, Ronald Schachter (2003, 20), a former high school teacher, describes the computer as "coaching" students.

Promotional material, thus, uses language sensitive to values common to classroom teachers in the field. Over the past thirty years process-writing approaches have made significant inroads into the teaching practices of K–16 teachers. Composition studies and literacy studies, along with the work of such initiatives as the National Writing Project, have been among the forces transforming the thinking and practices of K–16 writing teachers. Studies like the 1998 National Assessment of Educational Progress have shown persuasively that students who perform better on writing assessments engage in planning and produce multiple drafts, revising with the help of teacher and peer comments (National Writing Project and Nagin 2003, 43–44). Vantage Learning (2004d) implies that it shares such assumptions, describing writing as "a continuous, iterative process of writing and revising." Alongside this definition Vantage Learning provides a nonlinear diagram like those many process-minded instructors use when discussing with students the recursive nature of writing. A walk through the MY Access! demo (2004b) shows that when composing within the program, students are urged to begin by prewriting and provided with links to Venn Diagrams or Cluster Webs, which will stimulate their thinking. As in many a process-oriented writing workshop these days, students are also encouraged to use a journal writing space, or notepad, built into the program, where they may reflect on their own goals or development as writers.

The company assures the process-oriented instructor, furthermore, that the computer as coach is not concerned just with surface features. MY Access! uses IntelliMetric which, as Scott Elliot (2003, 72) notes in his chapter for Shermis and Burstein, "analyzes more than 300 semantic, syntactic, and discourse level features" which "fall into five categories," "Focus and Unity; Development and Elaboration; Organization and Structure; Sentence Structure; Mechanics and Conventions." (See Jones, chapter 6 in this volume, for an analysis of how IntelliMetric analyzes these features.) Vantage Learning (2004b) lets teachers know that when evaluating in the domain of focus and meaning, the computer looks at whether audience has been addressed; when evaluating organization, it asks whether the introduction is engaging and the conclusion "strong"; and when considering content and development, it considers whether the writer "explores many facets of the topic."

Finally, in reassuring potential users that the program is intended not to replace teachers but rather to serve as an instructional aid, Vantage (2004c) emphasizes that instructors may override scores. Teachers have access to a "flexible rubric" as well, allowing them to evaluate student writing using only a selection of the available domains (e.g., focus and sentence structure). Instructors may also embed their own comments within student essays or design their own prompts. Since IntelliMetric requires a large number of hand-scored essays on a particular topic in order to perform discursive operations, instructors who create their own prompts will need to evaluate the students' work themselves in most of the domains.

The National Writing Project and Nagin (2003, 10) suggest that process-oriented teachers work from a position articulated by scholar James Moffett: "Writing has to be learned in school very much the same way that it is practiced out of school. This means that the writer has a reason to write, an intended audience, and control of subject and form. It also means that composing is staged across various phases of rumination, investigation, consultations with others, drafting, feedback, revision, and perfecting."

Teachers are using varied technological resources such as blogs, listservs, and integrated writing environments to open up the spaces of learning—to widen the process of investigation and to bring students into contact with different audiences. Vantage Learning would likely assert that MY Access! should be included on that list of resources extending the realm of possibility. But a closer examination of the program suggests that rather than occupying a multidimensional space, MY Access! constricts and narrows the learning environment. In the words of Julie Cheville (2004, 47), such technologies are more likely to "impoverish students' understandings of language conventions and writing."

In "What Happens When Machines Read Our Students' Writing?" Anne Herrington and Charles Moran (2001, 497) discuss the ways in which, by demanding that students write to computers and not to people, computer assessment "sabotages many of our aims for our students' learning," in particular our desire to help them explore the role of context in their own writing. Meaningful explorations of context occur through engaged conversation between students and peers, students and teachers, and students and outside audiences. Miles Myers (2003, 11) claims that automated evaluation systems help students to publish their work, offering an "internet connection to an audience which will provide a score and possibly some other evaluative responses." But the responses offered by MY Access! are not the stuff of much conversation. The "hum of writing and thinking" that permeates the space comes from individuals entering data into a computer. What is lost is that noisy space of exchange (either online or in person) between writers and audiences—a space most process-oriented teachers see as critical to effective writing instruction.

Julie Cheville (2004, 51) shows effectively how Criterion Online subordinates meaning to "fixed linguistic and compositional features." By way of example, she notes that such programs fail to recognize either inventive or illogical essays, and cites Jill Burstein, a computational linguist for ETS Technologies, who admitted that e-rater "looks at an essay like a bag of words." (Cheville 2003, 50) MY Access! works in much the same way, reading against generic forms instead of in real-world contexts, and in doing so creating road blocks to rumination and investigation. The program does remind students that it is important to "stick to your main purpose when writing" and to "think of your audience as you write" (Vantage Learning 2004b). But it is unable to engage in the close kind of listening around which process-oriented classrooms are built. The program won't say back to the student in its own words what it thinks the student "means," nor will it comment on the voice projected by the piece or discuss with the student what more it would like to hear. It may underline phrases that are "nonstandard" or "colloquial," perhaps giving the student a chance to think about whether they are appropriate for a given audience, but then possibly marking the student off for their use when generating a score. And the program may underline what it perceives to be a student's thesis, but it will not play the believing and doubting game, thus helping students rethink underlying assumptions behind claims.

Herrington and Moran (2001) note the gamelike nature of their experiences writing to the computer. Interestingly, one California English teacher and assistant principal describes the reaction of a group of California English-language learner high school students using the program. "It's really a voyage of discovery. The kids log on, pull up their portfolios, write, rewrite, submit, rewrite, get their scores and then do it all over again. . . . It's like they're playing the game of writing. And they love to win." ("High Schools Plug into Online Writing Programs" 2003) Still, unlike many computer games today in which players actually construct rules together as they play, as happens in the real economic and social world in which these students will live and work, the game of MY Access! is a highly prescriptive one. Collaboration, cooperation, or contention are not among the classroom discourse practices promoted by this game.

When using MY Access! students do not compose and revise in relation to real-life learning communities. Their journey of discovery is
a solitary and linear one. For instance, features promoting online or
in-class discussion of their ideas with teachers or peers do not appear
to be built into the program—such discussion would certainly slow
down the students on their race to win. Promotional materials written for administrators construct the revision process differently from,
and more honestly than, the material available to teachers, noting that
students use the feedback to revise "as appropriate," not "where effective" ("High Schools Plug into Online Writing Programs" 2003) Results
from the assessments may, similarly, be used by teachers and the school
to "drill down on specific weak skills," and not as material for valuable classroom reflection on the processes of composing and revising
(Ezarik 2004).

The feedback MY Access! generates is formulaic and, as many critics
of computer assessment have pointed out, never speaks to elements of
surprise or spontaneity in a student's work, as do real-life readers during
face-to-face workshops or peer critique sessions. One program coordinator describing the use of the program in a California summer school
class would likely disagree. She suggests that the students using the program were becoming "wonderful peer editors. They were helping each
other, looking over each other's shoulders. Their buddy would come
over and say, 'Look at that. You only have two sentences in your second
paragraph. You have to write more stuff. Why don't you give an example
of something that happened to you'" (Schachter 2003, 22).

The student may indeed be offering his or her peer some valuable
advice, and yet the critique appears motivated more by an understanding of the mathematics behind the computer's evaluation than by a
desire to have his or her needs as a reader met. *Education Week* staff
writer Kathleen Kennedy Manzo (2003, 39) similarly observes that students in a class using Criterion Online had learned that if they included
"predictable words, phrases, or features in their paper, the computer
would view it favorably regardless of the quality of the work." Programs
like MY Access! fail to encourage students to become introspective readers of their own and others' writing.

Just as MY Access! impoverishes the work of the student, so it impoverishes the work of the teacher. The 1998 National Assessment of
Educational Progress linked higher levels of student performance with
such teaching practices as teacher-student discussion. "Students whose
teachers always spoke with them about their writing outperformed their

peers whose teachers sometimes spoke with them about their writing" (National Writing Project and Nagin 2003, 44). At first glance Vantage Learning appears to encourage such student-teacher interactions, arguing that the program is not meant to replace teachers but rather to liberate them from cumbersome tasks such as grading and record keeping. Teachers may then put their talents to work as coaches instead of judges—become, in the words of one California administrator, "collaborators" (Schachter 2003, 22). This administrator envisions these collaborations, however, as ones in which teachers help the students to interpret what the computer has said, and not ones where they provide their own, perhaps contradictory, feedback.

Miles Myers (2003, 16) provides a more complex picture of how computer-assisted instruction may aid the teacher in the response process, paraphrasing a teacher who had used e-rater. "The student and I can together consult the *e-rater* scoring and analysis of the essay giving us a third party with whom we can agree and disagree. The *e-rater* score and analysis can make clear that there is something in the world called Composition Knowledge, that evaluating essays is not just a personal whim in my head."

And yet many process-oriented instructors would argue that it is the job of the teacher to persuade students that the judgments of real-life readers, whether they be teachers or not, *matter*—that responses are rooted not in personal whim but in a complex web of social expectations and understandings that shift from one rhetorical situation to another. Granted, grading and responding to student writing is a process with which many teachers, especially beginning teachers, may feel uncomfortable, and yet that discomfort should feed a desire to model for students a process of judgment that is sensitive, multileveled, and aware of the landscape—the process that students themselves should adopt when reading their own and others' writing.

As noted, Vantage Learning (2004c) reminds potential users that teachers may embed their own comments or responses to student writing or even turn off certain features, rewarding students for keenness or complexity not measurable by the computer; and teachers are able to override computer evaluation but, as the preservice teachers taking my writing pedagogy class remarked when learning about the program, students may well see the computer's evaluation as carrying more weight than that of the teacher. One teacher using Criterion Online notes that students know the difference between what the computer tells them and what their veteran teacher has to say (Manzo 2003, 40). But it seems likely that less seasoned teachers, or those whose lack of confidence in their own expertise leads them to see their responses as arising from personal whim, will not convey to their students the same faith in their own judgments.

MY Access! takes authority away from the teacher/facilitator as reader and responder, rendering him or her not a coach but a translator. It also takes over the process of assignment construction, relying on prompts developed to work specifically with the program. Many of these prompts may be similar to ones already in use by teachers. But even if they invite students to write about interesting topics, they do not arise organically out of classroom discussions or other reading and writing activities done in relation to those topics; nor do prompts draw on the familiar and nuanced language of the teacher or make it clear to students how a writing assignment is sequenced in relation to an earlier assignment. While teachers might address these issues by elaborating on existing prompts, giving the student more background or supplying links to other lessons, the computer will certainly not take that added context into account when responding to the student writing. As noted, teachers may add their own prompts; but since one of the program's primary selling features is the feedback it provides, and given the expense incurred in adopting the program, teachers are likely to feel pressured to employ the program's prompts fully.

MY Access! claims to contribute to the professional development of writing teachers. Yet by removing the process of curriculum development from the hands of the teacher, teaching becomes no longer a multifaceted process that responds to the shifting needs and interests of a particular community of learners within a certain space. In "Crossing Levels: The Dynamics of K–16 Teachers' Collaboration," Western Massachusetts Writing Program affiliates Diana Callahan and others (2002, 205) assert that the most effective professional development models "assume . . . that teachers' knowledge is valuable—all teachers." MY Access! is built on no such assumption, instead channeling student and teacher reflection into narrow and predictable cycles.

The claims I have made about the ways in which MY Access! constructs learners, teachers, and the learning environment invite much more exploration. In criticizing programs such as MY Access! I do not want to ignore the very real burdens teachers and students of writing, particularly at the primary and secondary levels, confront. But we need to hear less from industry and more from actual students, teachers, and schools using programs like MY Access! As Carl Whithaus notes in chapter 12 of this collection, programs that read our students' work are already in use, and what is needed are more detailed discussions about how teachers actually approach such software. How widely used are MY Access! and programs like it? How much of a place are these programs given in the classroom or in learning centers? How is their use being funded? What is sacrificed in order to put money into using the program, in terms of teacher professional development, smaller class sizes, other technologies? What do students and teachers of varying backgrounds and needs actually think of the programs and their role in their development as writers and teachers? And how do students accustomed to using such programs respond to the far more complex rhetorical tasks and audiences that await them in actual professional and academic settings? For fuller answers to these questions, discussions must include administrators, teachers, and scholars working in varied disciplines and at different levels, from elementary to university.

As a faculty member working in teacher education, I would argue that preservice teachers must also play a pivotal role in our discussions. With this in mind, I am working on making this subject not only one of personal inquiry but one of interest for my students. Near the end of my semester-long inquiry-based course in writing pedagogy, and prior to a discussion of available technologies for writing instruction, I provided my students with a copy of the MY Access! promotional brochure sent to me in 2003 and asked them to imagine that the principal at their school had invited them to share their initial impressions of the program. Many of my fifteen students made revealing observations. Some were intrigued, recognizing the appeal computers might have for their future students. Well aware of the large numbers of students they were likely to have in their classes, some pointed out the value of providing students with feedback more quickly than they possibly could by hand. But several wondered about the impersonal nature of such experiences. One student noted that using the program "[t]ells students they are being handed over to machines." "Do the teachers even care about us anymore?" she imagined her future students asking. Other students saw the program as inviting formulaic or highly standardized writing, leaving little room for creativity. "This seems like all student essays will sound exactly the same," commented one, while another wrote "[t]his could stifle and misdirect development of writing skills." One made a direct connection to standardized testing: "Writing for the computer [is] just like writing for MCAS [the Massachusetts Comprehensive Assessment System, used to determine advancement and graduation]."

The above responses are anecdotal, growing out of a classroom exercise, and yet my students' insights have been useful to me in considering what subjects of inquiry we should take up in my writing pedagogy courses. In future semesters I see my classes doing more of the following:

- Discussing and evaluating various programs available to and in use by middle and secondary school teachers. This means examining programs like MY Access! while also investigating viable and less invasive technologies to aid in both teaching and learning.
- Exploring in even greater depth how human feedback and response matters to the classroom and student development as well as the significance of locally developed curricula and assessment systems.
- Helping future teachers grow and develop their confidence as writers and responders as well as investigating strategies for coping with a heavy teaching, and paper, load without resorting to computer grading.
- Considering the role of standardized testing in our curricula and the ways writing teachers prepare students for those assessments.
- Stressing the importance of advocacy and examining ways to participate in decision-making processes within our schools and school systems.
- And finally, in cases where teachers enter schools where programs like MY Access! are in use, generating strategies for being truthful about what the program in fact does—for helping our students to recognize its limitations. In such cases, teachers may use the program as an instructional opportunity, helping students to critically analyze and respond to what it means to have computers, instead of people, responding to their writing.

15

WHY LESS IS NOT MORE
What We Lose by Letting a Computer Score Writing Samples

William Condon

Earlier in this volume, Rich Haswell (chapter 4) questions the validity of machine scoring by tying it to holistic scoring methodologies—and I certainly agree with his critique of timed writings, holistically scored. However, I want to suggest that questions about machine scoring differ from questions about holistic readings. Machine scoring involves looking back even farther in the history of writing assessment—to indirect testing. Several essays in this collection describe the basic methodology behind machine scoring. The computer is programmed to recognize linguistic features of a text that correlate highly with score levels previously assigned a text by human raters. Thus "trained," the machine searches essays for those features, assigning them the score levels indicated by anywhere from thirty to fifty linguistic markers. In this way, the machine achieves as much as 98 percent agreement with human raters (which, of course, means that it is no better than 2 percent *less* reliable than human raters).

What we want to notice here is that the machine does not in any sense *read* a text. It simply searches for a feature (periodic sentences, conjunctive adverbs, topic-specific vocabulary, vocabulary or concept mapping, etc.) and assigns a score based on how many of those features it finds and how frequently it finds them. This is not really comparable to holistic scoring, since the machine is incapable of forming an overall impression of an essay—or, for that matter, any kind of *impression* about anything. As I have written elsewhere (Condon and Butler 1997), the machine is incapable of understanding the difference in meaning between these two sentences:

> The roast is ready to eat.
> The tiger is ready to eat. (2)

In other words, nothing in the machine's scoring process takes into account the content, the semantic effectiveness, or the rhetorical choices in the essay being scored. Instead, the machine looks at physical features of a text that, separately, are *associated* with a certain level of performance. This process more closely resembles the old multiple-choice question tests, which purported to judge writing proficiency by asking a set of questions that focused on a range of abilities associated with good writing: vocabulary, syntactic knowledge, error recognition, and the like. In other words, instead of a step forward, or even marking time, machine scoring represents a step backward, into an era when writing proficiency was determined by indirect tests.

For the moment, though, and just for the sake of argument, let us assume that machine scoring lives up to the representations of its various promoters. We can come back later in this essay to consider the more worthwhile assessment alternatives that machine-scored timed samples, because cheaply administered, threaten to displace. For now, let us *pretend* that the machine reads as human raters do, that it is capable of making fine judgments about writing ability as a whole construct, that its scores are just as good as those rendered by human raters. In fact, arguing over the claims advanced by the testing agencies may engage us in chasing after red herrings, since the real question is not whether machines can do what the agencies claim, but whether machine-scored timed samples are better than the alternatives—or at least whether a cost-benefit analysis would come out in favor of machine scoring. So we need to look first at the losses—the testing agencies have been quick to point out the gains—involved in using computers to score timed writings, and then, later in this essay, we need to consider the alternatives to stepping backward to indirect assessments of writing.

If we grant, *arguendo,* all the claims in favor of machine scoring as being similar to what human raters do, where does that leave us? If the machine can score as accurately as—and more efficiently than—human raters, that represents a gain. But what are the corresponding losses? We need to examine that list before we decide that machine scoring—even if it could be as good as advertised—should take the place of human raters.

First, and perhaps most basically, in any test type that is administered nationally, rather than locally, we lose control over the construct: *writing.* What we assess is dictated to us by an outside agency—and specifically, in this case, by the capacity of the rating machine. Second, samples must be short, thus preventing the writer from taking an original approach to a topic, coming up with a different approach, organizational pattern, or even vocabulary items, which would inhibit the machine's ability to fit the sample within its set of algorithms. So the writing sample is frequently limited to what a writer can produce in twenty minutes or half an hour.

Given the constraint of time, topics must be far simpler than the topics most teachers would use in class, even at the beginning of a term. Both these factors limit the face validity of the sample. In addition, fast, off-the-cuff writing typically cannot contain much depth or complexity of thinking; practically speaking, the writer simply has no time to do more than sprint to finish an essay that is on topic—and that is so short it hardly deserves to be called an essay. Such a sample, however it is scored, cannot tell us much about a student's writing ability, because the sample's validity is so narrow that it cannot test very much of the construct.

The limitations on face validity mean that we can draw only very limited conclusions from the sample. We can, for example, as Edward White (1994) has pointed out, tell whether the test taker can produce competently formed sentences. We can make some conclusions about the fluency of the writing and about the writer's ability, unassisted, to produce more or less mechanically correct prose. In other words, we can make the kinds of judgment that might allow us to place a writer into a very basic course that deals with sentence-level problems or a higher one that might begin with writing paragraphs or short simple essays. Such an assessment is not useful to most four-year colleges, which are typically prevented from offering such basic courses by legislatures that insist that four-year colleges and universities offer only "college-level" courses. In sum, then, four-year colleges lose the ability to make any sort of useful distinction or ranking among their entering students, since (1) all should be performing above the level that such a short timed machine-scored sample can measure; and (2) even if students perform at a lower level, the four-year school can offer no course to help those students. And the same problem faces the two-year college for all students who are ready for college-level writing: since the sample measures a construct that is significantly below what college-level courses offer, the institution can have little confidence in a decision that places a student into college composition or even into the foundational course immediately below college composition. Of course, community colleges are generally able to offer courses at a sufficiently low level that this distinction might apply—yet the number of such students is quite low, so the question of economics returns. But more to the point, sorting students by ability is supposed to result in classes where the range of ability varies but is manageable. Such short, limited samples cannot provide enough information to make such finer judgments. This latitude leaves teachers holding the bag, in classes where the range of students' abilities is potentially so broad as to make teaching more difficult than it needs to be—or should be.

If the machine could score longer, more topically complex samples, that would be an improvement, but really the objections above extend, to some degree, to even the best timed writing tests, scored by human raters. My own program offers students a choice of topics, all of which solicit more than one sample—one analytic or argumentative and another reflective—that respond to a short selection of text, and the testing session allows two hours for completion. Yet even this far more robust sample, as Diane Kelly-Riley and I have demonstrated elsewhere (2004), is not sufficient for test takers to incorporate critical thinking into their samples—at least not without cost. When we score a set of timed writings for placement and then again for critical thinking, the resulting scores actually show a negative correlation. In effect, if students choose to think, their placement scores suffer (see White 1994 for confirmation of this phenomenon). For several reasons, this negative correlation is not surprising, but it means that if we want to assess students' readiness for college writing—or, beyond that, whether they should be exempt from the course—even a much more robust sample than the computer can score is incapable of reaching the competencies involved in such a decision. Indeed, as I will discuss later in this essay, timed writing samples are themselves of such limited validity that their ability to provide this kind of information is low. The overwhelming majority of students simply cannot produce such evidence in such a limited sample of writing. To the extent that the placement decision depends on anything but the most basic aspects of good writing, these samples also lack predictive validity.

Losing control of the construct involves a second loss: the assessment inevitably takes place on a national level, rather than on the local level. Writing prompts are designed by experts at national, even international testing firms. Such prompts almost certainly have little to do with local curricula, and they may well be inappropriate for a local student population. In Washington State University's entry assessment, the prompt asks students to respond to a short argumentative reading because the ability to analyze and interpret a text, as well as join in conversation with the text, is central to the curriculum of English 101. Similarly, we demand that students summarize the author's position as context for the student's own position on the issue. This demand parallels the 101 curriculum, and it responds to an assignment type that many teachers of first-year students tell us they use, whether in English 101 or other courses across the curriculum. In the consideration of the diminished construct, we saw what we lose in decision-making ability. By using someone else's topics, we see what we lose in our ability to be sure that the instrument actually measures a construct that is relevant to local curriculum and expectations. In other words, by importing topics and judgments that are national, rather than local, we lose important aspects of systemic validity.

Of course, using a large-scale test that is national in scope means that the criteria used in judging the sample probably do not match local expectations either. While the testing services offer customized samples, these are far more expensive. The default test uses the testing agency's topic and the testing agency's raters to set the machine's parameters, so there is no relationship between the test's results and local curriculum, local standards, or local course sequences. In other words, local administrators are little better off than when they set a cutoff score in (mis)using the SAT verbal or the ACT English score for placement: beginning with a "best guess," the program administrator adjusts the cutoff, over time, until placements seem roughly to fit course levels. Such a procedure never results in placements that are as accurate as possible, and such a process mistreats several terms' worth of students, until the level stabilizes. The best assessments are local, since in the local context teacher/raters understand their curriculum and their expectations, so that they can make firmer judgments matching a particular sample to a particular level of instruction with which those teacher/raters have firsthand experience. Teacher/raters who actually teach in the program they place students into know what the beginning writing of successful students looks like, and they can make placements according to an "expert rater" system. The advantages of such local assessments have long been documented (see Haswell 2001 and Smith 1993 for examples at different institutions), so we should be reluctant to give up these benefits.

A third, and perhaps even more costly loss occurs when the machine stands in as one rater of two (one human score paired with one machine score, with disagreements resolved by a second human rater). In assessments that use two (or three) human raters, conversations about writing, about writing standards, about judgments of quality occur. In addition, when local assessments use writing teachers as raters, those teachers share a great deal of lore about course expectations, signs of student ability, curriculum, and so on. Teacher/raters bring their knowledge of the instructional context with them, and that knowledge aids in making more accurate decisions. During the assessment, they learn a great deal about incoming students, information that helps them as they move back into the classroom. This system is reiterative and cumulative, constantly feeding a rich knowledge set from instruction into assessment and from assessment back into instruction. These conversations serve a number of other purposes as well. Teacher/raters define the construct operationally for themselves, and they carry that common sense of the construct into planning their own course assignments and activities.

These sessions also serve as powerful faculty development. Teachers talk not only about quality but also about strategies: how might we handle this student in this course? Why should we realize that this student probably could not succeed at the assignments we typically offer in a particular course, while he or she might well succeed at the tasks offered in another? What sorts of assignment might result in more of these writers succeeding in our course?

Local assessments, which typically employ teachers as raters, produce more valuable and more interesting outcomes than merely a score with which to establish a ranking upon which a placement can be based. Move the assessment away from the instructional context *and* plug a machine in as one rater, and we break the cycle. Those interactions simply cannot happen. Taking the assessment out of its context drastically reduces the information available from the assessment. While we might argue that even a poor assessment, done locally, produces benefits that make it worth the trouble and expense, clearly we could not make such an argument in favor of machine-scored timed writings. If the scores themselves are not worth the expense and trouble, then the test also is not—because the scores are all we get from such an assessment.

Fourth, in various ways aside from those discussed above, a timed machine-scored sample takes away local agency. The shorter the sample, the lower the level of confidence that students and teachers have in it. Indeed, in my own experience working in four universities' assessment programs and consulting with dozens more, if the sample requires less than an hour to complete, teachers routinely administer a second sample on the first day of class in order to make a second judgment about whether a given student belongs in the course. This wastes time and effort, of course, but the point here is that if a more robust, human-scored sample is below the teachers' trust threshold, then all machine-scored timed samples are necessarily below this trust threshold, and so will create duplication of effort. In addition, students distrust and resent timed samples, even the ones that offer extended times and multiple topics and genres. Their level of confidence and investment being low, their performance may well suffer, but the main problem is that they begin the course resenting the assessment process and often convinced that they do not belong there, particularly if the course is at a lower level than they had hoped for or at a higher level than they had expected. The fact that the topic does not match the course's curriculum also saps agency from the teachers, who have been told, implicitly, that they are not qualified to make these judgments, that their institution does not trust them to make those judgments, or that their institution does not care enough about the students to pay the teachers to make those judgments. Any or all of these messages create an unhealthy level of cynicism and a sense of powerlessness among the teacher corps. No matter the economic benefit—even if machine scoring were free—these costs outweigh the advantages.

What we see in this cost-benefit analysis is that machine scoring's principal advantage—economy—comes at too great a cost. Institutions are tempted to adopt machine scoring because the cost of assessment is borne by the student, and that cost (most testing firms charge between $4 and $8 per sample) is lower than the cost of operating a local assessment (indeed, the institution's cost goes to zero). At my own institution, students pay a $12 fee for the Writing Placement Exam. In return, they sit for two hours and write two samples that are tailored to our English 101 curriculum. Such a test has higher face and systemic validity than a single sample written in only one-fourth of the time could possibly yield. Our students also move into classes in which instructors are better prepared, because the teachers know a great deal more about what students can do, what tasks they are ready for, where their zone of proximal development is. Thus, the higher fee comes with much higher value. Even if the institution must bear the cost—many are not allowed to charge separate fees for such an assessment—the payoff in faculty development alone seems worth the price and worth the trouble of offering a local assessment and using local faculty as raters. Machine scoring simply cannot compete economically, as long as we consider *all* the costs of employing it.

Aside from this cost-benefit analysis, another issue looms large: assessment has moved ahead since the advent of the timed writing sample in the late 1960s. Today, the demand for outcomes-based assessments that respond to benchmarked competencies drastically reduces the usefulness of any timed sample. For this and any number of other reasons, we can and should do better than timed writing tests, no matter how they are scored. Over the past two decades, since Belanoff and Elbow's (1986) landmark article on a system of programwide portfolio-based writing assessment, the field of writing assessment has developed a robust set of tools, from portfolios to various other kinds of performance assessment based on actual student learning outcomes.

Less robust forms of assessment entail losses. Indirect tests are context-free: they do not connect with a student's curriculum, nor do they take into account the learning that goes on in a given classroom. Direct tests are context-poor. While they are based on an actual sample of a student's writing, they are so tightly controlled—in topic, time for writing, genre, and so on—that they provide only the merest glimpse into a person's overall writing competencies. Various forms of performance assessment, in contrast, are context-rich (Hamp-Lyons and Condon 1993). They not only offer a far better survey of an individual's abilities, they also bring with them artifacts from the curriculum and the classroom (assignments, for example, as well as the writer's reflections on the learning process), so that we can begin to assess writing in ways that can feed back into the classroom, resulting in improved instruction. We can also use context richness to help us make judgments about where we might improve instruction, curriculum, and course design in order to boost student performance. These more robust assessments involve looking directly at the work products students create in their classes. Therefore, this class of assessment values, rather than undermines, what happens between student and teacher, between student and student. Outcomes assessment focuses directly on what students can or cannot do, and it emphasizes the importance of doing well in class, since the effort there translates directly to results on an assessment. Finally, the reverse is also true: students are clearly invested in earning a high grade in a course, so we need not question their effort on course assignments (or if we do, at least we can say that such a level of effort is typical of a given student). We know, on an outcomes-based performance assessment, that we are getting the best effort a student will give. The same is simply not true of timed writing samples.

Since the essays that computers are able to score must be short and tightly controlled by topic (else the correlations will be too low to produce a reliable score), the result is an even more limited sample than is collected in the usual direct test, holistically scored. Such a limited sample can provide a very rough—and not very fair—ranking of writing samples (note: not of writers by their abilities). This ranking tells a teacher almost nothing about a student's performance, so it provides no feedback into the writing classroom, no information that either the teacher or the student can use to improve. As Brent and Townsend (in chapter 13 of this volume) indicate, although there may be some tasks (i.e., short-answer exams, brief response papers) that may fall within the scope of the construct reached by machine-scored timed writings, these classroom tasks are typically not central to judging student performance there—and none require responses to topics of which students have no knowledge or for which students have had no chance to prepare. We should only use assessments for placement that for the most part address the kinds of task students will face in the classrooms for which they are headed. And any exit assessment or outcomes-based evaluation should of course depend primarily on work products central to evaluating whether students have achieved the expectations placed upon them in the course. Again, outcomes-based performance assessments address what teachers have actually asked students to learn, and these assessments provide information about whether teachers are asking students to address all they should be.

Portfolio-based writing assessments provide a clear example of these benefits, and since these assessments have been conducted successfully for almost two decades, they provide a realistic alternative for both larger- and smaller-scale assessments. Conversations around portfolios are rich and rewarding, again resulting in improved instruction both for individual teachers and across writing programs (Condon and Hamp-Lyons 1994). Performance assessments generally—and portfolios specifically—promote conversation about learning. As students assemble portfolios, they consult with their teachers and their peers. As teachers read and rate portfolios, they consult each other during norming sessions and, typically, while evaluating the difficult cases (Leonhardy and Condon 2001; Condon and Hamp-Lyons 1994). No automated-scoring program can assess a portfolio: the samples are too long, the topics often differ widely, and student writers have had time to think, to work up original approaches, and to explore source materials that help promote more complex thinking. Still, even if computers *could* make such judgments, these valuable conversations simply could not take place, so that the assessment process would exclude the one aspect that teachers—whether writing teachers or not—regularly report as the most valuable form of faculty development they have access to. (Compare Belanoff and Elbow 1986; and, to demonstrate that even ETS knows the value of these conversations, see Sheingold, Heller, and Paulukonis 1995; Sheingold et al. 1997.)

Beyond programmatic benefits, portfolios incorporate data that enable evaluation on the institutional level. Performance assessments provide artifacts that speak to the whole process of learning to write. We see multiple samples, produced under normal writing conditions. We can see assignments, syllabi, reflections about the learning process. These artifacts provide data for accreditation purposes, for far more robust accountability measures, and for a program's or an institution's internal evaluation processes. Such high-stakes assessments of student learning outcomes can be mounted separately from placement tests, exit assessments, and program evaluations, of course, but the most sensible and economical assessments take account of each other so that data from one can provide benchmarks for the next and so that, taken together, these assessments provide a look at a student's whole educational experience along a given dimension (e.g., writing, critical thinking, quantitative reasoning). Indirect tests of any kind—or even timed direct tests, whether scored by humans or by machines—provide none of these data.

These and other losses suggest that machine scoring takes us in several wrong directions. At the very moment when state and national legislatures and accrediting agencies are demanding greater accountability—and basing that accountability on student learning outcomes—the machine-scoring process robs us of the ability to provide the fuller and more complete information about students' learning and about their achievements. At the very moment when performance assessments are helping promote consistency in writing instruction across classrooms, machine scoring takes us back to a form of assessment that simply does not reach into the classroom. At the very moment when better, more valid, more thoughtful, more accessible forms of assessment have made assessment the teacher's friend, machine scoring promises to take us back to a time when assessment was nothing but a big stick for beating up on teachers. At the very moment when writing assessments have produced extremely effective engagements of assessment with instruction, machine scoring promises to take assessment back *out* of the learning process. Perhaps F. Scott Fitzgerald, in another context, has characterized the machine-scoring initiative best: "And so we beat on . . . borne back ceaselessly into the past."

16

MORE WORK FOR TEACHER?
Possible Futures of Teaching Writing in the Age of Computerized Assessment

Bob Broad

*[Household] labor-saving devices were invented and diffused through-
out the country during those hundred years that witnessed the first
stages of industrialization, but they reorganized the work processes of
housework in ways that did not save the labor of the average housewife.*

—Cowan

In her book *More Work for Mother: The Ironies of Household Technology
from the Open Hearth to the Microwave* (1983), Ruth Schwartz Cowan presents a feminist history of modern household technology. As the title of
her book emphasizes, her argument is that the hundreds of "gadgets"
invented with the purpose of easing the labor of "housewives" achieved
the net result of dramatically increasing the quantity and range of tasks
for which women were responsible in the American home. For example,
when the wood-burning stove replaced the open hearth as the home's
source of heat and the cooking apparatus, men and children (the
family's collectors of wood fuel) had much less work to do because the
stove consumed far less wood than did the open fireplace. However,
the stove made it possible, and shortly thereafter obligatory as a sign of
her family's increasing social status, for a woman to cook a much wider
range of foods, often all at the same time, and most often with no help
from anyone else in her household.

Likewise with the vacuum cleaner (which changed cleaning carpets
from a semiannual family task to a weekly solo task) and the washing machine (which allowed soap producers to convince women that
stained clothing was intolerable). In every case, the new technology
briefly fulfilled its labor-saving promise before the social system—within
which women's work was understood, negotiated, and shaped—quickly
and substantially increased its expectations for women's household
labor. The dramatic result of this dynamic was that numerous social
observers during the nineteenth and twentieth centuries commented

on how American women, surrounded by helpful technology, invariably appeared pale, exhausted, harried, and sick. One lesson Cowan wants us to draw from her analysis is that technological advances must be analyzed and acted upon with careful attention to the social, cultural, and political *systems* within which they will play out in people's lives. Often, technology will deliver very different results as it plays out *in the social and political system* from what its designers intend or predict.

As an admirer of Cowan's history of technology, I immediately thought of *More Work for Mother* when in fall 2003 I drew from my mailbox a postcard from the Educational Testing Service (ETS). The postcard's rhetorical purpose was to persuade me (presumably along with everyone else on the National Council of Teachers of English mailing list or those interested in writing assessment) to visit the Educational Testing Service booth at the council's annual conference with the specific purpose of learning more about—and subsequently buying—an ETS product called Criterion.

As readers of the current book are probably already aware, ETS Technologies, Inc. is "a for-profit, wholly-owned subsidiary of ETS" (Burstein 2003, 119), and Criterion Online Writing Evaluation is a computer program that claims to evaluate students' writing. Two distinct appeals on the postcard from ETS attempt to persuade teachers of writing to include Criterion in their teaching practices. The most direct appeal shrewdly targets the topic on which writing teachers are most sensitive and vulnerable: time starvation. The postcard generously offers that "Criterion™ gives teachers what they need most . . . time to teach." Thus we classroom teachers of writing are encouraged to outsource to Criterion our evaluations of students' writing, the part of our job that, following the logic of the postcard, takes valuable time away from the *teaching* of composition. In a moment, I will examine the implicit belief that writing assessment takes us away from teaching writing. First, however, let me offer some personal context for my analysis of the second, more diffuse, appeal made by ETS on behalf of Criterion.

In the late 1980s, I was teaching high school English in Washington, D.C. and resenting the influence of testing—primarily ETS testing in the form of Advanced Placement and SAT exams—on the learning and teaching in my classrooms, especially the learning and teaching of writing. One evening I stopped into a bookstore near Dupont Circle and discovered a volume that permanently changed my professional life. The book was *None of the Above: Behind the Myth of Scholastic Aptitude* by David Owen (1985). I recommend this book to everyone concerned with the effects of testing on education. Owen started out researching ETS in a quiet, journalistic fashion. Along the way, he was so horrified and outraged by the secretiveness, deceptions, and arrogant disregard for students and teachers demonstrated by those he dealt with at ETS that the book ended up as a blistering critique of the educational, political, and economic functions of ETS.

This is the right time to say that, as I've matured, my view of ETS has moderated to an extent. It has become clear to me that people at ETS are smart and dedicated, and furthermore that many of them do care about education. I have even met one ETS researcher in the past few years who shows a spirit of genuine intellectual inquiry (as opposed to the typical relentless ETS sales pitch) in his presentations at the Conference on College Composition and Communication. So my view of ETS is no longer as narrow or as fiery as Owen's. Nevertheless, it is clear to me that the *educational effects* of ETS products and services create serious educational difficulties and obstacles for students and teachers, difficulties I hope are unintended and unforeseen by the people of ETS but that teachers of writing must nevertheless vigorously oppose.

Now back to the postcard. The second appeal on the card has to do with the general character of the professional relationship between ETS and classroom teachers. Above, I have sketched my deeply skeptical, often angry, analysis of that relationship based on my reading of Owen and my twenty-five years teaching literacy to students from prekindergarten to doctoral studies. The postcard attempts to project exactly the opposite picture of that relationship under the headline "Working Together to Advance Learning" and "Listening. Learning. Leading." "At ETS we are committed to understanding the demands of the classroom by forming partnerships with educators. Your requirements drive us to develop products and services that help advance learning . . . . How long does it take you to evaluate an essay? Instantly . . . using Criterion™ Online Writing Evaluation."

In pitching Criterion as a solution to the brutal demands on writing teachers' time, ETS shows there is some truth to its claim to "understand the demands of the classroom." But in order to legitimately claim that they "listen," "learn," and "form partnerships with educators," ETS would have to do more than understand (and exploit) those classroom demands. They would also have to demonstrate understanding of the educational goals and values that shape classroom activities, and they would have to respond in some substantive way to teachers' concerns, expressed forcefully now for decades, about the detrimental effects on

U.S. education of ETS products and services. We are still waiting for such a listening and learning response from ETS, and we are still waiting for such a partnership.

The history of technology in general and of ETS's impact on teaching writing in particular make obvious that the time-saving claims ETS makes on behalf of Criterion are disingenuous at best. Cowan would warn that it is highly unlikely that outsourcing evaluation to ETS will result in teachers having more time to teach writing. To the contrary, writing teachers in institutions that purchase Criterion would almost surely be assigned more students or more classes, or both. Even more sinister than the implications for teacher workload and time is the quality or character of the educational impact programs like Criterion would have on the teaching of writing. Better than anyone in the world, the good people of ETS know that assessment drives instruction. A more candid motto for Criterion would be: "Teach your students to write like machines for a reader who is a machine."

PRESERVING THE PLACE OF ASSESSMENT WITHIN THE TEACHING OF WRITING

Let us now return to ETS's implicit claim that time writing instructors spend on assessment is time taken away from teaching. It is not difficult to see why a corporation that makes its money from the outsourcing of assessment would promote this view. The crucial question is whether students and teachers of writing, and the general public, ought to accept such a view and endorse it by purchasing products that help to separate teaching from assessment.

Evaluation of writing holds an undeniably murky and ambiguous place in the hearts of most writing teachers. Many of those teachers openly dread evaluating their students' writing, chiefly because it requires a tremendous investment of time and effort, yielding often dubious pedagogical benefits (see Belanoff 1991; Haswell, chapter 4 in this volume). However, this bleak scenario is not the only one possible for teachers of writing. In fact, many of us do some of our highest-quality teaching when responding to and evaluating our students' writing. And the core argument of one of our profession's most important recent books is that teachers of writing need to reclaim assessment as a crucial, powerful, and rewarding part of the process of teaching and learning writing.

Brian Huot's (Re)Articulating Writing Assessment (2002) urges teachers of writing to lay claim to evaluation and use its power to drive the best possible teaching and learning of composition. "Assessment can and should be . . . an important and vital part of the effective teaching of writing. One of the main goals of this book is to establish the importance of assessment to the teaching of writing and to connect the teaching of writing to what we now call writing assessment" (11).

Huot's insistence that composition instructors embrace and control the design and implementation of assessment as an integral part of their teaching practice obviously and directly contradicts the enthusiasm for outsourcing assessment evident in the postcard from ETS. But Huot goes even further than making claims for the pedagogical importance of understanding evaluation as part of teaching. Citing Beason, Huot also points openly to the power dynamics and ethics of the relationship between teaching and assessment. "Our profession's abandonment of assessment as a positive practice and its adoption of negative conceptions of assessment as punitive and counterproductive to fostering literate behavior in our students cannot but continue to put us in a position of powerlessness, while at the same time putting our students and programs in peril. To come to a new understanding of assessment is to not only become conscious of its importance, power, and necessity for literacy and its teaching, but also to understand assessment as one of our ethical and professional responsibilities (Beason 2000)" (13). Taking up the power inherent in evaluation is not only our pedagogical responsibility but also our political responsibility.

To cap off his proposed transformation of the relationship between evaluation and teaching writing, Huot even argues that teachers need to teach their students how to assess their own and each others' writing as part of the crucial set of rhetorical skills students need to be successful writers. "Being able to assess writing quality and to know what works in a particular rhetorical situation are important tools for all writers" (2002, 70).

As we contemplate the possible futures of teaching writing in the age of computer-assisted writing assessment, we—teachers, students, administrators, and the public that funds and benefits from our work—need to choose between a vision of literacy learning like Huot's that includes, embraces, and enhances the educational power of assessment or the ETS sales pitch suggesting that teachers and students will be better off when students' writing is evaluated by a computer instead of by themselves, peers, or teachers.

TEACHING WRITING IN THE AGE OF COMPUTER-ASSISTED WRITING ASSESSMENT

Current thinking in our field holds that outsourcing assessment comprises a seriously damaging loss to the teaching and learning of writing.

Chapters in the present volume (including this chapter) also view the use of computerized writing assessment as potentially damaging to students' rhetorical development. Here, I aim to develop further the argument against using computerized evaluation in teaching writing and to discuss what the history of technology and democracy have taught us about how to win that argument. I will also speculate methodically about what our future(s) might look like if we lose the argument and university and college administrators outsource writing assessment to dealers such as ETS, Vantage Learning, and Knowledge Analysis Technologies.

Though I have what I consider a satisfactory knowledge of the technical workings of products such as Intelligent Essay Assessor, Criterion and IntelliMetric my focus in this chapter is philosophical and strategic rather than technical. To help teachers of writing protect the integrity of their profession, I will apply lessons learned from the history and philosophy of technology to the emergence of new-generation computerized assessment, and I will apply lessons learned from past struggles between technocrats and the wider public for control over how technology is distributed and used in society. For support in these efforts, I will begin and end by looking to the work of Andrew Feenberg.

Feenberg's 1991 *Critical Theory of Technology* initiated his argument (carried forward in his subsequent work, to which I will turn later) regarding how societies might shape uses of technology for the common good as discerned through democratic processes. Feenberg insists that the typical dichotomy between technophobic and technocratic viewpoints will fail to serve this project. Instead, he suggests that we stay alert to technological developments and make, as a democratic society, well-reasoned decisions regarding how to handle those developments.

For the specific purposes of considering how teachers of writing might best respond to the emergent assessment technologies, I found Feenberg's thoughts on the interplay between technology and understandings of human capabilities especially helpful. "Roughly formulated, the problem concerns the similarities and differences between human thought and information processing. To the extent that similarities can be found, computerized automata can replace people for many sophisticated purposes. To the extent that differences are found, greater philosophical precision is introduced into the notion of human thinking, clearly distinguished from manmade simulacra" (96–97).

What I, as a teacher-scholar of composition, take from Feenberg's analysis is that insofar as my assessment processes match what a computer can do, it may be appropriate and helpful to use the computer in evaluating students' writing or shift my teaching to address other needs. And where my teaching practices offer students value that computers cannot reproduce, I should not only productively focus my professional energies for the sake of my students, but also strive to understand myself and my profession with greater insight and "precision."

One thing that makes the history and politics of technology exciting is that no one really knows where technological developments may take us. So while we might take heart from the humanistic undertones of Feenberg's approach to technology, not everyone is so kindly disposed toward the human side of the equation. Take, for example, Ray Kurzweil. In *The Age of Spiritual Machines: When Computers Exceed Human Intelligence* (1999), Kurzweil frankly and with tremendous enthusiasm predicts that humans will soon be reduced to the status of technology's mainly extraneous caretaker. "In the second decade of the [twenty-first] century, it will become increasingly difficult to draw any clear distinction between the capabilities of human and machine intelligence. The advantages of computer intelligence in terms of speed, accuracy, and capacity will be clear. The advantages of human intelligence, on the other hand, will become increasingly difficult to distinguish" (4). Kurzweil's extended analysis makes clear that, given sufficient enthusiasm for and faith in the rapid development of artificial intelligence, Feenberg's formulation could leave humans with nothing to offer, and nothing to do, that computers can't do better, quicker, and cheaper.

Luckily, the new generation of computerized assessment technologies, while undeniably impressive from the standpoint of artificial intelligence and language processing, leave human teachers of writing with plenty to do. More important, those technologies can help us better identify and understand what we human teachers of writing do best, especially writing assessment. For now, Feenberg's analysis still holds promise. But the future of our profession depends on how we understand and represent to ourselves and the general public what rhetoric and rhetorical instruction are.

PREDICTIONS AND QUESTIONS FOR THE FUTURE OF RHETORICAL ASSESSMENT IN "THE AGE OF SPIRITUAL MACHINES"

Fortunately, our most robust definitions of rhetoric promise to hold computerized evaluations at bay for some time. Consider James Berlin's 1996 description of rhetoric's dynamic and multidimensional processes.

"Thus, in composing or in interpreting a text, a person engages in an analysis of the cultural codes operating in defining his or her subject position, the positions of the audience, and the constructions of the matter to be considered. . . . The reader must also engage in this dialectical process, involving coded conceptions of the writer, the matter under consideration, and the role of the receiver in arriving at an interpretation of the message" (84). In Berlin's description, reading and writing involve complex interpretations of cultural codes. Berlin drills deep into rhetoric to find the most sophisticated and nuanced elements of the process.

In the world of computerized writing assessment, the usefulness of a definition of rhetoric like Berlin's is that evaluation software doesn't even begin or claim to assess these cultural and intellectual capabilities (see also Ericsson, chapter 2 in this volume). The theory of rhetoric underlying computerized evaluation is relatively rudimentary and reductive. Designers of such products as Intelligent Essay Assessor forthrightly admit that they are simply incapable of (and uninterested in) assessing rhetorical abilities. "Mr. Landauer says it [Intelligent Essay Assessor] is not intended to be used for English-composition or creative-writing assignments, in which a student is being graded more on writing skill than on knowledge of a subject. The essay assessor works best on essays assigned to check students' factual knowledge in such subjects as history, political science, economics, and the sciences" (McCollum 1998, A38; see also Landauer, Laham, and Foltz 2003).

Even the spokespeople for ETS's e-rater (the "scoring engine" for Criterion; see Burstein 2003, 119), which is designed and marketed (as we have seen) specifically for the assessment of rhetorical abilities, admit that their product cannot assess the stylistic and intellectual merits of texts. "[Richard] Swartz [of ETS] emphasized the modest goal of computerized scoring: to judge the structure and coherence of the writing, rather than the quality of the thoughts and originality of the prose. In college, he said, professors grade the development of ideas, while essay-rating computers 'are better suited to judgment about more basic-level writing'" (Matthews 2004).

The point here is not the limitations of a particular computerized evaluation system, nor even whether we agree with Berlin's definition of rhetoric. The point, following Feenberg, is that understanding what artificial intelligence can do should and will shape our conception of what human intelligence can do. In this way, mechanical assessment promises to help us clarify and refresh our understanding of what we do when we teach and assess writing by distinguishing what humans can do from what computers can do.

PREDICTIONS

The history of technology suggests that the continued growth and evolution of artificial intelligence will privilege what humans alone can do and commodify (and thereby devalue) what computers can do. Based on the capabilities and limits of artificial intelligence in relation to the practice of teaching and assessing writing, we should expect that computerized assessment will lead us to privilege several specific features of writing instruction.

- *Rhetoric* (see Berlin 1996) as a process so complex and multiply context-dependent that only human beings can successfully perform and analyze it
- *Feeling* (curiosity, humor, irony, pleasure, desire) in evaluating writing
- Human *relationships* in the learning and teaching of writing: teachers and students working, negotiating, and creating knowledge collaboratively
- *Diverse kinds of readings*: poetic, perfunctory, generous, mean-spirited, imaginative, critical
- *Validity* and *educativeness* (see Wiggins 1998) of evaluations

Meanwhile, by handling the following aspects of writing instruction competently, computerized assessment will commodify them, and so lead us to devalue them as processes a mere machine can perform.

- The composition and evaluation of *standardized timed impromptu essays* and essays written chiefly to show *content knowledge*
- Quick, cheap, quantitative *grading* or *scoring*
- Numerical *agreement* ("reliability") as a feature of multiple evaluations

PROMISING AVENUES OF INQUIRY

In addition to shifting how we value different elements of writing assessment, emerging evaluative technologies also raise interesting new questions in the field of teaching and assessing writing.

- Given a choice between human and computer evaluation of their writing, which will students choose, and why? (In their preliminary inquiries, Baron 1998 and Foltz 1998 came up with conflicting answers to both the "which" and the "why" questions.)
- What do students learn about writing when their performances are evaluated by a computer? How does the expectation of computerized grading shape students' writing processes and products?
- As more computerized assessment programs enter the marketplace, how will they compete against one another? What features will distinguish one computerized evaluator from another? Will the effort to compete through emphasizing such differences undercut mechanized assessment's claims to objectivity and neutrality?

FIGHTING TO PRESERVE HUMAN WRITING ASSESSMENT

In spring 2004, the Conference on College Composition and Communication issued its "Position Statement on Teaching, Learning, and Assessing Writing in Digital Environments" (2005). The statement presents a number of thoughtful observations and guidelines for teachers and administrators of writing programs using digital technology. Near the end of the document, the position statement addresses computerized writing assessment. Under the heading "A Current Challenge: Electronic Rating," the statement makes this unambiguous assertion: "Because all writing is social, all writing should have human readers, regardless of the purpose of the writing" (789).

For those of us committed to rhetorical education, this bold, clear statement from the conference in support of human readers is very welcome. To prove effective in protecting writing classrooms from efforts to outsource assessment, however, the statement will need further support and development. For starters, we will need to follow the advice of the conference statement itself: it states that decisions about teaching and assessment practices must be justified with direct reference to learning goals or outcomes.

> As with all teaching and learning, the foundation for teaching writing digitally must be university, college, department, program, and course learning goals or outcomes. These outcomes should reflect current knowledge in the field (such as those articulated in the WPA [Writing Program Administrators] Outcomes Statement), as well as the needs of students,

who will be expected to write for a variety of purposes in the academic, professional, civic, and personal arenas of life. Once programs and faculty have established learning outcomes, they then can make thoughtful decisions about curriculum, pedagogy, and assessment. (786)

The conference position statement aptly suggests the WPA Outcomes Statement (Harrington et al. 2001) as just the sort of outcome statement that can best guide our assessment decisions. Yet in rejecting computerized evaluation in favor of human evaluation, the conference statement does not support or justify this particular position with reference to the WPA statement or other specific learning outcomes.

The simultaneous emergence of commercial computerized assessment and the bold but as yet unsupported stance of the Conference on College Composition and Communication statement in favor of human assessment creates the perfect opportunity for those in our profession to articulate how human writing assessment better supports our desired outcomes for rhetorical education than does mechanical evaluation. Therefore the area of future struggle will be over which outcomes (that is, which kinds of learning, skill, and knowledge) are valued most highly. If we sincerely believe it—and I hope we do—we need to emphatically argue exactly how human instructor-evaluators provide superior educational experiences over the unarguably cheaper, faster computerized evaluation.

Fortunately, the WPA Outcomes Statement provides a vision of and mission for rhetorical learning, teaching, and assessment that strongly supports human evaluation. Perhaps the greatest threat to the century-old project of standardized writing assessment is the fact that rhetorical processes are highly varied and context-sensitive. Because standardized writing assessment has always relied on a theory of classical psychometrics (now outdated in the field of psychometrics), it has always emphasized standardization and consistency over the variation and difference that are the marks of rhetorical exchange. The Outcomes Statement boldly foregrounds the need for our students to learn to respond to "the needs of different audiences" and "different kinds of rhetorical situations." Note that computerized assessment's distinguishing feature is decontextualized and generic (i.e., standardized) rhetorical tasks, and its main point of pride is the sameness and consistency of the scores it awards to student texts. The Outcomes Statement helps clarify that the overwhelming uniformity inherent in mechanical assessment undermines our efforts to prepare students to compose, assess, and succeed in complex and varied rhetorical scenarios.

The Outcomes Statement also highlights such complex skills as select-ing, evaluating, and using sources; thinking critically and creatively; and mastering various modes, phases, and strategies of the composing pro-cess. These are yet more areas in which artificial intelligence has not even claimed the right to encroach on human teaching and assessment, much less proven itself worthy to do so. So this is the terrain on which we will struggle to preserve and privilege human judgment in teaching writing.

In his 1999 *Questioning Technology*, Feenberg points to historical examples of people rejecting technocratic control of technology in favor of democratic control of technology. In the cases of AIDS drug treat-ments, computer networks, and various environmental threats, people saw technology playing out in society in ways they determined harmed their values and their goals, and they organized politically to change their course.

Luckily, those of us concerned with teaching and assessing writing do not have to look far for examples of how we have successfully sup-planted destructive assessment practices with constructive ones. Both in 1943 and in 2004, on the eve of the unveiling of SAT II, the Educational Testing Service bowed to pressure from writing teachers and, contrary to its best technocratic and classical psychometric judgment, included an actual writing sample in its assessments. Commentators like ETS's Hunter Breland (1996) have fumed over the ignorance and stubborn-ness of writing teachers in insisting on making people write when assess-ing writing ability, but writing teachers have nevertheless (so far) carried the day.

In our current efforts to understand computerized assessment and determine its appropriate place in the realm of rhetorical learning, we can follow these historical examples from within and outside of rheto-ric and composition. First, as McAllister and White argue in chapter 1 of this volume, we have the responsibility to educate ourselves about the features and implications of various mechanical-assessment appli-cations. Next, we have the solemn responsibility to study and predict the impact on rhetorical learning of these various applications. If we, as professional educators, determine that a particular use of artificial intelligence helps students and teachers meet established learning goals, then we should support and invite that use of technology. Where we determine that use of computerized evaluation would trivialize and denude rhetorical instruction and experience, we must fight it and pre-vent it from being used.

Victory in this struggle will depend on our ability to link the pedagogical (including assessment) practices we promote to a compelling portrait of what rhetoric is, why rhetorical arts are important to our society, and what it means to be human and literate, a portrait that clearly demonstrates the necessity of human relationships and interactions in the evaluation of rhetorical abilities. Human writers need human readers, not software. Students need responses from peers and teachers, not computers. The teaching of writing needs to include the assessment of writing, not outsource it.

In defense of these principles and practices we will need to educate ourselves, argue our case to the world, and be ready to fight those who would put their profit before our students' learning.

17

A BIBLIOGRAPHY OF MACHINE SCORING OF STUDENT WRITING, 1962–2005

Richard H. Haswell

This bibliography focuses on the theory, design, application, and implications of automated or machine rating of extended student writing. It covers the literature in English that speculates and reports on the success of computers in scoring "free text" or essaylike compositions of students. The writing scored may range from paragraphs answering examination questions to drafts for course papers to timed extemporaneous essays written under formal assessment conditions.

As such, the bibliography treats only incidentally other areas of machine analysis of writing: application of readability formulas, text mining, information retrieval, computer-assisted instructional feedback systems, programmed learning systems, automatic text generation, machine translation, computerized record keeping, and spelling-, grammar-, and style-checkers. The bibliography also eschews conference papers that are not accessible through libraries or the Internet, journalistic items such as press releases and news stories, and product ads and plugs.

The terminus ad quo is 1962, with Walter R. Reitman's thoughts on the possibility of machine grading at a conference on needed research in the teaching of English. The terminus ad quem is 2005, although the representation of work from that year is thin. None of the contributions to this present volume are included here.

Ajay, Helen Beuck. 1973. Strategies for Content Analysis of Essays by Computer. Ph.D. diss., University of Connecticut, Storrs.

Ajay, Helen Beuck, and Ellis Batten Page. 1973. *Analysis of Essays by Computer (AEC-II)*. Final report to the National Center for Educational Research and Development. Washington, DC: Office of Education, Bureau of Research.

Anderson, C. W., and G. E. McMaster. 1982. Computer Assisted Modeling of Affective Tone in Written Documents. *Computers and the Humanities* 16:1–9.

Andeweg, Bas A., J. C. de Jong, and R. Natadarma. 1996. Improving Writing Skills through Ganesh. In *Effective Teaching and Learning of Writing: Current Trends in Research*, edited by Gert Rijlaarsdam, Huub van den Bergh, and Michel Couzijn. Amsterdam: Amsterdam University Press.

Anson, Chris M. 2002. Responding to and Assessing Student Writing: The Uses and Limits of Technology. In *Teaching Writing with Computers: An Introduction,* edited by Pamela Takayoshi and Brian Huot. Boston: Houghton Mifflin.

Attali, Yigal. 2004. *Exploring the Feedback and Revision Features of Criterion.* Princeton, NJ: Educational Testing Service. www.ets.org/research/dload/NCME_2004-Attali.pdf.

Baron, Dennis. 1998. When Professors Get A's and the Machines Get F's. *Chronicle of Higher Education,* November 20, A56.

Barth, Rodney J. 1979. ERIC/RCS Report: An Annotated Bibliography of Readings for the Computer Novice and the English Teacher. *English Journal* 68 (1): 88–92.

Bejar, Isaac I. 1996. *Generative Response Modeling: Leveraging the Computer as a Test Delivery Medium.* English Report No. ETS-RR-96-13. Princeton, NJ: Educational Testing Service. ERIC Document Reproduction Service, ED 401 302.

Bennett, Randy Elliott 1993. Toward Intelligent Assessment: An Integration of Constructed-Response Testing, Artificial Intelligence, and Model-Based Measurement. In *Test Theory for a New Generation of Tests,* edited by Norman Frederiksen, Robert J. Mislevy, and Isaac I. Bejar. Hillsdale, NJ: Lawrence Erlbaum.

Bennett, Randy E., and Isaac I. Bejar. 1998. Validity and Automated Scoring: It's Not Only the Scoring. *Educational Measurement: Issues and Practice* 14 (4): 9–12.

Bereiter, Carl. 2003. Foreword to Shermis and Burstein 2003, vii x.

Bergler, Sabine. 1995. From Lexical Semantics to Text Analysis. In *Computational Lexical Semantics,* edited by Patrick Saint-Dizier and Evelyne Viegas. Cambridge: Cambridge University Press.

Breland, Hunter M. 1996. Computer-Assisted Writing Assessment: The Politics of Science versus the Humanities. In *Assessment of Writing: Politics, Policies, Practices,* edited by Edward M. White, William D. Lutz, and Sandra Kamusikiri. New York: MLA.

Breland, Hunter M., and Eldon G. Lytle. 1990. Computer-Assisted Writing Skill Assessment Using WordMAP. Paper presented at the American Educational Research Association, Boston, April. www.writinglab.com/brelandlytle.html.

Brock, Mark N. 1995. Computerised Text Analysis: Roots and Research. *Computer Assisted Language Learning* 8 (2–3): 227–258.

Burstein, Jill. 1999. Enriching Automated Essay Scoring Using Discourse Marking. In *COLING-ACL '98: Proceedings of the 36th Annual Meeting of the Association for Computational Linguistics and 17th International Conference on Computational Linguistics, Aug. 10–14, 1998.* Montreal: Association for Computational Linguistics.

———. 2003. The E-rater Scoring Engine: Automated Essay Scoring with Natural Language Processing. In Shermis and Burstein 2003.

Burstein, Jill, and Martin Chodorow. 1999. Automated Essay Scoring for Nonnative English Speakers. In *37th Annual Meeting of the Association for Computational Linguistics: Proceedings of the Conference: 20–26 June 1999, University of Maryland, College Park, Maryland, USA.* New Brunswick, NJ: Association for Computational Linguistics. www.ets.org/research/dload/acl99rev.pdf.

Burstein, Jill, Lawrence T. Frase, April Ginther, and Leslie Grant. 1996. New Technologies for Language Assessment. In *Annual Review of Applied Linguistics,* vol. 16, edited by Robert B. Kaplan, Charles A. Ferguson, Henry G. Widdowson, Richard Tucker, and Merrill Swain. Cambridge: Cambridge University Press.

Burstein, Jill, and Derrick Higgins. 2005. Advanced Capabilities for Evaluating Student Writing: Detecting Off-Topic Essays without Topic-Specific Training. Paper presented at the International Conference on Artificial Intelligence in Education, July 2005, Amsterdam, www.ets.org/Media/Research/pdf/erater_burstein_higgins_CR.pdf.

Burstein, Jill, and Randy M. Kaplan. 1995. On the Application of Context to Natural Language Processing Applied to the Analysis of Test Responses. In *IJCAI: Proceedings from the Workshop on Context in Natural Language Processing.* Montreal: International Joint Conference on Artificial Intelligence.

Burstein, Jill, Karen Kukich, L. Braden-Harder, Martin Chodorow, S. Hua, and Bruce Kaplan. 1998. *Computer Analysis of Essay Content for Automatic Score Prediction: A Prototype Automated Scoring System for GMAT Analytical Writing Assessment.* Research Report 98-15. Princeton, NJ: Educational Testing Service.

Burstein, Jill, Karen Kukich, Susanne Wolff, Chi Lu, and Martin Chodorow. 1998. *Computer Analysis of Essays.* Princeton, NJ: Educational Testing Service.

———. 1998. Enriching Automated Scoring Using Discourse Marking. Paper presented at the workshop on discourse relations and discourse marking at the annual meeting of the Association for Computational Linguistics, Montreal. www.ets.org/research/erater.html.

Burstein, Jill, Karen Kukich, Susanne Wolff, Chi Lu, Martin Chodorow, L. Braden-Harder, and M. D. Harris. 1998. Automated Scoring Using a Hybrid Feature Identification Technique. In *Proceedings of the Annual Meeting of the Association for Computational Linguistics.* Montreal: Association for Computational Linguistics. www.ets.org/research/erater.html.

Burstein, Jill, and Daniel Marcu. 2000. Benefits of Modularity in an Automated Essay Scoring System. Paper presented at the Workshop on Using Toolsets and Architectures to Build NLP Systems, 18th International Conference on Computational Linguistics, Luxembourg, August 2000. ftp.ets.org/pub/res/erater_colinga4.pdf.

———. 2000. Toward Using Text Summarization for Essay-Based Feedback. Paper presented at the Conference TALN 2000, Lausanne. www.isi.edu/~marcu/papers/taln-sum2000.pdf.

———. 2003. Automated Evaluation of Discourse Structure in Student Essays. In Shermis and Burstein 2003.

———. 2004. A Machine Learning Approach for Identification of Thesis and Conclusion Statements in Student Essays. *Computers and the Humanities* 37 (4): 455–467.

Burstein, Jill, Daniel Marcu, S. Andreyev, and Martin Chodorow. 2001. Towards Automatic Classification of Discourse Elements in Essays. In *Proceedings of the 39th Annual Meeting of the Association for Computational Linguistics.* Montreal: Association for Computational Linguistics.

Burstein, Jill, Susanne Wolff, and Chi Lu. 1999. Using Lexical Semantic Techniques to Classify Free-Responses. In *Breadth and Depth of Semantic Lexicons,* edited by Evelyne Viegas, 227–246. Dordrecht and Boston: Kluwer Academic Press.

Byerly, Gayle A. 1978. CAI in College English. *Computers and the Humanities* 12 (3): 281–285.

Calfee, Robert. 2000. To Grade or Not to Grade. *IEEE Intelligent Systems* 15 (5): 35–37. www.knowledge-technologies.com/papers/IEEEdebate.pdf.

Chase, Clinton I. 1999. *Contemporary Assessment for Educators.* New York: Addison-Wesley Longman.

Cheville, Julie 2004. Automated Scoring Technologies and the Rising Influence of Error. *English Journal* 93 (4): 47–52.

Chodorow, Martin, and Claudia Leacock. 2000. An Unsupervised Method for Detecting Grammatical Errors. In *Proceedings of the First Conference of the North American Chapter of the Association for Computational Linguistics.* ACM International Conference Proceedings Series, Vol. 4. New Brunswick, NJ: Association of Computational Linguistics.

Chung, Gregory K. W. K., and Eva L. Baker. 2003. Issues in the Reliability and Validity of Automated Scoring of Constructed Responses. In Shermis and Burstein 2003.

Chung, Gregory K. W. K., and Harold F. O'Neil, Jr. 1997. *Methodological Approaches to Online Scoring of Essays.* Report No. CSE-TR-461. Los Angeles: University of California, Center for the Study of Evaluation, Standards, and Student Testing. ERIC Document Reproduction Service, ED 418 101.

Cizek, Gregoy J., and Bethany A. Page. 2003. The Concept of Reliability in the Context of Automated Essay Scoring. In Shermis and Burstein 2003.

Clauser, Brian E., P. Harik, and Stephen G. Clyman. 2000. The Generalizability of Scores for a Performance Assessment Scored with a Computer-Automated Scoring System. *Journal of Educational Measurement* 37:245–261.

Clauser, Brian E., Melissa J. Margolis, Stephen G. Clyman, and Linette P. Ross. 1997. Development of Automated Scoring Algorithms for Complex Performance Assessments: A Comparison of Two Approaches. *Journal of Educational Measurement* 34:141–161.

Clauser, Brian E., R. G. Subhiyah, Ronald J. Nungester, D. R. Ripkey, Stephen G. Clyman, and D. McKinley. 1995. Scoring a Performance-Based Assessment by Modeling the Judgments of Experts. *Journal of Educational Measurement* 32:397–415.

Clauser, Brian E., D. B. Swanson, and Stephen G. Clyman. 1999. A Comparison of the Generalizability of Scores Produced by Expert Raters and Automated Scoring Systems. *Applied Measurement in Education* 12:281–299.

Cole, Jason C., and Anthony D. Lutkus. 1997. Score Comparisons of ACCUPLACER (Computer-Adaptive) and COMPANION (Paper) Reading Tests: Empirical Validation and School Policy. *Research in the Schools* 4 (2): 65–70.

College Entrance Examination Board, ed. 1991. *Computerized Placement Tests: Background Readings.* ERIC Document Reproduction Service, ED 339 728.

Conference on College Composition and Communication Committee (Kathleen Yancey, Chair). 2004. Position Statement on Teaching, Learning, and Assessing Writing in Digital Environments. *College Composition and Communication,* 55 (4): 785–789. www.ncte.org/groups/cccc/positions/115775.htm.

Coombe, Christine A., ed. 1998. *Current Trends in English Language Testing: Conference Proceedings for CTELT 1997 and 1998.* Vol. 1. ERIC Document Reproduction Service, ED 428 574.

Coombs, Don H. 1969. Review of *The Analysis of Essays by Computer,* by Ellis B. Page and Dieter H. Paulus. *Research in the Teaching of English* 3 (2): 222–228.

Cooper, Charles R. 1974. Research Roundup: Oral and Written Composition: Henry Slotnick, A Model of Computer Essay Grading. *English Journal* 63: 103–104.

Daigon, Arthur. 1966. Computer Grading of English Composition. *English Journal* 55 (1): 46–52.

Dale, Robert, and Shona Douglas. 1997. Two Investigations into Intelligent Text Processing. In *The New Writing Environment: Writers at Work in a World of Technology,* edited by Mike Sharples and Thea van der Geest. Berlin: Springer-Verlag.

Davies, Roy. 1989. The Creation of New Knowledge by Information Retrieval and Classification. *Journal of Documentation* 45 (4): 273–301.

Deerwester, Scott, Susan T. Dumais, George W. Furnas, Thomas K. Landauer, and Richard Harshman. 1990. Indexing by Latent Semantic Analysis. *Journal of the American Society for Information Science* 41:391–407.

Dieterich, Daniel J. 1972. Composition Evaluation: Options and Advice. *English Journal* 61 (8): 1264–1271.

Dobrin, David N. 1985. *Limitations on the Use of Computers in Composition.* ERIC Document Reproduction Service, ED 261 395.

Drechsel, Joanne. 1999. Writing into Silence: Losing Voice with Writing Assessment Technology. *Teaching English in the Two Year College* 26:380–387.

Elliot, Scott. 2003. IntelliMetric™: From Here to Validity. In Shermis and Burstein 2003.

Felix, Uschi. 1993. Marking: A Pain in the Neck! The Computer to the Rescue. *Babel: Australia* 28 (3): 15–15.

Finn, Patrick J. 1977. Computer-Aided Description of Mature Word Choices in Writing. In *Evaluating Writing: Describing, Measuring, Judging,* edited by Charles R. Cooper and Lee Odell. Urbana, IL: NCTE.

Fitzgerald, Kathryn R. 1994. Computerized Scoring? A Question of Theory and Practice. *Journal of Basic Writing* 13 (2): 3–17.

Foltz, Peter. 1990. Using Latent Semantic Indexing for Information Filtering. In *Proceedings of the Conference on Office Information Systems,* edited by R. B. Allen. New York: Association for Computing Machinery.

———. 1996. Latent Semantic Analysis for Text-Based Research. *Behavior Research Method, Instruments, and Computers* 28:197–202.

————. 1998. Quantitative Approaches to Semantic Knowledge Representations. *Discourse Processes* 25 (2–3): 127–130.

Foltz, Peter W., Darrell Laham, and Thomas K. Landauer. 1999. Automated Essay Scoring: Applications to Educational Technology. In *Ed Media 1999: World Conference on Educational Multimedia, Hypermedia, and Telecommunications, Seattle, Washington, USA, June 19–24, 1999,* edited by Betty Collis and Ron Oliver. Charlottesville, VA: Association for the Advancement of Computing in Education.

Forehand, Garlie A. 1987. Development of a Computerized Diagnostic Testing Program. *Collegiate Microcomputer* 5 (1): 55–59.

Forehand, Garlie A., and Myrtle W. Rice. 1987–1988. Diagnostic Assessment in Instruction. *Machine-Mediated Learning* 2 (4): 287–296.

Hake, Rosemary. 1977. A Test to Teach to: Composition at Chicago State University. *ADE Bulletin* 52:31–37.

Hartnett, Carolyn G. 1978. *Measuring Writing Skills.* ERIC Document Reproduction Service, ED 170 014.

Hearst, Marti A. 2000. The Debate on Automated Essay Grading. *IEEE Intelligent Systems* 15 (5): 22–35. www.knowledge-technologies.com/papers/IEEEdebate.pdf.

Herrington, Anne, and Charles Moran. 2001. What Happens When Machines Read Our Students' Writing? *College English* 63 (4): 480–499.

Hiller, Jack H. 1998. Applying Computerized Text Measurement Strategies from Project Essay Grade (PEG) to Military and Civilian Organizational Needs. ERIC Document Reproduction Service, ED 418 995.

Hirschman, Lynette, Eric Breck, Marc Light, John D. Burger, and Lisa Ferro. 2000. Automated Grading of Short-Answer Tests. *IEEE Intelligent Systems* 15 (5): 31–35.

Hock, Dennis J. 1990. A Correlational Study of Computer-Measured Traits and Holistic Assessment Ratings of First-Year College Students' Essays. Ph.D. diss., Indiana University of Pennsylvania.

Huot, Brian. 1996. Computers and Assessment: Understanding Two Technologies. *Computers and Composition* 13 (2): 231–244.

Jobst, Jack. 1984. Computer-Assisted Grading of Essays and Reports. *Computers and Composition* 1 (2): 5.

————. 1984. Computer-Assisted Grading: The Electronic Handbook. *Journal of Teaching Writing* 3 (2): 225–235.

Johnson, Valen E. 1996. On Bayesian Analysis of Multirater Ordinal Data: An Application to Automated Essay Grading. *Journal of the American Statistical Association* 91 (433): 42–51.

Jones, Brett D. 1999. Computer-Rated Essays in the English Composition Classroom. *Journal of Educational Computing Research* 20 (2): 169–187.

Kaplan, Randy M., and Randy E. Bennett. 1994. *Using the Free-Response Scoring Tool to Automatically Score the Formulating-Hypothesis Item.* ETS Technical Report GRE No. 90-02b. Princeton, NJ: Educational Testing Service.

Kaplan, Randy M., Susanne Wolff, Jill Burstein, Chi Lu, and Bruce Kaplan. 1998. *Scoring Essays Automatically Using Surface Features.* GRE Report No. 94-21P. Princeton, NJ: Educational Testing Service.

Keith, Timothy Z. 2003. Validity of Automated Essay Scoring Systems. In Shermis and Burstein 2003.

Kelly, P. Adam. 2001. *Computerized Scoring of Essays for Analytical Writing Assessments: Evaluating Score Validity.* ERIC Document Reproduction Service, ED 458 296.

Klein, Davina C. D., Gregory K. W. K. Chung, Ellen Osmundson, Howard E. Herl, and Harold F. O'Neil, Jr. 2001. *Examining the Validity of Knowledge Mapping as a Measure of Elementary Students' Scientific Understanding.* CSE Technical Report No. 557. Los Angeles: University of California, National Center for Research on Evaluation, Standards, and Student Testing (CRESST).

Koether, Mary, and Esther Coke. 1973. *A Scheme for Text Analysis Using FORTRAN.* ERIC Document Reproduction Service, ED 074 152.

Kukich, Karen. 2000. Beyond Automated Essay Scoring. *IEEE Intelligent Systems* 15 (5): 22–27.

Landauer, Thomas K., and S. T. Dumais. 1997. A Solution to Plato's Problem: The Latent Semantic Analysis Theory of Acquisition, Induction, and Representation of Knowledge. *Psychological Review* 104:211–240.

Landauer, Thomas K., Peter W. Foltz, and Darrell Laham. 2000. Introduction to Latent Semantic Analysis. *Discourse Processes* 25:259–284.

Landauer, Thomas K., Darrell Laham, and Peter W. Foltz. 2000. The Intelligent Essay Assessor. *IEEE Intelligent Systems* 15:27–31.

———. 2003. Automated Scoring and Annotation of Essays with the Intelligent Essay Assessor™. In Shermis and Burstein 2003.

Landauer, Thomas K., Darrell Laham, Bob Rehder, and M. E. Schreiner. 1997. How Well Can Passage Meaning Be Derived without Using Word Order? A Comparison of Latent Semantic Analysis and Humans. In *Proceedings of the Nineteenth Annual Meeting of the Cognitive Science Society: August 7–10, 1997, Stanford University, Stanford, CA*, edited by Michael G. Shafto and Pat Langley. Mahwah, NJ: Lawrence Erlbaum

Larkey, Leah S. 1998. Automatic Essay Grading Using Text Categorization Techniques. In *SIGIR Ninety-Eight: Proceedings of the 21st Annual International ACM SIGIR Conference on Research and Development in Information Retrieval, August 24–28, 1998, Melbourne, Australia*, edited by W. Bruce Croft. New York: Association for Computing Machinery.

Larkey, Leah S., and W. Bruce Croft. 2003. A Text Categorization Approach to Automated Essay Grading. In Shermis and Burstein 2003.

Leacock, Claudia, and Martin Chodorow. 2003. Automated Grammatical Error Detection. In Shermis and Burstein 2003.

Lee, Yong-Won. 2001. *The Essay Scoring and Scorer Reliability in TOEFL CBT*. ERIC Document Reproduction Service, ED 455 253.

Lee, Yong-Won, Hunter Breland, and Eiji Muraki. 2002. *Comparability of TOEFL CBT Essay Prompts for Different Native Language Groups*. ERIC Document Reproduction Service, ED 464 963.

Legg, Sue M., and Dianne C. Buhr. 1992. Computerized Adaptive Testing with Different Groups. *Educational Measurement: Issues and Practice* 11 (2): 23–27.

Lemaire, Benoit, and Philippe Dessus. 2001. A System to Assess the Semantic Content of Student Essays. *Journal of Educational Computing Research* 24 (3): 305–320.

Levy, Lynn B., and Kentner V. Fritz. *Status Report on the Computer Grading of Essays*. Counseling Center Reports, Vol. 5, No. 10. Madison: University of Wisconsin, Counseling Center. ERIC Document Reproduction Service, ED 069 759.

Macrorie, Ken. 1969. Review of *The Analysis of Essays by Computer*, by Ellis B. Page and Dieter H. Paulus. *Research in the Teaching of English* 3 (2): 228–236.

———. 1970. Percival. In *Uptaught*. New York: Hayden.

Manzo, Kathleen Kennedy. 2003. Essay Grading Goes Digital: But Critics Question the Use of Software to Assess Writing. *Education Week* 22 (35): 39–43.

Martinez, M. E., and Randy E. Bennett. 1992. A Review of Automatically Scorable Constructed-Response Item Types for Large-Scale Assessment. *Applied Measurement in Education* 5 (2): 151–169.

Matalene, Carolyn B., and Nancy Barendse. 1989. Transaction in Holistic Scoring: Using a Computer to Understand the Process. *Journal of Teaching Writing* 8 (2): 87–107.

McCollum, Kelly. 1998. How a Computer Program Learns to Grade Essays. *Chronicle of Higher Education*, September 4: A37 A38.

———. 1999. Computers Will Help Grade Essays on Graduate Management Admission Test. *Chronicle of Higher Education*, January 29, A30.

McCurry, Niki. 1992. *The Computerized Inventory of Developmental Writing Traits*. ERIC Document Reproduction Service, ED 357 375.

McCurry, Niki, and Alan McCurry. 1992. Writing Assessment for the Twenty-First Century. *Computing Teacher* 19 (7): 35–37.

Millman, Jason, and Ronald S. Westman. 1989. Computer-Assisted Writing of Achievement Test Items: Toward a Future Technology. *Journal of Educational Measurement* 26 (2): 177–190.

Moon, Okhee. 1992. An Application of Computerized Adaptive Testing to the Test of English as a Foreign Language. Ph.D. diss., State University of New York at Albany.

Morgan, Bradford A. 1984. Evaluating Student Papers with a Word Processor. *Research in Word Processing Newsletter* 2 (6): 1–6.

Myers, Miles 2003. What Can Computers and AES Contribute to a K–12 Writing Program? In Shermis and Burstein 2003.

Myford, Carol M., and Frederick Cline. 2002. Looking for Patterns in Disagreements: A Facets Analysis of Human Raters' and E-rater's Scores on Essays Written for the Graduate Management Admissions Test (GMAT). Paper presented at the annual meeting of the American Educational Research Association. www.ets.org/research/dload/ AERA2002-myf.pdf.

Mzumara, Howard R., Mark D. Shermis, and Jason M. Averitt. 1999. *Predictive Validity of the IUPUI Web-Based Placement Test Scores for Course Placement at IUPUI: 1998–1999.* Indianapolis: Indiana University Purdue University, Testing Center. www.assessment. iupui.edu/report/VAL1999.pdf.

Mzumara, Howard R., Mark D. Shermis, and M. Fogel. 1999. *Predictive Validity of the IUPUI Web-Based Placement Test Scores for Course Placement at IUPUI: 1997–1998.* Indianapolis: Indiana University Purdue University, Testing Center

Nancarrow, Paula Reed, Donal Ross, and Lillian Bridwell-Bowles. 1984. *Word Processors and the Writing Process: An Annotated Bibliography.* Westport, CT: Greenwood.

Ohlsson, Stellan. 1986. *Computer Simulation and its Impact on Educational Research and Practice.* ERIC Document Reproduction Service, ED 282 521.

Ott, Christopher. 1999. Essay Questions: How Well Can Computers Judge Prose—And Would You Want One Grading Your Exam? *Salon.com,* May 25. www.salonmag.com/ tech/feature/1999/05/25/computer_grading/.

Page, Ellis B. 1966. Grading Essays by Computer: Progress Report. In *Proceedings of the Invitational Conference on Testing Problems, October 29, 1966, New York City.* Princeton, NJ: Educational Testing Service.

———. 1966. The Imminence of Grading Essays by Computer. *Phi Delta Kappan* 48:238–243.

———. 1967. Statistical and Linguistic Strategies in the Computer Grading of Essays. In *Proceedings of the Second International Conference on Computational Linguistics, Grenoble, France, August 24.* Yorktown Heights, NY: IBM Research Center.

———. 1968. Analyzing Student Essays by Computer. *International Review of Education* 14:210–225.

———. 1985. Computer Grading of Student Essays. In *International Encyclopedia of Educational Research: Research and Studies,* edited by Torsten Husen and T. Neville Postlethwaite. Oxford: Pergamon.

———. 2003. Project Essay Grade: PEG. In Shermis and Burstein.

Page, Ellis B., G. A. Fisher, and M. A. Fisher. 1968. Project Essay Grade: A FORTRAN Program for Statisticval Analysis of Prose. *British Journal of Mathematical and Statistical Psychology* 21:139.

Page, Ellis B., and Dieter H. Paulus. 1968. *The Analysis of Essays by Computer.* Final Report of U.S. Office of Education Project No. 6-1318.Washington, DC: Department of Health, Education, and Welfare. ERIC Document Reproduction Service, ED 028 633.

Page, Ellis B., and Nancy S. Petersen. 1995. The Computer Moves into Essay Grading: Updating the Ancient Test. *Phi Delta Kappan* 76:561–565.

Page, Ellis B., John P. Poggio, and Timothy Z. Keith. 1997. Computer Analysis of Student Essays: Finding Trait Differences in Student Profile. Paper presented at the AERA/ NCME Symposium on Grading Essays by Computer. ERIC Document Reproduction Service, ED 411 316.

Page, Ellis B., P. I. Tillett, and Helen Beuck Ajay. 1989. Computer Measurement of Subject-Matter Tests: Past Research and Future Promises. In *Proceedings of the First Annual Meeting of the American Psychological Society.* Alexandria, VA: American Psychological Society.

Palmer, John, Robert Williams, and Heinz Dreher. 2002. Automated Essay Grading System Applied to a First Year University Subject—Can We Do It Better? InformingScience. org. proceedings.informingscience.org/IS2002Proceedings/papers/Palme026Autom. pdf.

Pedersen, Elray L. 1983. Computer-Assisted Evaluation of Student Papers: I Can Write Anything You Can Write—Faster And Better. *CALICO Journal* 1 (2): 39–42.

Ponisciak, Steve, and Valen Johnson. 2003. Bayesian Analysis of Essay Grading. In Shermis and Burstein.

Powers, Donald E., Jill C. Burstein, Martin S. Chodorow, Mary E. Fowles, and Karen Kukich. 2001. *Stumping E-rater: Challenging the Validity of Automated Essay Scoring.* GRE Board Research Report No. 98-08bP. Princeton, NJ: Educational Testing Service.

———. 2002. Comparing the Validity of Automated and Human Scoring of Essays. *Journal of Educational Computing Research* 26 (4): 407–425.

Reid, Stephen, and Gilbert Findlay. 1986. Writer's Workbench Analysis of Holistically Scored Essays. *Computers and Composition* 3 (2): 6–32.

Reitman, Walter R. 1962. Computer Models of Psychological Processes and Some Implication for the Theory and Practice of Writing. In *Needed Research in the Teaching of English: Proceedings of a Project English Research Conference, May 5–7, 1962,* edited by Erwin Ray Steinberg. Washington, DC: U.S. Department of Health, Education, and Welfare, Office of Education.

Roberts, Carl W., and Roel Popping. 1993. Computer-Supported Content Analysis: Some Recent Developments. *Social Science Computer Review* 11:283–291.

Rounds, Jeanine C., Martha J. Kanter, and Marlene Blumin. 1987. Technology and Testing: What Is Around the Corner? In *Issues in Student Assessment,* edited by Dorothy Bray and Marcia J. Belcher. San Francisco: Jossey-Bass.

Roy, Emil. 1990. A Decision Support System for Improving First-Year Writing Courses. *Computer-Assisted Composition Journal* 4 (3): 79–86.

———. 1993. Computerized Scoring of Placement Exams: A Validation. *Journal of Basic Writing* 12 (2): 41–54.

———. 1992. Evaluating Placement Exams with a Structured Decision System. *Computers and Composition* 9 (2): 71–86.

Roy, Sandra, and Emil Roy. 1992. Direct Mail Letters: A Computerized Linkage between Style and Success. *Journal of Business and Technical Communication* 6 (2): 224–234.

Rudner, Lawrence M. 2001. Bayesian Essay Test Scoring System—Betsy. ericae.net/betsy/.

———. 2001. Responding to Testing Needs in the 21st Century with an Old Tool, a Very Old Tool. In *Assessment: Issues and Challenges for the New Millennium,* edited by Garry Richard Walz and Jeanne Bleuer. Greensboro, NC: ERIC Clearinghouse on Counseling and Student Services.

Rudner, Lawrence, and Phil Gagné. 2001. An Overview of Three Approaches to Scoring Written Essays by Computer. *Practical Assessment Research and Evaluation* 7(26). ericae. net/pare/getvn.asp?v=7&n=26

Russell, Michael. 2000. *It's Time to Upgrade: Tests and Administration Procedures for the New Millennium.* ERIC Document Reproduction Service, ED 452 833.

Russell, Michael, and Walt Haney. 2000. Bridging the Gap between Testing and Technology in Schools. *Education Policy Analysis Archives* 8 (19). epaa.asu.edu/epaa/v8n19.html.

Salton, Gerald, and Anita Wong. 1976. On the Role of Words and Phrases in Automatic Text Analysis. *Computers and the Humanities* 10:69–87.

Sampson, James P., Jr. 1998. *Using the Internet to Enhance Test Interpretation.* ERIC Document Reproduction Service, ED 426 329.

Schachter, Ronald. 2003. A.I.: Something to Build on. *District Administration* 39 (July): 20–24.

Schuemann, Cynthia M. 1998. An Investigation into the Comparable Effectiveness of Two Tests of Writing Administered to College-Level English as a Second Language Students: The Computerized Placement Test and Holistically Scored Essay Exams. Ph.D. diss., Florida International University, University Park.

Segall, Michaela. 1991. Holistic Assessment of Writing. In *Project Synergy: Software Support for Underprepared Students,* edited by Kamala Anandam. Software Implementation Report, September. ERIC Document Reproduction Service, ED 345 803.

Shermis, Mark D., and Fellicia D. Barrera, eds. 2002. *Automated Essay Scoring for Electronic Portfolios.* San Francisco: Wiley. [Special issue of *Assessment Update* 14 (4), 2002.]

Shermis, Mark D., and Jill Burstein, eds. 2003. *Automated Essay Scoring: A Cross-Disciplinary Perspective.* Mahwah, NJ: Lawrence Erlbaum.

Shermis, Mark D., and Kathryn E. Daniels. 2003. Norming and Scaling for Automated Essay Scoring. In Shermis and Burstein 2003.

Shermis, Mark D., Chantal Mees Koch, Ellis B. Page, Timothy Z. Keith, and Susanne Harrington. 2002. Trait Ratings for Automated Essay Grading. *Educational and Psychological Measurement* 62 (1): 5–18.

Shermis, Mark D., Howard Mzumara, Mike Brown, and Clo Lillig. 1997. *Computerized Adaptive Testing through the World Wide Web.* ERIC Document Reproduction Service, ED 414 536.

Shukur, Zarina, Edmund Burke, and Eric Foxley. 1999. Automatically Grading Customer Confidence in a Formal Specification. *Journal of Computing in Higher Education* 11 (1): 86–119.

Sirc, Geoffrey. 1989. Response in the Electronic Medium. In *Writing and Response: Theory, Practice, and Research,* edited by Chris M. Anson. Urbana, IL: NCTE.

Sireci, Stephen G., and Saba Rizavi. 2000. *Comparing Computerized and Human Scoring of Students' Essays.* ERIC Document Reproduction Service, ED 463 324.

Slotnick, Henry Barry. 1971. An Examination of the Computer Grading of Essays. Ph.D. diss., University of Illinois at Urbana-Champaign.

——. 1971. *An Examination of the Computer Grading of Essays.* ERIC Document Reproduction Service, ED 074 504.

——. 1972. Toward a Theory of Computer Essay Grading. *Journal of Educational Measurement* 9 (4): 253–263.

——. 1974. Computer Scoring of Formal Letters. *Journal of Business Communication* 11 (2): 11–19.

Slotnick, Henry B., and John V. Knapp. 1971. Easy Grading by Computers: A Laboratory Phenomenon? *English Journal* 60 (1): 75–87.

Slotnick, Henry B., John V. Knapp, and Rodney L. Bussell. 1971. Bits, Nybbles, Bytes: A View of Electronic Grading. *Journal of Business Communication* 8 (2): 35–52.

Stansfield, Charles W., ed. 1986. *Technology and Language Testing: A Collection of Papers from the 7th Annual Colloquium on Language Testing Research, Princeton, New Jersey, April 6–9, 1985.* ERIC Document Reproduction Service, ED 365 142.

Starr, Douglas. 1993. Paper Grading on Single Disc Preferable to Multi-Disc Way. *Community College Journalist* 21 (4): 4–6.

Stephens, Derek. 2001. Use of Computer Assisted Assessment: Benefits to Students and Staff. *Education for Information* 19:265–275.

Stewig, John Wren. 1984. The Key to Improving Education. *Education Digest* 49 (May): 10–13.

Streeter, Lynn, Joseph Psotka, Darrell Laham, and Don MacCuish. 2004. The Credible Grading Machine: Automated Essay Scoring in the DOD [Department of Defense]. www.knowledge-technologies.com/papers/essayscoring.pdf.

Takayoshi, Pamela. 1996. The Shape of Electronic Writing: Evaluating and Assessing Computer-Assisted Writing Processes and Products. *Computers and Composition* 13 (20): 245–258.

Thompson, Clive. 1999. The Attack of the Incredible Grading Machine. *Lingua Franca* 9 (5). www.linguafranca.com/9907/nwo.html.

United States Distance Learning Association. 2002. Underachiveing Schools to Receive Online Development Tool. *USDLA Journal* 16 (July). www.usdla.org.

Wainer, Howard, and Neil J. Dorans. 1990. *Computerized Adaptive Testing: A Primer.* Hillsdale, NJ: Lawrence Erlbaum.

Weigle, Sara Cushing. 2002. *Assessing Writing.* Cambridge Language Assessment Series. Cambridge: Cambridge University Press.

Whalen, Thomas E. 1971. *The Analysis of Essays by Computer: A Simulation of Teachers' Ratings.* ERIC Document Reproduction Service, ED 048 352.

———. 1971. *Assessment of Language Ability by Computer.* ERIC Document Reproduction Service, ED 052 206.

Whithaus, Carl. 2004. The Development of Early Computer-Assisted Writing Instruction (1960–1978): The Double Logic of Media And Tools. *Computers and the Humanities* 38 (2): 149–162.

Whittington, Dave, and Helen Hunt. 1999. Approaches to the Computerized Assessment of Free Text Responses. In *Proceedings of the Third Annual Computer Assisted Assessment Conference.* Loughborough, UK: Loughborough University. cvu.strath.ac.uk/dave/publications/caa99.html.

Williams, Robert 2001. Automated Essay Grading: An Evaluation of Four Conceptual Models. In *Expanding Horizons in Teaching and Learning: Proceedings of the 10th Annual Teaching Learning Forum, February 7–9, 2001,* edited by A. Herrmann and M. M. Kulski. Perth, Australia: Curtin University of Technology. cea.curtin.edu.au/tlf/tlf2001/williams.html.

Williamson, David M., Isaac I. Bejar, and A. S. Hope. 1999. "Mental Model" Comparison of Automated and Human Scoring. *Journal of Educational Measurement* 36:158–184.

Williamson, Michael. 2004. Validity of Automated Scoring: Prologue for a Continuing Discussion of Machine Scoring Student Writing. *Journal of Writing Assessment* 1 (2): 85–104.

Wirth, Susan Katherine. 1972. A Paraphrasing Strategy in the Content Grading of Essay Examinations by Computer, Ph.D. diss., University of Connecticut, Storrs.

Wonnberger, Carl G. 1955. Judging Compositions—Machine Method. *English Journal* 44 (8): 473–475.

Woods, Elinor M. 1970. Recent Applications of Computer Technology to School Testing Programs. *Review of Educational Research* 40 (4): 525–539.

Wresch, William. 1988. Six Directions for Computer Analysis of Student Writing. *Computing Teacher* 15 (7): 13–16.

———. 1993. The Imminence of Grading Essays by Computer—25 Years Later. *Computers and Composition* 10 (2): 45–58.

Wresch, William, and Helen Schwartz. 1988. The Uses of Computers in the Analysis and Assessment of Writing [conference presentation synopsis]. *Notes from the National Testing Network in Writing* 8:26–27.

Yang, Yongwei, Chad W. Buckendahl, Piotr J. Juszkiewicz, and Dennison S. Bhola. 2002. A Review of Strategies for Validating Computer Automated Scoring. *Applied Measurement in Education* 15 (4): 391–412.

GLOSSARY OF TERMS

ACCUPLACER. College Board's suite of placement tests, administered via the Internet. Includes placement tools for reading, math, and writing, the writing assessed through WritePlacer Plus based on the IntelliMetric Essay Scoring Engine.

ACT. Testing corporation founded in 1959, originally known as the American College Testing Program, now known only as ACT.

AES. Automated essay scoring, a phrase often used in the computing industry to refer to software, such as e-Write or Intelligent Essay Assessor, that renders a score or rate from a naturally written extended piece of discourse.

Algorithm. Sequence of commands that allows a computer to accomplish a task in a finite number of steps.

Artificial intelligence (AI). Construction of machines such that they can solve humanlike problems in a humanlike way.

CAWA. Computer-assisted writing assessment, referring to any computer program that analyzes and judges written language, from spell-checkers to essay scorers.

College Board. Corporation that owns the SAT and the Advanced Placement Program, originally established as the College Entrance Examination Board (CEEB) in 1900.

COMPASS. ACT's essay-scoring machine, based on the IntelliMetric Essay Scoring Engine, also known as COMPASS e-Write.

Criterion. ETS's essay-scoring machine, based on e-rater technology (developed by ETS).

e-rater. ETS' essay-assessment program.

ETS. Testing corporation founded in 1947 as the Educational Testing Service, now popularly known as ETS.

e-Write. ACT's scoring machine, based on the IntelliMetric Essay Scoring Engine, also known as COMPASS e-Write.

GMAT. Graduate Management Admissions Test, owned by the Graduate Management Admission Council, a standard entrance examination for business graduate schools. In 1999 it became the first large-scale test to have examinee essays machine scored (by ETS's e-rater).

Grammar- and style-checkers. Computer programs that detect deviations from algorithms having to do with punctuation, subject-verb agreement, frequency of passive constructions, and other "rules" of standard written language.

Intelligent Essay Assessor. Essay-assessment machine based on latent semantic analysis, originally developed by Knowledge Analysis Technologies, now purveyed by Pearson Knowledge Technologies

IntelliMetric Essay Scoring Engine. Essay-assessment machine developed by Vantage Technologies, used in COMPASS e-Write, ACCUPLACER, MY Access! and other scoring programs.

Knowledge Analysis Technologies. Original developer and purveyor of the Intelligent Essay Assessor, now known as Pearson Knowledge Technologies.

Latent semantic analysis (LSA). Computer-based language-analysis program used in the Intelligent Essay Assessor; uses mathematical and statistical techniques to extract information and make content inferences about texts.

MY Access! Online essay-scoring and feedback system, based on the IntelliMetric Essay Scoring Engine, a Vantage Learning product.

Natural-language processing. Capability of computers to decode and encode meaningfully the language normally used by humans to communicate among themselves (not language formatted into some computer code).

Parser. Machine capability to translate a source code into an object code. In computer language processing this might entail identifying grammatical parts in natural texts.

Pearson Knowledge Technologies. Purveyor of automated essay-assessment applications including the Intelligent Essay Assessor and Summary Street, formerly known as Knowledge Analysis Technologies; part of Pearson Education.

Reliability. Degree to which a test, repeated again under similar conditions, produces the same outcome. Different components of a test have different reliabilities. *Writer reliability* is how closely repeated performances of a student on a test match the previous performances of the student. *Rater reliability* is how consistent an examiner is on scoring or rating a test. *Interrater reliability* is the degree to which one rater matches the score or rate of another rater, or of a group of raters, on the same test performance.

SAT. Test of academic knowledge often used in college admissions decisions, originally standing for "Scholastic Aptitude Test," then changed to "Scholastic Achievement Test," then to "Scholastic Assessment Test," and now, according to the College Board, not standing for anything.

Spell-checker. Computer program, often a part of word-processing software, that compares input words against an internal dictionary and flags mismatches.

Summary Street. Online essay-scoring and feedback system based on latent semantic analysis, purveyed by Pearson Knowledge Technologies.

Text mining. Capability of computers automatically to extract information from text, usually by detecting patterns—morphological, lexical, or syntactic—in large databases.

Validity. How well a test functions as a test. There are many kinds of validity, all expressed as a relative degree. *Concurrent validity* is the degree to which a test correlates with a different test purporting to measure the same ability. *Construct validity* is the degree to which parts of the test further the goal of the test—perhaps how well one half of the test integrates the other half, or how well one item avoids merely duplicating another item. *Criterion-related validity* judges a test by comparing its outcomes with a comparable test. *Face validity* is the functionality of a test as judged by experts. *Instructional validity* is the degree to which a test serves the curriculum in which it functions. *Predictive validity* is the degree of accuracy with which the test predicts some future performance of the test taker, perhaps course grade or teacher-judged writing ability.

Vantage Learning. Vantage Laboratories division that programs Web-based tools for writing assessment and feedback, developer and purveyor of the IntelliMetric Essay Scoring Engine.

Washback. Effects of a test or a testing system upon instruction.

WebCT. Computer support system for educators, including chat, e-mail, exam-marking, and grade-book features, marketed by WebCT, Inc.

WritePlacer Plus. Writing-assessment portion of ACCUPLACER, based on the IntelliMetric Essay Scoring Engine.

NOTES

CHAPTER 1 (MCALLISTER AND WHITE)

1. While the term "automated-essay scoring" (AES) is also frequently used, we prefer "computer-assisted writing assessment" because it more accurately reflects the current (and previous) state of this discipline. Virtually none of the work in computer-assisted writing assessment is automatic to the point of being autonomous yet, but rather requires numerous human-computer interactions; thus, computers are *assisting* in the partially automated writing-assessment process. It is also worth noting that "automation" does not necessarily involve computers. For example, Henry Ford and Elihu Root—Samuel Colt's lead engineer—both developed highly automated production systems long before the development of the computer.

2. A notable example of such articulate writing teachers are those who wrote the official position statement on computer-assisted writing assessment for the Conference on College Composition and Communication (2004):

    > Because all writing is social, all writing should have human readers, regardless of the purpose of the writing. Assessment of writing that is scored by human readers can take time; machine-reading of placement writing gives a quick, almost instantaneous scoring and thus helps provide the kind of quick assessment that helps facilitate college orientation and registration procedures as well as exit assessments.
    >
    > The speed of machine-scoring is offset by a number of disadvantages. Writing-to-a-machine violates the essentially social nature of writing: we write to others for social purposes. If a student's first writing experience at an institution is writing to a machine, for instance, this sends a message: writing at this institution is not valued as human communication—and this in turn reduces the validity of the assessment. Further, since we can not know the criteria by which the computer scores the writing, we can not know whether particular kinds of bias may have been built into the scoring. And finally, if high schools see themselves as preparing students for college writing, and if college writing becomes to any degree machine-scored, high schools will begin to prepare their students to write for machines.
    >
    > We understand that machine-scoring programs are under consideration not just for the scoring of placement tests, but for responding to student writing in writing centers and as exit tests. We oppose the use of machine-scored writing in the assessment of writing. (798)

3. Ellis Page (2003) proposes a somewhat more broad set of categories into which critics of computer-assisted writing assessment fall: humanist (only humans can judge what humans have written); defensive (the testing environment is too complex for a computer to assess it correctly); and construct (computers can't accurately identify all the "important" variables that determine "good" writing) (51–52).

4. There are many examples of pre computer age stylistic analyses. See, for example, Charles Bally's *Traité de stylistique française* (1909), Caroline Spurgeon's *Shakespeare's Imagery and What it Tells Us* (1935), and Wolfgang Clemen's *Development of Shakespeare's Imagery* (1977). Wainer (2000) cites perhaps two of the most ancient

examples, one from around 2200 BCE, when a Chinese emperor implemented official testing procedures for his officials in a variety of disciplines including writing, and the second taken from the Hebrew Bible (Judges 12:4–6), in which people in a fleeing crowd were asked to say the word *shibboleth*; those who mispronounced it were suspected to be Ephraimites—a group prohibited from leaving—and were punished very harshly indeed (2).

5. Vantage Learning, the maker of IntelliMetric, includes this information on its Web site (2005a): "We take pride in our ability to develop and implement high-quality, large-scale online assessment programs. . . . Vantage Commercial's Language Recognizer™ uses natural language parsers to index documents in multiple languages, while our rule compilers parse the very specific rule specification languages used in our rule bases."

6. For refinements in Sager's work see *Foundational Issues in Natural Language Processing*, edited by Sells, Shieber, and Wasow (1991); *The Core Language Engine*, edited by Alshawi (1992); and *Machine Learning of Natural Language*, edited by Powers and Turk (1989).

7. Roy Davies (1989) recounts and expands upon Swanson's notion that "[k]nowledge can be created by drawing inferences from what is already known," for example, in published articles and books.

8. After Knowledge Analysis Technologies was purchased by Pearson Education, Landauer was named to his current position of executive vice president of Pearson Knowledge Technologies.

CHAPTER 2 (ERICSSON)

1. Although a foray into the meaning of *wisdom* is tempting here, I will resist the temptation and leave it to readers to ponder what Elliot might consider "wisdom" and how a computer program might attain or "internalize" that noble trait.

2. Their claim that "writing teachers are critical to the development of the technology because they inform us how automated essay evaluations can be most beneficial to students" (xv) is disingenuous in that it assumes that writing teachers accept this technology as something that could be beneficial to students—many teachers disagree with this assumption. This claim also leaves out writing scholars—the people who study writing and composition.

3. For proof of this claim, see McGee, chapter 5 in this volume.

4. Speculation on what happens to student writing when this "partner" is a computer is well worth consideration, but beyond the scope of this chapter.

CHAPTER 4 (HASWELL)

1. According to Dr. Nancy Drew's Web site, the Triplet Ticket proposes to make life easier for "today's over-burdened teachers." The promo repeats three classic warrants for machine scoring of student essays: eliminate human reader bias, reduce paper load, and provide immediate feedback. Next to a photograph filled with nothing but stacked essays is this text: "Assigning electronically graded essays as an instructional alternative counteracts the tendency for teachers to stop giving written essays because of grading overload" (Drew 2004). When I e-mailed her (August 2004), pointing out that her stated criteria for rating essays—spelling, sentence length, and essay length—could be calculated with count and find functions of any word-processing program, she answered that the statement was a mistake of her Web page writer, that there were other criteria, and that she could not divulge them because of a pending patent.

2. In 1985, Quintilian Analysis required the student or the teacher to enter the essay via line editing (no word wrap) and to insert special coding characters marking end of paragraph and parts of speech. The output included gentle advice worthy of Mr. Chips: "Your sentences run to the short side, typical of popular journalism

or writing for audiences unwilling to cope with longer sentence constructions. Are you using such short sentences for some particular effect? Are you trying to outdo Hemingway?" It sold for $995. The author, Winston Weathers, is better known for his theory and pedagogy of alternative styles.

3. At this point in reading my essay my daughter Elizabeth, a plant biologist, had had enough, commenting: "Familiarity also breeds efficiency. No scientist wants or needs to test every claim that is published by others; trust in the work of others is required for scientific advances." Agreed—and a truth that applies to all labor, not just scientific, including the labor of writing teachers. So the issue is not just what's the efficiency, but whom do you trust and when do you question. The example of *Arabidopsis* is my own, by the way, not Latour's, whose analysis of many other black boxes is hard to beat (21–62).

4. Other programs achieve similar rates. IntelliMetric's performance is exact agreement 57 percent of the time, adjacent agreement 41 percent (Elliott 2003). That's a very profitable 2 percent third-reading rate with the usual definition of "agreement," and a costly 43 percent third-reading rate with an exact agreement definition. In selling the software today, while the standard magic formula is "the machine agrees with human raters as well as human raters agree with each other," some promoters go further. IntelliMetric, according to Scott Elliot, "will typically outperform human scorers" (75), and Ellis Page makes the same claim for Project Essay Grade (Page and Petersen 1995). They can say that because their machine scores correlate better with the *mean* score of a group of raters than any one of the rater's scores do with that average. They don't say what is so good about an average score. Another black box.

5. GIGO: garbage in, garbage out. Again, in 1966 Arthur Daigon got it right, or almost right. After his prediction that computer grading would first be used in "large scale testing of composition," he shrewdly added that this "would merely require simulation of the single evaluative end product of enlightened human judgment. Is the composition *unacceptable, fair, good,* or *excellent?*" (47). The question is whether reducing a piece of writing to a "single evaluative end product" (i.e., rate), with a discrimination no more informative than 1, 2, 3, and 4, constitutes human judgment that one can call "enlightened."

6. "Pitiful" is not an exaggeration. Technically speaking, holistic score explains around 9 percent of the total variance of the target criterion. That's an average of many studies (for a review, see McKendy 1992). Educational Testing Service's own researchers have improved this predictive power by creating optimal conditions, and then only minimally. The best Breland et al. (1987) could achieve was 33 percent on essays written at home on announced topics. In the customary short, impromptu, sit-down conditions of Educational Testing Service testing, Brent Bridgeman (1991), another Educational Testing Service researcher, found that a holistically scored essay added zero to a prediction of freshman grades, a prediction formula combining high school GPA, SAT scores, and a multiple-choice test of writing-skill knowledge. For Educational Testing Service this is truly being hoist by your own petard. The higher Educational Testing Service achieves a correlation with machine scores and human holistic scores, the less grounds—by their own research—they have to argue that machine scores should serve for placement. And what's true of Educational Testing Service is equally true of the other automatic rating enterprises. It's no surprise that Shermis and Burstein's *Automated Essay Scoring* (2003), that book-length argument for machine scoring from the industry side, reports not one completed study of the *instructional* validity of machine scores. On the crucial distinction between old-fashioned test validity (to which commercial validation of machine scoring sticks) and current contextual or instructional or decision validity, see Williamson 2004.

7. The art of validating one poor method of writing assessment by equating it with another poor method has been long practiced on the commercial side. For a typical example, see Weiss and Jackson's conclusion to their College Board study (1983)

that found an indirect measurement of writing proficiency, the Descriptive Tests of Language Skills, predicting college writing-course performance (final grade and post-essay) as badly as did a pre-essay. The predictive coefficient for all was terrible, around .4, but they still say, "In fact, each of the Descriptive Tests of Language Skills scores was found to predict posttest essay scores about as well as pretest essay scores did and somewhat better than self-reported high school English grades did. Thus, these results lend support to the use of the Descriptive Tests of Language Skills as an aid in making decisions about the placement of students in introductory level college composition courses" (8). On the instructional side, the rationale that validates a new computer-aided method of instruction because it is no worse than a previous computerless method is standard in defense of online distance-learning courses. See Russell 1999.

CHAPTER 5 (MCGEE)

1. This and subsequent quotations were taken from the Knowledge Analysis Technologies Web site in April 2001. The site has since undergone a major revision, and while some of the promotional copy from the earlier version persists unchanged, the seemingly hyperbolic claims about understanding "the meaning of written essays" no longer appear.

2. In a 2002 memo to the provost requesting funds to administer the test, an economics professor asserted that the "ETS test is a cheap and effective way to get reliable third-party assessments of our students' writing skills" (Vandegrift).

3. In his "Apologia for the Timed Impromptu," Edward White (1995) concedes many weaknesses of timed impromptus and lists the kinds of advanced composing skills that short impromptu essay tests are "unlikely . . . [to] provide us with much useful information about" (34). Consequently, invoking sophisticated text-analytical approaches to the scoring of such essays seems like analytical overkill.

4. That belief was later ratified when I had an opportunity to compare the scores Criterion awarded to the essays by students whose "diagnostic essays" I had already scored holistically. There was one malfunction, one higher than expected, one lower than expected, and the remaining thirty-three matched very closely with the scores I had awarded.

5. In a 1950 paper, Alan Turing proposed a test of a computer's ability to produce humanlike conversation, asserting that a machine that could pass such a test deserved to be called intelligent. One source describes the test as follows: "a human judge engages in a natural language conversation with two other parties, one a human and the other a machine; if the judge cannot reliably tell which is which, then the machine is said to pass the test" ("The Turing Test" 2005)

6. Cynics may find something distasteful in the testing corporations' assertion that a fair assessment of their machines depends upon students having made a "good faith effort " and suggest that students attempting to psyche out a scoring machine did not initiate the cycle of bad faith.

7. My understanding of cohesion is informed largely by Joseph Williams's *Style: Ten Lessons in Clarity and Grace* (2000). Having used that text on multiple occasions, I found his treatment of the related principles of cohesion and coherence particularly useful when teaching college students who crafted decent sentences but didn't do enough to ease the cognitive burden on readers attempting to make meaning of new information.

8. The original essay included multiple references to Huey Long, whose name I considered reversing to "Huey Short," but decided, instead, to revise it to Huey Newton.

CHAPTER 6 (JONES)

1. The relationships between ACCUPLACER, WritePlacer *Plus*, Vantage Learning, and IntelliMetric can be confusing. ACCUPLACER is the company that

purveys online placement testing. WritePlacer *Plus* is the essay test portion within ACCUPLACER. It uses the technology called IntelliMetric, created by the Vantage Learning Company.

2.   All student names are pseudonyms.

3.   Fifty-six essays from 2004 were chosen to represent students who had the widest possible range of sentence skills and reading scores. Eight-two essays from 2002 were random in that I just picked essays from the first ten students in an alphabetized list of students within each score level. These two batches comprise the "more or less randomly picked essays." Another eleven essays had already been identified as potentially anomalous by Nancy Enright and me.

4.   All analyses were significant at the $p < .001$ level, meaning that the odds of this finding having resulted from a random distribution are less than one in a thousand.

5.   It may be that the capacity of IntelliMetric to distinguish more subtle aspects of writing has improved some since 2002. The variance in essay scores explained by length alone was 90 percent in 2002. In 2003, the percentage was 82 percent, while in 2004 the percentage was 84 percent.

CHAPTER 7 (HERRINGTON AND MORAN)

1.   In addition to products for writing placement at college entry level, the products include programs for high-stakes statewide assessment: for example, Vantage Technologies lists the Oregon Department of Education as a client for its Technology Enhanced Student Assessment, a "high-stakes statewide assessment system," also the Pennsylvania Department of Education for its statewide assessment system, and a product for CTB/McGraw Hill for "direct assessment for use by K–12 institutions" (Vantage Learning 2005a). The capability of standardized assessment and record keeping to track that assessment become bases for marketing products for use in the classroom for assessing writing, tracking performance, and even providing feedback on writing: for example, Vantage Learning's Learning Access, a comprehensive program marketed as helping K–9 teachers "meet the challenges of No Child Left Behind," MY Access! an "Online Writing Development Tool," developed in partnership with the Massachusetts Department of Education and designed for classroom use, and ETS's Criterion, for "online writing evaluation in college classrooms." Another type of product, in which KAT has taken the lead, is aimed at content assessment, using the Intelligent Essay Assessor program. KAT's Web site lists such clients as the U.S. Air Force Research Laboratories for a Career Map Occupational Analysis Program; Prentice Hall for a companion Web site to the text *Keys to Success*; the University of Colorado for the Colorado Literacy Tutor, designed for "individualized, computer-aided reading instruction"; and Florida Gulf Coast University for an automated essay-assessment program for a large online course, Understanding the Visual and Performing Arts.

CHAPTER 14 (ROTHERMEL)

1.   This promotional brochure has been replaced by the online Product Sheet (Vantage Learning 2004d).

REFERENCES

ACT. 2001. *COMPASS E-Write Direct Writing Assessment from ACT.* Iowa City, IA: ACT.
———. 2003. COMPASS/ESL. In *E-Write Reference Manual*, 3:2. Iowa City, IA: ACT.
———. 2005. COMPASS/E-Write. www.act.org/e-write/scoring.html.

Alshawi, Hiyan, ed. 1992. *The Core Language Engine.* Cambridge: MIT Press.

Anson, Chris M. 1984. *Composition and Communicative Intention: Exploring the Dimensions of Purpose in College Writing.* Ph.D. Dissertation, Indiana University.

Anson, Chris M., Leonhard E. Bernold, Cathy Crossland, Joni Spurlin, Molly McDemott, and Stacy Weiss. 2003. Empowerment to Learn in Engineering: Preparation for an Urgently-Needed Paradigm Shift. *Global Journal of Engineering Education* 7 (2): 145–155.

Attali, Yigal, and Jill Burstein. 2004. Automated Essay Scoring with e-rater v.2.0. Paper presented at the International Association for Educational Assessment, Philadelphia, PA.

Baker, Tracy, and Peggy Jolly. 1999. The "Hard Evidence": Documenting the Effectiveness of a Basic Writing Program. *Journal of Basic Writing* 18 (1): 27–39.

Bally, Charles. 1909. *Traité de stylistique française.* Stuttgart: Winter.

Baron, Dennis. 1998. When Professors Get A's and Machines Get F's. *Chronicle of Higher Education*, November 20, A56.

Barritt, Loren, Patricia T. Stock, and Francelia Clark. 1986. Researching Practice: Evaluating Placement Essays. *College Composition and Communication* 37 (3): 315–327.

Bartholomae, Diavid 1985. Inventing the University. In *When a Writer Can't Write*, edited by Mike Rose, 134–165. New York: Guilford.

Bass, Elisabeth. 2000. Writing Program Administrators Listserve, December 7.

Bazerman, Charles. 1981. What Written Knowledge Does: Three Examples of Academic Discourse. *Philosophy of the Social Sciences* 11:361–387.

Beach, Richard. 1993. *A Teacher's Introduction to Reader-Response Theories.* Urbana, IL: NCTE.

Bean, John C. 1996. *Engaging Ideas: The Professor's Guide to Integrating Writing, Critical Thinking, and Active Learning in the Classroom.* San Francisco: Jossey-Bass.

Beason, Larry. 2000. Composition as Service: Implications of Utilitarian, Duties, and Care Ethics. In *The Ethics of Writing Instruction: Issues in Theory and Practice*, edited by Michael Pemberton, 105–137. Stamford, CT: Ablex.

Bedore, Pamela, and Deborah F. Rossen-Knill. 2004. Informed Self-Placement: Is Choice Offered a Choice Received? *Writing Program Administration* 28 (1–2): 55–78.

Belanoff, Patricia 1991. The Myths of Assessment. *Journal of Basic Writing* 10:54–66.

Belanoff, Patricia, and Peter Elbow. 1986. Using Portfolios to Increase Collaboration and Community in a Writing Program. *Journal of Writing Program Administrators* 9 (3): 27–39.

Bennett, Randy E., and William C. Ward, eds. 1993. *Construction Versus Choice in Cognition Measurement: Issues in Constructed Response, Performance Testing, and Portfolio Assessment.* Hillsdale, NJ: Lawrence Erlbaum.

Bereiter, Carl. 2003. Foreword to Shermis and Burstein 2003, vii x.

Berlin, James. A. 1996. *Rhetorics, Poetics, and Cultures: Refiguring College English Studies.* Urbana, IL: NCTE.

Berthoff, Ann E. 1981. *The Making of Meaning: Metaphors, Models, and Maxims for Writing Teachers.* Portsmouth, NH: Boynton/Cook Heinemann.

———. 1988. Democratic Practice, Pragmatic Vistas. *Reader* 20:40–47.

Beshur, Alison. 2004. Software Grades Essays: From One Teacher to Others, a Program to Make Life Easier. *Corpus Christi Caller-Times,* June 2, C1, C10.

Bishop, Robert L. 1974. Computing in the Teaching of Journalistic Skills. *On-Line* 3 (3): 5–12.

Bizell, Patricia, and Bruce Herzberg. 1990. *The Rhetorical Tradition: Readings form Classical Times to the Present.* New York: Bedford/St. Martins.

Black, John B., Deanna Wilkes-Gibbs, and Raymond W. Gibbs, Jr. 1982. What Writers Need to Know That They Don't Know They Need to Know. In *What Writers Know: The Language, Process, and Structure of Written Discourse,* edited by Martin Nystrand, 325–343. New York: Academic.

Bloom, Bob. 2003. *What We Really Value: Beyond Rubrics in Teaching and Assessing Writing.* Logan, UT: Utah State University Press.

Boden, Margaret. 1977. *Artificial Intelligence and Natural Man.* New York: Basic Books.

Borja, Rhea R. 2003. Educators Go High-Tech to Check Essay Exams. *USA Today,* January 16. www.usatoday.com/tech/news/2003-01-15-essay-grader_x.htm (accessed May 8, 2005).

Boylan, Hunter R. 1999. Demograpics, Outcomes, and Activities. *Journal of Developmental Education* 23 (2): 2–8.

Boylan, Hunter R., Barbara Bonham, Charles Claxton, and Leonard B. Bliss. 1992. The State of the Art in Developmental Education: Report of a National Study. Paper presented at the First National Conference on Research in Developmental Education, Charlotte, NC.

Breland, Hunter M. 1996. Computer-Assisted Writing Assessment: The Politics of Science versus the Humanities. In *Assessment of Writing: Politics, Policies, Practices,* edited by Edward M. White, William D. Lutz, and Sandra Kamusikiri, 249–256. New York: MLA.

Breland, Hunter M., Roberta Camp, Robert J. Jones, Margaret M. Morris, and Donald A. Rock. 1987. *Assessing Writing Skill.* ETS Research Monograph No. 11. ERIC Document Reproduction Service, ED 286 920.

Bridgeman, Brent. 1991. Essays and Multiple-Choice Tests as Predictors of College Freshmen GPA. *Research in Higher Education* 32 (3): 319–332.

Bridwell-Bowles, Lillian. 1989. Designing Research on Computer-Assisted Writing. *Computers and Composition* 7 (1): 81–94.

Britton, James, Tony Burgess, Nancy Martin, Andrew McLeod, and Harold Rosen. 1975. *The Development of Writing Abilities (11–18).* London: Macmillan.

Broad, Bob. 2003. *What We Really Value: Beyond Rubrics in Teaching and Assessing Writing.* Logan: Utah State University Press.

Burns, Hugh. 1987. Computers and Composition. In *Teaching Composition: Twelve Bibliographical Essays,* edited by Gary Tate, 378–400. Fort Worth: Texas Christian University Press.

Burstein, Jill. 2003. The *E-rater* Scoring Engine: Automated Essay Scoring with Natural Language Processing. In Shermis and Burstein 2003, 113–121.

Burstein, Jill, and Daniel Marcu, 2004. A Machine Learning Approach for Identification of Thesis and Conclusion Statements in Student Essays. *Computers and the Humanities* 37 (4): 455–467.

Byerly, Gayle A. 1978. CAI in College English. *Computers and the Humanities* 12 (3): 281–285.

Callahan, Diana, Charles Moran, Mary-Ann DeVita Palmieri, and Bruce Penniman. 2002. Crossing Levels: The Dynamics of K–16 Teachers' Collaboration. In *Teaching Writing in High School and College: Conversations and Collaborations,* edited by Thomas C. Thompson, 203–213. Urbana, IL: NCTE.

Campbell, R. Sherlock, and James W. Pennebaker. 2003. The Secret Life of Pronouns: Flexibility in Writing Style and Physical Health. *Psychological Science* 14:60–65.

Cannon, Walter W. 1981. *Terrors and Affectations: Students' Perceptions of the Writing Process.* ERIC Document Reproduction Service, ED 199 720.

Carlson, Sybil, and Brent Bridgeman. 1986. Testing ESL Student Writers. In *Writing Assessment: Issues and Strategies*, edited by Karen L. Greenberg, Harvey S. Wiener, and Richard A. Donovan, 126–152. New York: Longman.

Carrell, Patricia L., and Laura Monroe. 1993. Learning Styles and Composition. *Modern Language Journal* 77:148–62.

Centra, John A. 1993. *Reflective Faculty Evaluation: Enhancing, Teaching, and Determining Faculty Effectiveness*. San Francisco: Jossey-Bass.

Chase, Richard. 1957. *The American Novel and Its Tradition*. Baltimore: Johns Hopkins University Press.

Cheville, Julie. 2004. Automated Scoring Technologies and the Rising Influence of Error. *English Journal* 93 (4): 47–52.

Chodorow, Martin, and Jill Burstein. 2004. *Beyond Essay Length: Evaluating e-rater's Performance on TOEFL Essays*. Princeton, NJ: Educational Testing Service.

Choueka, Yaacov, and Serge Lusignan. 1985. Disambiguation by Short Contexts. *Computers and the Humanities* 19 (3): 147–157.

Clemen, Wolfgang. 1977. *Development of Shakespeare's Imagery*. Oxford: Routledge.

College Board. 2005. Fact sheet: ACCUPLACER. www.collegeboard.com/prod_downloads/highered/apr/ACCUPLACER.pdf.

College Entrance Examination Board. 2001. *ACCUPLACER: WritePlacer* Plus [brochure]. New York: College Board.

Condon, William, and Wayne Butler. 1997. *Writing the Information Superhighway*. Boston: Allyn and Bacon.

Condon, William, and Liz Hamp-Lyons. 1994. Maintaining a Portfolio-Based Writing Assessment: Research That Informs Program Development. In *New Directions in Portfolio Assessment*, edited by Donald A. Daiker and Laurel Black, 277–285. New York: Heinemann-Boynton/Cook.

Condon, William, and Diane Kelly-Riley. 2004. Assessing and Teaching What We Value: The Relationship between College-Level Writing and Critical Thinking Abilities. *Assessing Writing* 9 (1): 56–75.

Conference on College Composition and Communication. 1995. Writing Assessment: A Position Statement. *College Composition and Communication* 46 (3): 430–437.

Conference on College Composition and Communication Committee (Kathleen Yancey, Chair). 2004. Position Statement on Teaching, Learning, and Assessing Writing in Digital Environments. *College Composition and Communication* 55 (4): 785–789. www.ncte.org/groups/cccc/positions/115775.htm.

Connors, Robert J. 1997. *Composition-Rhetoric: Backgrounds, Theory, and Pedagogy*. Pittsburgh: University of Pittsburgh Press.

Cooper, Charles R. 1983. Procedures for Describing Written Texts. In *Research on Writing: Principles and Methods*, edited by Peter Mosenthal, Charles Tamor, and Sean A. Walmsley, 287–313. New York: Longman.

Cope, Bill, and Mary Kalantzis. 2000. *Multiliteracies: Literacy Learning and the Design of Social Futures*. New York: Routledge.

Council of Writing Program Administrators. 2000. WPA Outcomes Statement for First-Year Composition. www.ilstu.edu/~ddhesse/wpa/positions/outcomes.htm (accessed May 8, 2005).

Cowan, Ruth Schwartz. 1983. *More Work for Mother: The Ironies of Household Technology from the Open Hearth to the Microwave*. New York: Basic Books.

Cronbach, Lee J. 1988. Five Perspectives on Validity Argument. In *Test Validity*, edited by Harold Wainer, 3–17. Hillsdale, NJ: Lawrence Erlbaum.

Crowley, Sharon. 1998. *Composition in the University: Historical and Polemical Essays*. Pittsburgh: University of Pittsburgh Press.

Cunningham, James M. 1983. *An Evaluation of English Placement Instruments for First Time Freshmen at Embry-Riddle Aeronautical University*. Ph.D. diss., Florida Atlantic University and University of Central Florida.

Daigon, Arthur. 1966. Computer Grading of English Composition. *English Journal* 55 (1): 46–52.

Davies, Roy. 1989. The Creation of New Knowledge by Information Retrieval and Classification. *Journal of Documentation* 45 (4): 273–301.

Deerwester, Scott, Susan T. Dumais, George W. Furnas, Thomas K. Landauer, and Richard Harshman. 1990. Indexing by Latent Semantic Analysis. *Journal of the American Society for Information Science* 41:391–407.

Dethier, Brock. 1983. In Defense of Subjective Grading. *North Carolina English Teachers* 40 (4): 3–6.

Diederich, Paul B. 1974. *Measuring Growth in English.* Urbana, IL: National Council of Teachers of English.

Dobrin, David N. 1985. *Limitations on the Use of Computers in Composition.* ERIC Document Reproduction Service, ED 261 395.

Doris, Bernardette. 1947. A Practical Proposal to Take the Drudgery out of the Teaching of Freshman Composition and to Restore to the Teacher His Pristine Pleasure in Teaching. *College English* 8 (7): 383–384.

Dorough, C. Dwight, Martin M. Shapiro, and Jeanette P. Morgan. [1963?]. *Automated Instruction of Remedial English.* Vol. 1. U.S. Department of Health, Education, and Welfare Title VII Project No. 551. Houston: University of Houston.

Drechsel, Joanne. 1999. Writing into Silence: Losing Voice with Writing Assessment Technology. *Teaching English in the Two Year College,* 26:380–387.

Dressman, Michael R. 1986–1987. The Junior-Level Writing Proficiency Examination at the University of Houston Downtown. *CEA Forum* 16 (4) 17 (1): 14–15.

Drew, Nancy. 2004. The Triplet Ticket. www.tripletticket.com/wiki/TT/PurchsingInformation (accessed August 2004).

Educational Testing Service. 2004. Criterion. www.ets.org/criterion/.

Elliot, Scott 2003. IntelliMetric™: From Here to Validity. In Shermis and Burstein 2003, 71–86.

Emig, Janet. 1971. *The Composing Processes of Twelfth Graders.* Urbana, IL: NCTE.

———. 1977. Writing as a Mode of Learning. *College Composition and Communication* 28:122–128.

Ezarik, Melissa 2004. Vantage Learning. *District Administration* 40 (February): 72.

Fassler [Walvoord], Barbara E. 1978. The Interdepartmental Composition Program at Central College. In *Options for the Teaching of English: Freshman Composition,* edited by Jasper Neel, 84–89. New York: MLA.

Feenberg, Andrew. 1991. *Critical Theory of Technology.* New York: Oxford University Press.

———. 1999. *Questioning Technology.* New York: Routledge.

Finn, Patrick J. 1977. Computer-Aided Description of Mature Word Choices in Writing, In *Evaluating Writing: Describing, Measuring, Judging,* edited by Charles R. Cooper and Lee Odell, 69–90. Urbana, IL: NCTE.

Florida Gulf Coast University. 2005. Pew Grant in Course Redesign. knowledge-technologies.com/fgcu.shtml.

Foltz, Peter. 1990. Using Latent Semantic Indexing for Information Filtering. In *Proceedings of the Conference on Office Information Systems,* edited by R. B. Allen, 40–47. New York: ACM.

———. 1998. Quantitative Approaches to Semantic Knowledge Representations. *Discourse Processes* 25 (2–3): 127–130.

Foltz, Peter W., M. A. Britt, and C. A. Perfetti. 1994. Where Did You Learn That? Matching Student Essays to the Texts They Have Used. Paper presented at the Fourth Annual Conference of the Society for Text and Discourse, Washington DC.

Foltz, Peter W., Walter Kintsch, and Thomas K. Landauer. 1993. An Analysis of Textual Coherence Using Latent Semantic Indexing. Paper presented at the Third Annual Conference of the Society for Text and Discourse. Boulder, CO.

Foster-Smith, M. Cassandra. 1980. Efficiency Tools In the Speeches of Martin Luther King, Jr. In *8th International Conference on Computational Linguistics, Proceedings of COLING '80,* 167–173. Yorktown Heights, NY: Association for Computational Linguistics.

Fowles, Mary E. 2001. Challenging "E-rater": Efforts to Refine Computerized Essay Scoring. Paper presented at the annual meeting of the Conference on College Composition and Communication, Denver.

Freedman, Sarah Warshauer. 1984. The Registers of Student and Professional Expository Writing: Influences on Teachers' Responses. In *New Directions in Composition Research*, edited by Richard Beach and Lillian Bridwell, 334–347. New York: Guilford.

Fulwiler, Toby. 1984. How Well Does Writing across the Curriculum Work? *College English* 46 (2): 113–125.

Gage, John T. 1978. Conflicting Assumptions about Intention in Teaching Reading and Composition. *College English* 40 (3): 255–263.

Glau, Gregory R. 1996. The "Stretch Program": Arizona State University's New Model of University-Level Basic Writing Instruction. *Writing Program Administration* 20 (1–2): 79–91.

Hackman, Judith D., and Paula Johnson. 1981. Using Standardized Test Scores for Placement in College English Courses: A New Look at an Old Problem. *Research in the Teaching of English* 15 (3): 275–279.

Hamp-Lyons, Liz, and William Condon. 1993. Questioning Assumptions about Portfolio-Based Assessment. *College Composition and Communication* 44 (2): 176–190.

Harrington, Susanmarie, Rita Malencyzk, Irv Peckham, Keith Rhodes, and Kathleen Blake Yancey. 2001. WPA Outcomes Statement for First-Year Composition. *College English* 63 (3): 321–325.

Haswell, Richard H. 1983. Minimal Marking. *College English* 45 (6): 600–604.

———. 2001. The Two-Tiered Rating System: The Need for Ongoing Change. In *Beyond Outcomes: Assessment and Instruction within a University*, edited by Richard H. Haswell, 39–52. Westport, CT: Ablex.

———. 2002. Researching Teacher Evaluation of ESL Writing via Prototype Theory. Paper presented at the Third Second-Language Writing Conference, Purdue University, Purdue, IN.

Hawisher, Gail E., Cynthia I. Selfe, Charles Moran, and Paul LeBlanc. 1996. *Computers and the Teaching of Writing in American Higher Education, 1979–1994: A History*. Norwood, NJ: Ablex.

Henry, Alex, and Robert L. Roseberry. 1999. Raising Awareness of the Generic Structure and Linguistic Features of Essay Introduction. *Language Awareness* 8 (3): 190–200.

Herrington, Anne, and Charles Moran. 2001. What Happens When Machines Read Our Students' Writing? *College English* 63 (4): 480–499.

High Schools Plug into Online Writing Programs. 2003. *District Administration* 39 (November): 11.

Hoyt, Jeff E. 1998. Factors Affecting Student Retention at UVSC. Office of Institutional Research and Management Studies, Utah Valley State College at Orem. www.uvsc.edu/ir/research.html.

Huot, Brian. 1996. Computers and Assessment: Understanding Two Technologies. *Computers and Composition* 13 (2): 231–243.

———. 2002. *(Re)Articulating Writing Assessment for Teaching and Learning*. Logan: Utah State University Press.

Hutchinson, Mary Anne. 1993. *The Composition Teacher as Drudge: The Pitfalls and Perils of Linking across the Disciplines*. ERIC Document Reproduction Service, ED 359 533.

Jones, Brett. 1999. Computer-Rated Essays in the English Composition Classroom. *Journal of Educational Computing Research* 20 (2): 169–187.

Jones, Ed. 2002. Apparent Anomalies in ACCUPLACER Essay Scoring. Paper presented at the fall meeting of the New Jersey Testing Administrators Special Interest Group, Rutgers, NJ.

Joyce, James. 1982. UNIX Aids for Composition Courses. In *Computing in the Humanities*, edited by Richard W. Bailey, 33–38. Amsterdam: North-Holland.

Kaufer, David, Cheryl Geisler, Suguru Ishizaki, and Pantelis Vlachos. 2005. Textual Genre Analysis and Identification. In *Ambient Intelligence for Scientific Discovery*, edited by Yang Cai, 129–151. New York: Springer.

Kaufer, David, Cheryl Geisler, Pantelis Vlachos, and Suguru Ishizaki. In press. Mining Textual Knowledge for Writing Education and Research: The DocuScope Project.

Keith, Timothy Z. 2003. Validity of Automated Essay Scoring Systems. In. Shermis and Burstein 2003, 147–167.

Kemp, Fred. 1992. Who Programmed This? Examining the Instructional Attitudes of Writing Support Software. *Computers and Composition* 10 (1): 9–24.

Kiefer, Kathleen. 1983. Testing Basic Writers' Proficiency: An Effective Model. Paper presented at the annual meeting of the Wyoming Conference on Freshman and Sophomore English, Laramie, WY.

Klein, Davina C. D., Gregory K. W. K. Chung, Ellen Osmundson, Howard E. Herl, and Harold F. O'Neil, Jr. 2001. *Examining the Validity of Knowledge Mapping as a Measure of Elementary Students' Scientific Understanding.* CSE Technical Report No. 557. Los Angeles: University of California, National Center for Research on Evaluation, Standards, and Student Testing (CRESST).

Knowledge Analysis Technologies. 2001. Home page. www.knowledge-technologies.com (accessed April 15, 2001).

———. 2003. *Intelligent Essay Assessor.* www.k-a-t.com/ (accessed January 2004).

———. 2004a. Intelligent Essay Assessor. Demo. www. knowledge-technologies.com/ IEAdemo.shtml (accessed September 1, 2004).

———. 2004b. A World Leader in Automated Essay Assessment and Text Analysis. www. k-a-t.com/.

Koether, Mary, and Esther Coke. 1973. *A Scheme for Text Analysis Using FORTRAN.* ERIC Document Reproduction Service, ED 074 152.

Kohut, Gary F., and Kevin J. Gorman. 1995. The Effectiveness of Leading Grammar/Style Software Packages in Analyzing Business Students' Writing. *Journal of Business and Technical Communication* 9 (3): 341–361.

Kosinski, Wanda. 2003. *Placement Tests and Cut Scores.* Ramapo: Ramapo College of New Jersey.

Kucera, Henry W. 1967. The Innocent Linguistic and the Unresentful Drudge. In *Computers in Humanistic Research: Readings and Perspectives*, edited by W. Nelson Francis, 153–159. Englewood Cliffs, NJ: Prentice-Hall.

Kukich, Karen. 2000. Beyond Automated Essay Scoring. *IEEE Intelligent Systems* 15 (5): 22–27. www.computer.org/intelligent/ex2000/pdf/x5022.pdf.

Kurzweil, Raymond. 1999. *The Age of Spiritual Machines: When Computers Exceed Human Intelligence.* New York: Viking.

Landauer, Thomas K. 2004. Pearson Education to Acquire Knowledge Analysis Technologies. Press release from Knowledge Analysis Technologies/Pearson Education, June 29, 2004. www.knowledge-technologies.com.

Landauer, Thomas K., Darrell Laham, and Peter W. Foltz. 2003. Automated Scoring and Annotation of Essays with the Intelligent Essay Assessor™. In Shermis and Burstein 2003, 87–112.

Landauer, Thomas K., Darrell Laham, Bob Rehder, and M. E. Schreiner. 1997. How Well Can Passage Meaning be Derived without Word Order? A Comparison of Latent Semantic Analysis and Humans. In *Proceedings of the 19th Annual Conference of the Cognitive Science Society*, edited by M, G. Shafto and P. Langley, 412–417. Mahwah, NJ: Lawrence Erlbaum.

Landow, George. 1992. "Ms. Austen's Submission." In *Hypertext: The Convergence of Contemporary Critical Theory and Technology.* Baltimore: Johns Hopkins University Press.

Lankshear, Colin, and Michele Knobel. 2003. *New Literacies: Changing Knowledge and Classroom Learning.* Buckingham, UK: Open University Press.

Larkey, Leah S., and W. Bruce Croft. 2003. A Text Categorization Approach to Automated Essay Grading. In Shermis and Burstein 2003, 55–70.

Latour, Bruno. 1987. *Science in Action: How to Follow Scientists and Engineers through Society.* Cambridge, MA: Harvard University Press.

Leacock, Claudia, and Martin Chodorow. 2003. Automated Grammatical Error Detection. In Shermis and Burstein 2003, 195–208.

Lemke, Jay. 1995. *Textual Politics: Discourse and Social Dynamics.* Bristol, PA: Taylor and Francis.

Leonhardy, Galen, and William Condon. 2001. Exploring the Difficult Cases: In the Cracks of Writing Assessment. In *Beyond Outcomes: Assessment and Instruction within a University,* edited by Richard H. Haswell, 65–80. Westport, CT: Ablex.

Lerner, Neal. 1998. Drill Pads, Teaching Machines, and Programmed Texts: Origins of Instructional Technology in Writing Centers. In *Wiring the Writing Center,* edited by Eric H. Hobson, 119–136. Logan: Utah State University Press.

Lugo, Angela. 2005. Personal e-mail, May 27.

Macrorie, Ken. 1969. Review of *The Analysis of Essays by Computer,* by Ellis B. Page and Dieter H. Paulus. *Research in the Teaching of English* 3 (2): 228–236.

Maid, Barry. 1996. The T-F Opposition in Writing Development. In *Most Excellent Differences: Essays on Using Type Theory in the Composition Classroom,* edited by Thomas C. Thompson, 35–46. Gainesville, FL: Center for Applications of Psychological Type.

Maik, Linda L., and Thomas A. Maik. 1987. Perceptions of Word Processing in Composition Classes: First-Year and Upper-Level Students Compared. *Computers and Composition* 4 (3): 7–16.

Maimon, Elaine P. 1981. *Writing in the Arts and Sciences.* Cambridge, MA: Winthrop.

Manzo, Kathleen Kennedy. 2003. Essay Grading Goes Digital. *Education Week on the Web,* May 8, 39–43. counts.edweek.org/sreports/tc03/article.cfm?slug=35essays.h22 (accessed May 8, 2005).

Markel, Mike. 1991. Criteria Development and the Myth of Objectivity. *Technical Writing Teacher* 18 (1): 37–48.

Markovic, Mihailo. 1984. *Dialectical Theory of Meaning.* Translated by David Rougé and Joan Coddington. New York: Springer. [Originally published Belgrad: Noit, 1961.]

Marling, William. 1984. Grading Essays on a Microcomputer. *College English* 46 (8): 797–810.

Matthews, Jay. 2004. Computers Weighing In on the Elements of Essay Programs Critique Structure, Not Ideas. *Washington Post,* August 1, A01.

Matzen, Richard N., Jr., and Jeff E. Hoyt. 2004. Basic Writing Placement with Holistically Scored Essays: Research Evidence. *Journal of Developmental Education* 28 (1): 2–4, 6, 8, 10, 12–13, 34.

McCollum, Kelly. 1998. How a Computer Program Learns to Grade Essays. *Chronicle of Higher Education,* September 4: A37 A38.

McDaniel, Ellen. 1985. A Bibliography of Text-Analysis and Writing-Instruction Software. *Computers and Composition* 2 (3): 8–9.

McGee, Tim, and Patricia Ericsson. 2002. The Politics of the Program: MS WORD as the Invisible Grammarian. *Computers and Composition* 19 (4): 453–470.

McGregor, Ellen N., and Lousi Attinasi, Jr. 1996. *Developmental Course-Taking and Subsequent Academic Performance at Pima Community College.* Tucson, AZ: Office of Institutional Research, Pima Community College at Tucson.

McKendy, Thomas. 1992. Locally Developed Writing Tests and the Validity of Holistic Scoring. *Research in the Teaching of English* 26 (2): 148–166.

Meehan, James. 1976. The Metanovel: Writing Stories by Computer. Ph.D. diss., Yale University, New Haven, CT.

Messick, Samuel. 1989. Validity. In *Educational Measurement,* edited by Robert L. Linn, 13–103. New York: American Council on Education and Macmillan.

Morgan, Bradford A. 1984. Evaluating Student Papers with a Word Processor. *Research in Word Processing Newsletter* 2 (6): 1–6.

Murphy, Suzanne. 2004. Personal e-mail, October 28.

Myers, Miles 2003. What Can Computers and AES Contribute to a K–12 Writing Program? In Shermis and Burstein 2003, 3–17.

Nancarrow, Paula Reed, Donal Ross, and Lillian Bridwell-Bowles. 1984. *Word Processors and the Writing Process: An Annotated Bibliography*. Westport, CT: Greenwood.

National Commission on Writing in America's Schools and Colleges. 2003. The Neglected "R": The Need for a Writing Revolution. New York: College Board.

National Language Software Registry. 2000.What Is the National Language Software Registry? January 11, 2000. registry.dfki.de.

National Writing Project and Carl Nagin. 2003. *Because Writing Matters: Improving Student Writing in Our Schools*. San Francisco: Jossey-Bass.

Newkirk, Thomas. 1984. Anatomy of a Breakthrough: Case Study of a College Freshman Writer. In *New Directions in Composition Research*, edited by Richard Beach and Lillian S. Bridwell, 131–148. New York: Guilford.

Nystrand, Martin. 1982. Rhetoric's "Audience" and Linguistic's "Speech Community": Implications for Understanding Writing, Reading, and Texts. In *What Writers Know: The Language, Process, and Structure of Written Discourse*, edited by Martin Nystrand, 1–28. New York: Academic.

Owen, David. 1985. *None of the Above: Behind the Myth of Scholastic Aptitude*. Boston: Houghton Mifflin.

Page, Ellis B. 1966. The Imminence of Grading Essays by Computer. *Phi Delta Kappan* 48:238–243.

———. 1968. Analyzing Student Essays by Computer. *International Review of Education* 14: 210–225.

———. 2003. Project Essay Grade: PEG. In Shermis and Burstein 2003, 43–54.

Page, Ellis B., and Dieter H. Paulus. 1968. *The Analysis of Essays by Computer*. Final Report of U.S. Office of Education Project No. 6-1318. Washington, D.C.: Department of Health, Education, and Welfare. ERIC Document Reproduction Service, ED 028 633.

Page, Ellis B., and Nancy S. Petersen. 1995. The Computer Moves into Essay Grading: Updating the Ancient Test. *Phi Delta Kappan* 76:561–565.

Palmer, John, Robert Williams, and Heinz Dreher. 2002. Automated Essay Grading System Applied to a First Year University Subject—How Can We Do It Better? Informing Science InSITE Conference Proceedings. proceedings.informingscience. org/IS2002Proceedings/papers/Palme026Autom.pdf.

Palomba, Catherine A., and Trudy W. Banta. 1999. *Assessment Essentials: Planning, Implementing, and Improving Assessment in Higher Education*. San Francisco: Jossey-Bass.

Pedersen, Elray L. 1989. The Effectiveness of Writer's Workbench and MacProof. *Computer-Assisted Composition Journal* 3 (2): 92–100.

Pennington, Martha C. 1993. Computer-Assisted Writing on a Principled Basis: The Case against Computer-Assisted Text Analysis for Non-proficient Writers. *Language and Education* 7 (1): 43–59.

Phelan, Greg. 2003. For Student Essayists, an Automated Grader. *New York Times,* September 4, G5, late edition.

Pianko, Sharon A. 1979. A Description of the Composing Processes of College Freshmen Writers. *Research in the Teaching of English* 13 (1): 5–22.

Plato. 1987. *Theaetetus*. Translated by Robin A. H. Waterfield. New York: Viking Penguin.

Potter, Rosanne G. 1991. Statistical Analysis of Literature: A Retrospective on *Computers and the Humanities*, 1966–1990. *Computers and the Humanities* 25:401–429.

Powers, Christopher, and David M. W. Turk, eds. 1989. *Machine Learning of Natural Language*. New York: Springer-Verlag.

Powers, Donald E., Jill C. Burstein, Martin Chodorow, Mary E. Fowles, and Karen Kukich. 2001. *Stumping E-rater: Challenging the Validity of Automated Essay Scoring*. Graduate Record Examination Board Professional Report No. 98-08bP. Princeton, NJ: Educational Testing Service.

———. 2002. Comparing the Validity of Automated and Human Scoring of Essays. *Journal of Educational Computing Research* 26 (4): 407–425.

Pratt, Mary Louise. 1977. *Toward a Speech-Act Theory of Literary Discourse.* Bloomington: Indiana University Press.

Raymond Walters College of the University of Cincinnati. 2002. *English Composition Placement.* Cincinnati: University of Cincinnati. www.uc.edu/EnglishPlacement/rwc_entryasp.

Reising, Robert W., and Benjamin J. Stewart. 1984. Grading and Evaluation. In *Research in Composition and Rhetoric: A Bibliographic Sourcebook,* edited by Michael G. Moran and Ronald F. Lunsford, 211–218. Westport, CT: Greenwood.

Reitman, Walter R. 1962. Computer Models of Psychological Processes and Some Implication for the Theory and Practice of Writing. In *Needed Research in the Teaching of English: Proceedings of a Project English Research Conference, May 5–7, 1962,* edited by Erwin R. Steinberg, 98–106. Washington, DC: U.S. Department of Health, Education, and Welfare.

Rice, Joseph A. 1977. The University Drags Its Feet over the Illiterate. In *Focus '77: 24th International Technical Communication Conference Proceedings,* edited by Norm Linsell, 188–190. Milwaukee: Ken Cook/Society for Technical Communication.

Richards, I. A. 1936. *The Philosophy of Rhetoric.* London: Oxford University Press.

Richards, I. A., and C. K. Ogden. 1923. *The Meaning of Meaning: A Study of the Influence of Language upon Thought and on the Science of Symbolism.* New York: Harcourt Brace.

Rickert, Hilary. 2002. Personal e-mail (June).

Rosenblatt, Louise. 1978. *The Reader, the Text, the Poem: The Transactional Theory of the Literary Work.* Carbondale: Southern Illinois University Press.

Roy, Emil. 1990. A Decision Support System for Improving First-Year Writing Courses. *Computer-Assisted Composition Journal* 4 (3): 79–86.

———. 1993. Computerized Scoring of Placement Exams: A Validation. *Journal of Basic Writing* 12 (2): 41–54.

Royer, Daniel J., and Roger Gilles. 1998. Directed Self-Placement: An Attitude of Orientation. *College Composition and Communication* 50 (1): 54–70.

———. 2002. Placement Issues. In *The Writing Program Administrator's Resource,* edited by Stuart C. Brown, Theresa Enos, and Catherine Chaput, 263–274. Mahwah, NJ: Lawrence Erlbaum.

Rudner, Lawrence, and Phil Gagné. 2001. An Overview of Three Approaches to Scoring Written Essays by Computer. *Practical Assessment, Research, and Evaluation* 7(26). ericae.net/pare/getvn.asp?v=7&n=26.

Russell, Thomas L. 1999. *The No Significant Difference Phenomenon: As Reported in 355 Research Reports, Summaries, and Papers.* Raleigh: North Carolina State University.

Sager, Naomi. 1981. *Natural Language Information Processing: A Computer Grammar of English and Its Applications.* Boston: Addison-Wesley Longman.

Salton, Gerald, and Anita Wong. 1976. On the Role of Words and Phrases in Automatic Text Analysis. *Computers and the Humanities* 10:69–87.

Schachter, Ronald 2003. A.I.: Something to Build On. *District Administration.* 39 (July): 20–24.

Schank, Roger C. 1984. *The Cognitive Computer: On Language, Learning, and Artificial Intelligence.* New York: Addison Wesley.

Schank, Roger C., and Robert P. Abelson. 1977. *Scripts, Plans, Goals, and Understanding: An Inquiry into Human Knowledge Structures.* Hillsdale, NJ: Lawrence Erlbaum.

Selber, Stuart. 2004. *Multiliteracies for a Digital Age.* Carbondale: Southern Illinois University Press.

Sells, Peter, Stuart M. Shieber, and Thomas Wasow, eds. 1991. *Foundational Issues in Natural Language Processing.* Cambridge: MIT Press.

Sheingold, Karen, Joan I. Heller, and Susan T. Paulukonis. 1995. *Actively Seeking Evidence: Teacher Change through Assessment Development.* MS#94-04. Princeton, NJ: Educational Testing Service.

Sheingold, Karen, Barbara A. Storms, William H. Thomas, and Joan I. Heller, 1997. *Pacesetter English Portfolio Assessment: 1995 Report*. Princeton, NJ: Center for Performance Assessment, Educational Testing Service.

Shermis, Mark D., and Jill Burstein, eds. 2003. *Automated Essay Scoring: A Cross-Disciplinary Perspective*. Mahwah, NJ: Lawrence Erlbaum.

Slotnick, Henry B., and John Knapp. 1971. Essay Grading by Computer: A Laboratory Phenomenon? *English Journal* 60 (1): 75–87.

Smith, William L. 1993. Assessing the Reliability and Adequacy of Using Holistic Scoring of Essays as a College Composition Placement Technique. In *Validating Holistic Scoring for Writing Assessment: Theoretical and Empirical Foundations*, edited by Michael M. Williamson and Brian A. Huot, 142–205. Cresskill, NJ: Hampton.

Snowdon, David A., Susan J. Kemper, James A. Mortimer, Lydia H. Greiner, David Wekstein, and William R. Markesbery. 1996. Linguistic Ability in Early Life and Cognitive Function and Alzheimer's Disease in Late Life: Findings from the Nun Study. *Journal of the American Medical Association* 275:528–532.

Soldofsky, Alan. 1982. Comment on "Memoirs and Confessions of a Part-Time Lecturer" [by Cara Chell]. *College English* 44 (8): 864–866.

Spurgeon, Caroline. 1935. *Shakespeare's Imagery and What It Tells Us*. Cambridge: Cambridge University Press.

Stormzand, Martin J., and M. V. O'Shea. 1924. *How Much English Grammar: An Investigation of the Frequency of Usage of Grammatical Constructions in Various Types of Writing Together with a Discussion of the Teaching of Grammar in the Elementary and the High School*. Baltimore: Warwick and York.

Streeter, Lynn, Joseph Psotka, Darrell Laham, and Don MacCuish. 2002. The Credible Grading Machine: Automated Essay Scoring in the DOD. Paper presented at Interservice/Industry Simulation and Education Conference (I/ITSEC), Orlando, FL. www.k-a-t.com/papers/essayscoring.pdf.

Swanson, Don R. 1986. Fish Oil, Raynaud's Syndrome, and Undiscovered Public Knowledge. *Perspective in Biology and Medicine* 30(1):7–18.

TextAI. 2005. About. *Text Analysis International*, February 8. www.textanalysis.com/About/about.html.

Tombeur, Paul. 1971. Research Carried Out at the Centre de Traitement Electronique des Documents of the Catholic University of Louvain. In *The Computer and Literary Studies*, edited by A. J. Aitken, Richard W. Bailey, and Neil Hamilton-Smith, 335–340. Edinburgh: Edinburgh University Press.

Trilling, Lionel. 1950. Reality in America. In *The Liberal Imagination*, 3–22. New York: Viking.

Turing, Alan. 1950. Computing Machinery and Intelligence. *Mind* 59 (236): 433–460.

The Turing Test. 2005. en.wikipedia.org/wiki/Turing_Test (accessed August 2005).

United States Distance Learning Association. 2002. Underachiveing Schools to Receive Online Development Tool. *USDLA Journal* 16 (July). www.usdla.org (accessed January 21, 2004).

University of Houston. 2003. Online Writing Assessment Enables Effective, Efficient Testing. *Syllabus* (January): 31–32.

Vandegrift, D. 2002. Re: Criterion Experience. Personal e-mail, October 30.

Vantage Learning. 2000. *A Study of WritePlacer* Plus™ *Electronic Scoring for College-Level Placement; RB-380*. Yardley, PA: Vantage Learning.

———. 2003a. Birmingham Case Study. www.vantagelearning.com/product_pages/assessmentcart.html (accessed August 2005).

———. 2003b. *MY Access!*™ [brochure].

———. 2004a. IntelliMetric™. www.vantagelearning.com (accessed August 2005).

———. 2004b. MY Access!™ Demo. www.vantagelearning.com/ (accessed August 2005).

———. 2004c. MY Access!™ FAQ. www.vantagelearning.com/content_pages/myaccess-faq.html (accessed August 2005).

————. 2004d. MY Access! Product sheet. www/vantage.com/pdfs/product_pages/full-myaccess.html/content_pages/full-myaccess.html (accessed August 13, 2004).

————. 2005a. Home page. www.vantagelearning.com/.

————. 2005b. Vantage Learning Extends MY Access!™ Writing Program with Alignment of 25 Writing Prompts to Open Court Reading™. *Gregory FCA Communications,* April 11. www.gregoryfca.com/prvantage041505.html (accessed May 8, 2005).

Vernon, Alex. 2000. Computerized Grammar Checkers 2000: Capabilities, Limitations, and Pedagogical Possibilities. *Computers and Composition* 17 (3): 329–349.

Wagman, Morton. 1998. *Language and Thought in Humans and Computers: Theory and Research in Psychology, Artificial Intelligence, and Neural Science.* Westport, CT: Praeger.

Wainer, Howard. 2000. Introduction and History. In *Computerized Adaptive Testing: A Primer,* edited by Howard Wainer, 1–21. Mahwah, NJ: Lawrence Erlbaum.

Webb, Jackson E. 1973. *Assisted Instruction Program in Writing.* Olympia, WA: Evergreen State College, Department of Applied Linguistics.

Weiss, David, and Rex Jackson. 1983. *The Validity of the Descriptive Test of Language Skills: Relationship to Direct Measures of Writing Ability and to Grades in Introductory College English Courses.* College Board Report No. 83-4. New York: College Entrance Examination Board.

White, Edward M. 1994. *Teaching and Assessing Writing.* 2nd ed. San Francisco: Jossey-Bass.

————. 1995. Apologia for the Timed Impromptu Essay Test. *College Composition and Communication* 46 (1): 30–45.

Whithaus, Carl. 2004. The Development of Early Computer-Assisted Writing Instruction (1960–1978): The Double Logic of Media and Tools. *Computers and the Humanities* 38 (2): 149–162.

Wiggins, Grant. 1998. *Educative Assessment: Designing Assessments to Inform and Improve Student Performance.* San Francisco: Jossey-Bass.

Williams, Joseph. 2000. *Style: Ten Lessons in Clarity and Grace.* New York: Longman.

Williamson, Michael M. 1993. The Worship of Efficiency: Untangling Theoretical and Practical Considerations in Writing Assessment. *Assessing Writing* 1 (2): 147–174.

————. 2004. Validity of Automated Scoring: Prologue for a Continuing Discussion of Machine Scoring Student Writing. *Journal of Writing Assessment* 1 (2): 85–104.

Wohlpart, Jim. 2004a. Personal interview, July 1.

————. 2004b. The Use of Technology to Redesign a Humanities Class: Strategies for Reducing Costs and Increasing Learning. Paper presented at the Course Redesign Symposium, Seton Hall University, South Orange, NJ.

Wresch, William. 1993. The Imminence of Grading Essays by Computer—25 Years Later. *Computers and Composition* 10 (2): 45–58.

Yang, Yongwei, Chad W. Buckendahl, and Piotr J. Juszkiewicz. 2001. A Review of Strategies for Validating Computer Automated Scoring. Paper presented at the annual meeting of Midwestern Educational Research Association, Chicago.

INDEX

CONTRIBUTORS

PATRICIA FREITAG ERICSSON, Assistant Professor at Washington State University and Coordinator of the Digital Technology and Culture degree, researches critical technology theory, techno-rhetoric and composition, and technical writing. She has recently published on standards in English education, the effects of word processing on composition teaching, and integrating oral communication in technical writing courses.

RICH HASWELL, Professor Emeritus at Texas A&M University–Corpus Christi, began teaching composition at the University of Missouri in 1962. He has written or co-edited six books and nearly fifty articles of research findings. Currently he works on CompPile, his online inventory of composition scholarship, and refines his technique of peeling mangoes.

CHRIS ANSON is Professor of English and Director of the Campus Writing and Speaking Program at North Carolina State University. His research interests, on which he has published widely, include writing across the curriculum, writing to learn, and response to writing.

ED BRENT is Professor of Sociology, President of Idea Works, Inc., and author of the SAGrader program. He has twice served as Chair of the Section on Communication and Information Technology in the American Sociological Association and won a career award for his contributions to social science computing.

BOB BROAD teaches, researches, consults, and directs the Writing Program at Illinois State University. He authored *What We Really Value: Beyond Rubrics in Teaching and Assessing Writing* and articles in the journals *Research in the Teaching of English, Assessing Writing,* and *The Journal of Writing Assessment.*

WILLIAM CONDON has been faculty member and Writing Program Administrator at a wide variety of institutions and is currently Director of Campus Writing Programs and Professor of English at Washington State University. Co-author of *Writing the Information Superhighway* and *Assessing the Portfolio: Principles for Theory, Practice, and Research,* he has published articles about writing assessment, program evaluation, and computers and writing.

GAIL S. CORSO, Associate Professor of English and Communication & Media Arts, coordinates writing, and chairs the Core Assessment Task Force at Neumann College. She recently presented and co-authored an article on developing a model information literacy program at the small college. She facilitated the design of two majors: Arts Production and Performance and Communication and Media Arts.

ANNE HERRINGTON is Professor of English at the University of Massachusetts at Amherst. Her scholarly work includes *Writing, Teaching, and Learning in the Disciplines* and *Genres across the Curriculum,* both co-edited with Charles Moran; and *Persons in Process: Four Stories of Writing and Personal Development in College,* co-authored with Marcia Curtis.

ED JONES directs the basic skills program in the English Department at Seton Hall University. His research interests include the reading-writing connection, articulation of high school and college writing goals, and the role of self-beliefs, race, and class in writing achievement. Currently, he is piloting a system for online directed self-placement.

TERI THOMSON MADDOX is the Director of Developmental Studies and Professor of English and Speech at Jackson State Community College in Jackson, Tennessee. She received an EdD in Higher and Adult Education at the University of Memphis and Developmental Education Specialist Certification at Appalachian State University.

RICHARD N. MATZEN is the Director of the Writing Center and Composition Programs at Woodbury University in Burbank, California. He has published in the *Journal of Developmental Education* and is a co-editor of the forthcoming book, *Reformation: The Teaching and Learning of English in Electronic Environments.*

KEN S. MCALLISTER is an Associate Professor of Rhetoric, Composition, and the Teaching of English at the University of Arizona where he co-directs the Learning Games Initiative, an interdisciplinary, inter-institutional research group that studies, teaches with, and builds computer games. He has published and spoken widely in the fields of game studies and the cultural history of technology and recently published *Game Work: Language, Power, and Computer Game Culture.*

TIM MCGEE is an Associate Professor and Director of Graduate Programs in Philadelphia University's School of Design and Media where he pursues his interests in multiliteracy, computer-based rhetorical pedagogy, argument from the locus of quantity, and the intersections of Artificial Intelligence and Language Arts curricula.

CHARLES MORAN is Professor of English (Emeritus) at the University of Massachusetts at Amherst. With Anne Herrington he co-edited *Genre Across the Curriculum* and *Writing, Teaching, and Learning in the Disciplines.* With Gail Hawisher, Paul LeBlanc, and Cynthia Selfe, he is co-author of *Computers and the Teaching of Writing in American Higher Education, 1979-1994: A History.*

BETH ANN ROTHERMEL is associate professor of English and Coordinator of Composition at Westfield State College in Westfield, Massachusetts. She teaches courses in first-year writing, writing pedagogy, and ethnography. She has published articles on the history of writing instruction at normal schools and on writing instruction in Sweden.

COLLEEN SORENSON is Director of Student Assessment at Utah Valley State College.

MARTHA TOWNSEND is Associate Professor of English and Director of the University of Missouri's twenty-year-old Campus Writing Program. Her publications include numerous chapters and articles on WAC/WID. Her research interests have taken her to universities across the U. S. as well as Romania, Korea, Thailand, South Africa, China, and Costa Rica.

EDWARD M. WHITE has written or edited eleven books and about 100 articles or book chapters on writing instruction and writing assessment. His best-known books are *Teaching and Assessing Writing* and *Assessment of Writing: Politics, Policies, Practices.* He is a visiting professor of English at the University of Arizona.

CARL WHITHAUS is Coordinator of Professional Writing and an Assistant Professor of English at Old Dominion University. He is the author of *Teaching and Evaluating Writing in the Age of Computers and High-Stakes Testing.* He has also published work on writing assessment and pedagogy, computer-mediated communication, and writing in the sciences.

WILLIAM W. ZIEGLER is associate professor of English and developmental writing coordinator at J. Sargeant Reynolds Community College in Richmond, Virginia. His interests include the assessment of writing and teaching English to speakers of other languages.